WHEN THEY CAME FOR ME

Other books by John R. Schlapobersky

Author:
From the Couch to the Circle: Group-Analytic Psychotherapy in Practice
    (Routledge, 2016)

Editor:
Selected Papers of Robin Skynner
    Vol. 1: Explorations with Families: Group Analysis and Family Therapy
        (Routledge, 1990)
    *Vol. 2: Institutes and How to Survive Them: Mental Health Training and
    Consultation*
        (Routledge, 1990)
Selected Papers of Malcolm Pines
        (Routledge, 2020: In Press)

WHEN THEY CAME FOR ME

The Hidden Diary of an Apartheid Prisoner

John R. Schlapobersky

berghahn
NEW YORK · OXFORD
www.berghahnbooks.com

First published in 2021 by
Berghahn Books
www.berghahnbooks.com

© 2021 John R. Schlapobersky

Foreword © 2021 Albie Sachs

Library of Congress Cataloging-in-Publication Data

Names: Schlapobersky, John R., author. | Sachs, Albie, 1935– writer of foreword.
Title: When they came for me : the hidden diary of an apartheid prisoner / John R.
 Schlapobersky.
Description: New York : Berghahn Books, 2021. | Includes bibliographical references
 and index.
Identifiers: LCCN 2020042164 (print) | LCCN 2020042165 (ebook) |
 ISBN 9781789209068 (hardback) | ISBN 9781789209082 (paperback) |
 ISBN 9781789209075 (ebook)
Subjects: LCSH: Schlapobersky, John R. | Political prisoners—South Africa—
 Biography. | Anti-apartheid activists—South Africa—Biography.
Classification: LCC DT1949.S35 A3 2021 (print) | LCC DT1949.S35 (ebook) |
 DDC 968.05092—dc23
LC record available at https://lccn.loc.gov/2020042164
LC ebook record available at https://lccn.loc.gov/2020042165

British Library Cataloguing in Publication Data

A catalogue record for this book is available from the British Library

ISBN 978-1-78920-906-8 hardback
ISBN 978-1-78920-908-2 paperback
ISBN 978-1-78920-907-5 ebook

This book is dedicated to the memory of my parents, Ruth (née Romm) and Archie Schlapobersky, who gave me life twice over; to all who have had to face their inquisitors; to those who passed through the gates of Pretoria Prison, the Compol Building and other places of confinement during the years of South Africa's apartheid government; and to those who did not come out alive or intact.

Each one of us is as intimately attached to the soil of this beautiful country as are the famous jacaranda trees of Pretoria and the mimosa trees of the bushveld. Each time one of us touches the soil of this land, we feel a sense of personal renewal. The national mood changes as the seasons change. We are moved by a sense of joy and exhilaration when the grass turns green and the flowers bloom ... The time for the healing of the wounds has come. The moment to bridge the chasms that divide us has come. The time to build is upon us ... Never, never and never again shall it be that this beautiful land will again experience the oppression of one by another.

—President Nelson Mandela, Inaugural Address, 10 May 1994

CONTENTS

ILLUSTRATIONS

FOREWORD

ALBIE SACHS

Beating Swords into Ploughshares

John Schlapobersky is a world-renowned author and pioneer of group psychotherapy. Half a century ago he was made to stand without sleep on a brick in an apartheid prison for five days and nights. Then he was incarcerated in solitary confinement in what we called 'The Hanging Jail' for weeks, and he never went home again. What can we learn now about human endurance, survival, repair and transcendence from this experience? John's exquisitely written memoir tells us.

John comes from a long line of storytellers. He now earns his living from encouraging people injured in their souls to find a road to healing through telling their stories to each other. In group psychotherapy, he tells us, the psychotherapist gets close to people whose souls have been maimed by violence in the state or family, by loss or by injury, and he hears thunder as they recount their nightmares. John is at last telling his own story. He is letting out and hearing the thunder that for fifty years has lain silent in his own soul. The book is quite beautiful. In the first part of this Foreword, I offer the counterpoint voice of my own experience. There is considerable overlap in what we each went through, but also great differences. What unites them, I believe, is that in both cases we sought and managed to turn negativity into positivity. We have beaten the swords of oppression into the ploughshares of hope.

In the second part of this Foreword I will discuss the different ways in which we have gone about this. In John's case it has been through his life's work as a psychotherapist. He concludes this memoir with an Epilogue he calls 'The Years After' in which the words of fellow survivors whom he has worked with, from different parts of the world, tell their own healing stories of survival and recovery. In my case, the theme of soft vengeance has been with me ever since I was blown up by a bomb placed in my car by South African security agents

(Sachs 1990). In broad terms it took the form of helping to write South Africa's new democratic constitution. It involved voting as an equal for the first time. It meant being sworn in in front of President Nelson Mandela as a Justice of South Africa's first Constitutional Court. It manifested itself in our decision to construct our court right in the heart of the Old Fort Prison, where MK Gandhi, Robert Sobukwe, Oliver Tambo and Nelson and Winnie Mandela had been imprisoned. It signified being party to decisions of the court that forbade the whipping of juveniles; declared that, under the constitution, living customary law abolished patriarchal rules that bore unjustly against women; upheld the right of same-sex couples to marry; underlined the importance of participatory democracy as a supplement to representative democracy; vindicated the right of prisoners to vote and of soldiers to form a trade union that would be able to negotiate conditions of employment and work; and, with direct relevance to John's story, outlawed capital punishment (Currie and de Waal 2005; de Vos and Freedman 2014; Brand and Gevers 2015).[1]

Looking back, it is clear that at the time of his incarceration John was innocent. By this I do not only mean that he was being mercilessly interrogated by apartheid Security Police for political crimes he had not actually committed. I am recording that, compared to those of us who regarded ourselves as dedicated revolutionary freedom fighters, he was an innocent. Unlike us, he was bare of any preparation for how to conduct himself when captured by the enemy. And what makes *When They Came for Me: The Hidden Diary of an Apartheid Prisoner* such an astonishingly readable piece of literature is precisely the grace and sophistication with which this innocence is preserved and captured. In almost poetically cadenced language, it reveals a pure – at times unbearably pure – naivety, which made him extremely vulnerable to his Security Police interrogators and yet at the same time gave him an extraordinary resilience. His interrogators did not know how to deal with the fact that he was unprogrammed politically; they had virtually no record of him in their files; he managed to deceive them even as they were beating him down. This innocence was to remain unabated. It now invests this account of pain, recovery and transcendence with a truly lyrical tone. And it carried him into a career – as a psychotherapist – in which he has pioneered healing principles for fellow survivors.

In John's Introduction, which he calls 'The Years Before', he describes the outlook of his own family, who had been far from apolitical. John's father, who had fought in Italy against Mussolini and Hitler, had returned to South Africa and been appalled by the fact that the Afrikaner National Party, which had in large part longed for a Hitler victory, had now been put into government by the whites-only electorate. He had supported the public demonstrations of the Torch Commando, which had been set up by ex-servicemen to oppose the extreme racism of the new apartheid government. John's mother, raised in a Jewish family in an Afrikaans farming community, was also appalled when her neighbours turned against her as an '*uitlander*', an outsider, after their election victory in 1948. She found a new association amongst socialists and communists in Johannesburg where she had played the piano at meetings of the Congress movement, and would sing 'The Internationale' in private. She later became an active member of an anti-apartheid grouping of white women called the Black Sash, who with silent dignity registered their repudiation of apartheid. But active as they had been in their different ways, even to the extent of leaving the country for Swaziland, they had not been involved in any underground activity. And John had not grown up in a world like mine; his imagination as a young boy had not been suffused with ideas of preparing for the revolutionary overthrow of an unjust racist state.

How different it was for people like me. I had never known political innocence – I had been born into the struggle. We did not celebrate birthdays, but we knew the date of the Russian Revolution. As a child growing up during the Second World War, I could tell you the number of Nazi soldiers who had been captured after the Battle of Stalingrad, as well as the dates of their surrender. The adventure stories we loved the most were about young boys and girls who had helped the partisans in occupied France, in Italy and the Soviet Union. My mother, Ray Sachs, would say to little me and my even littler brother, 'Tidy up, tidy up, Uncle Moses is coming!' Uncle Moses was not Moses Cohen or Moses Levine, but Moses Kotane, the general secretary of the Communist Party of South Africa and a member of the National Executive of the African National Congress. In the natural world of our infancy, a black man was at the centre, and our mother felt proud to be working with him, assisting him in achieving his goals. Quietly brave, diffident yet dogged, and humorous in her own way, Ray raised us alone after separating from my father, Solly Sachs. Solly, as the general secretary of the Garment Workers' Union, was constantly in the news, calling workers out on strike and being subjected to various restrictions and bitter attacks by the apartheid government. Although I felt some awkwardness in being known as the son of a public figure, I had immense admiration and respect for both him and our mother. All I asked was for them not to expect me to follow automatically in their political footsteps. I was a dreamer, a lover of literature; for me, characters in novels were much more real than any people I actually knew.

And, as it turned out, it was something that I had in common with John that was to draw me into active politics... a love of poetry. I went to a lecture by the Afrikaans writer Uys Krige on the Spanish poet Federico Lorca (Krige 2010). I did not even know that Spain had poets. Uys spoke almost non-stop for three hours about his own experiences in the last months of Republican Spain.[2] And he recited the great Lorca poem about the death of a bullfighter, '*A las cinco de la tarde*' [At five in the afternoon]. He went on to tell us of Lorca's execution by Franco's Nationalist soldiers in 1936, reciting Pablo Neruda's ode to his memory in Spanish, and then giving us an English translation of this extraordinary poem: 'If I could cry out of fear in a lonely house/if I could take out my eyes and eat them/I would do it for your mournful orange-tree voice/ and for your poetry that comes out screaming' (Beissert 2013).

What that did for me was to connect the soulfulness, the inwardness and the yearning of poetry with the great public events of the world and with the struggle for social justice. And a few weeks later, with my heart surging with a longing for justice and my mind filled with newly found political savvy, I was volunteering to join the Defiance of Unjust Laws Campaign. Everyone remembers their first kiss, and many can recall their first protest march. I remember the first time I went to jail. Unlike John at a similar age, I was consciously arming myself for the rigours of struggle (Thompson 2000).[3]

Once you are involved in the struggle, everything about you changes. You realize that prison and the possibility of death await you. You read books about life in prison. Your heroes are no longer daring pilots of Spitfire aeroplanes seeking to down Nazi Messerschmitts, but men and women in jail. We passed the books on. Amongst our favourites were beautiful eulogies to freedom and love by the imprisoned Turkish poet Nazim Hikmet (Hikmet 2002) and *Notes from the Gallows* by the Czech writer Julius Fučik (Fučik 1947), intensely succinct and eloquent reportage about the last days of his life, smuggled out by a sympathetic guard before he was executed in a Gestapo prison in Prague. From Algeria there was *La Question* [*The question*], a powerful book by Henri Alleg (Alleg 1958), a French-born man who had sided with the Algerian independence fighters and had been subjected to severe torture by the French security forces. Jean-Paul Sartre had written a particularly resonant introduction to this book, explaining how the torturers had sought not only to secure information but to destroy the humanity of those they were torturing, believing that the latter were lesser human beings, thus meriting the pain they were receiving. Reading these books, we felt that we were girding ourselves emotionally and intellectually for the battles that lay ahead. We sang ballads by Pete Seeger and Paul Robeson from the United States, and songs from the International Brigades that had volunteered for battle in Spain in support of the Republican forces.

It was touching to read in John's account that he had himself actually sung some of these songs during his detention. Yet they had come to him not as part of the struggle in South Africa but during a sojourn as an exchange student in the USA, at a time when that country was being torn apart by the Vietnam War. On his return home he had not been recruited into the underground resistance. He had not become part of our world of secrecy governed by the rules of clandestinity. He had not been given a code name, nor had he worked with comrades whom he only knew by these false names. He had not been told that if you are captured and the enemy tries to break you down, you must refuse to answer any of their questions – none whatsoever, full stop. In a struggle where on the one side were ideologically driven professionals paid by the state to hunt you down, and on the other were political groupings investing themselves in a culture of resistance, John had to interpret his experiences by himself, and invent his own stratagems for muteness, deceit and survival. Although each one of us in captivity faced his or her captors alone, those of us who belonged to the resistance movement had the comfort of knowing that we belonged to an organization that cared about what was happening to us. In this sense, John was even more solitary in his solitary confinement than we were.

White bodies matter. All bodies matter, yet whiteness both aggravated and mitigated the ferocity of the Security Police attack on John. There was a special venom directed at him because, in the eyes of his interrogators, people like him were traitors. We were seen to be those individuals who were 'stirring up the blacks' who would otherwise have been content with their lives. After all, our tormentors loved to say, why would blacks from all over the continent seek to stream into South Africa if life was so difficult for them here? And the fact that in most cases we were far better educated than our interrogators seemed to stimulate in them a special desire to humiliate us and show us who was really in charge. Our white skins, then, did not protect us from harsh repression, they did not save us from pain, and they did not allow us to avoid brutal or traumatic experiences.

And yet for all this special hatred, the fact that we were white would almost certainly have had some inhibitory effect on the savagery of the means they used against us. It would have protected some of us from having electrodes attached to our genitals, from having smothering wet bags placed over our heads, from being hung out of windows, and from simply being punched and kicked in the manner in which our black comrades or associates would be treated. They did not attack our bodies directly: they assaulted our bodies through attacking our minds and our wills by means of sleep deprivation and punctuated bouts of shouting followed by silence. In the case of John and many other captives, they added further agony by making them stand on a brick for five days and nights.

It was evident, too, that in addition to seeing John and me as whites, the interrogators saw us as Jews. As the vivid opening pages of the book show, John lived all the contradictions of being a Jew in a society based on the principle of white supremacy. He was a child of a community that had fled from vicious antisemitic persecution in Lithuania, and they had subsequently learnt of the loss in the Holocaust of huge numbers of their family who had stayed behind. Yet the paradox was that the persecuted Jews who had emigrated to South Africa had gone on to become privileged beneficiaries of the racism that went with their whiteness. Amongst the things that John and I shared, then, was that although we both came from a community that had historically suffered extreme oppression, we had actually grown up in a world where everything had been open to us. We could dream of being scientists, explorers, sports stars, writers, engineers or, for that matter, freedom fighters. The choice was ours. We were volunteers in the anti-racist struggle, and had to bear its consequences, whatever they might turn out to be.

In John's case, being a Jew was to give an extra twist to the course of his incarceration. Israel was selling arms to and exchanging security information with bitter antisemites in the South African state security system. And the antisemitic interrogators who referred to John with the derisory Afrikaans word *Joodjie* (little Jewboy) were eager to please officials of the State of Israel who, with his parents' support, were enquiring about arranging his deportation to that country. And even that twist had a twist to it: the interrogators' antisemitism was tempered by their even deeper hatred of the British who had conquered the Boer Republics. John was South African by birth but was naturalized as a British subject in Swaziland where he had grown up. On deporting him, the Security Police only allowed him to go to Israel.

Tolstoy told us that 'happy families are all alike; every unhappy family is unhappy in its own way' (Tolstoy 1873: 1). The same varied and distinctive unhappiness, I believe, applies to those who experience solitary confinement and torture. Each one suffers in his or her own specific, subjective way. The experience of being depersonalized is unbearably personal. John's descriptions of his torment are utterly his and his alone. His thoughts about his increasingly weird relationship with the brick on which he was compelled to stand for days on end; the extraordinarily rich portraits he paints of his two chief interrogators, Swanepoel and Coetzee; the stratagems that he developed at times to deceive them; his joy at hearing men's voices singing beautifully through the night, only to discover later to his horror that these songs were to support and console the men who were to be hanged in the prison at dawn – all these were unique to his experience, and totally different to anything that I could have written about in my *Jail Diary* (Sachs 1969).

And yet on reading this book I found myself amazed at how similar some of the less dramatic details of our experiences had been. We had both been engulfed by the same sense of surprise at the emotion we felt when simply being driven through town from one place of confinement to another. The astonishment had not come from gliding as a captive through the streets with everybody walking on the pavement or crossing the road without sparing a thought for us; this was something that just made us feel angry and sad. It came from the fact that a car could simply stop at traffic lights, without anybody issuing a command. The experience for both of us was strange and somnambulistic. We had completely forgotten what it was like to live in a world where human beings conducted themselves according to codes that were not based on dominance and submission, but where people were simply living together in a community. It was weird, and a startling reminder of how in a matter of days normality and abnormality had been inverted. Years apart and in different cities, John and I both realized from this experience how thoroughly we had been infantilized during our captivity. We had completely internalized living in a world of command and obey, something we had last experienced as toddlers. But then when we had been tiny tots the commands of our parents would have been associated with love and nurturing. Now we were grown people in grown bodies with grown minds and grown senses, but each with a will that had been reduced to that of a dependent infant.

A second source of amazement for me came from the similarity of our respective responses to reading the Old Testament. Although John had grown up as a believer, by the time he was imprisoned he had lost his faith and would only recover it quite a few years later. I had grown up in a strongly secular home where my parents had, as part of their new internationalist and scientific worldview, consciously and affirmatively rejected the religious beliefs of their parents. For the first weeks of our solitary confinement, the Bible was the only reading matter that we had. We devoured it with special intensity, looking for messages of consolation and hope. And in our different prison cells in different cities in different years we both felt the same disappointment and dismay at the harshness of the story. The relentless order of the day was to smite or be smitten. We wanted to read about love and music and happiness and transcendence, not about constant war and submission to an overpowering command to be obedient to the deity. We believed in all humankind, not a chosen race. By the same token, however, we were both enraptured by the Song of Songs from the time of Solomon, and both of us are inspired to this day by the beautiful millenarian visions of the prophets, especially of Isaiah:

> And he shall judge among the nations, and shall rebuke among the people; and they shall beat their swords into ploughshares and their spears into pruning hooks; nation shall not lift up sword against nation, neither shall they learn war any more. (Isaiah 2: 3–4)

It was beautiful and inspiring to read these words then, and it is beautiful and inspiring to reread them now as I write this Foreword. These little moments and incidents in *When They Came for Me* became vividly alive for me, because John was describing actual remembered experience. There was a special intensity in the reading; each incident was remembered and written down by John and then read, remembered and re-experienced by me. Yet I have no doubt that for readers who have never themselves come close to being in captivity there will be no difficulty in absorbing and marvelling at the literary power and emotional authenticity of the detail he provides.

And this brings me to a third source of amazement at the discovery of an unanticipated moment of congruence between John's experience and mine. It relates to the impact of solitary confinement as such. His story is primarily about a relentless barrage of castigatory actions happening to him. My *Jail Diary*, on the other hand, was basically about how to survive the emotional and psychological punishment of being in total isolation with nothing at all happening. Yet the few paragraphs in *When They Came for Me* that he devotes to the period of solitary confinement as such, where nothing was happening to him all day long, are suffused with intense pain and disorientation. As I was later told by an Italian senator who had been imprisoned in the time of Mussolini, and as I was told thereafter by Huey Newton, the Black Panther leader who had been locked up at the behest of the FBI, you never fully get over solitary confinement.

I do not believe that John had any idea of the risks he was taking by choosing to offer help to a young black man whom he had simply seen as a friend, as someone who needed his assistance. In my case, I knew full well that sooner or later the Security Police would crack down on me. My home had been raided before dawn several times; I had been placed under various restrictions, called 'banning orders', which had severely limited my movements and activities. The crackdown was getting closer. Laws were being changed to further empower the security forces. Meetings in the underground were becoming increasingly difficult to organize. People were being arrested, many of them my clients.

And then I myself was detained without trial twice. My experiences were horrid beyond imagining, but puny when compared to what happened to John. The first detention involved 168 days of solitary confinement. The punishment was the solitary confinement itself, an unnatural state for human beings to be in. The sense of desolation was extreme, beyond anything that I had anticipated. None of the books I had read about imprisonment or torture helped me. On a good day I would simply be depressed. On a bad day I would feel unmitigated despair.

But somehow, for all the despair I felt throughout, I did manage to survive my first detention without answering any of the questions put to me. And when I was eventually released, as suddenly and with as little explanation as had been given when I was locked up in the first place, I ran for miles and miles through Cape Town to the sea, and flung myself fully clothed into the waves. While I appeared to be triumphant, something inside me had been deeply undermined. I resumed my life as an advocate (barrister) in Cape Town, but no longer had the strength to continue with underground work.

On the occasion of my second detention, a team headed by Swanepoel was flown down from Pretoria especially, to accomplish what the Cape Town interrogators had failed to do. Some five years later, it was also Swanepoel, risen now to chief interrogator of the Security Police, who had responsibility for John's interrogation; which brings me to yet another moment of astonishment on learning about something shared by John and me – namely, the acute awkwardness that we both felt at writing about Swanepoel's physical ugliness. When dealing with my second detention in my book *Stephanie on Trial*, I had felt it necessary to refer to Swanepoel's ugly appearance but had experienced a great deal of discomfort at doing so (Sachs 1968). We spent our lives fighting against judging people in terms of their looks – were they attractive or not? We wanted to go beyond the outer mask and discover the human being under the skin. To say that someone was ugly seemed cheap, as though heroes were beautiful and villains ugly. But I had felt that Swanepoel's ugliness was a weapon that he loved to use. Instead of hiding it, he had cultivated it, with his short-cropped hair and bloodshot eyes, his thick neck and heavy hands, which he would slam down on the table as he glared and shouted at you with full force. We human beings spend so much of our lives concealing blemishes and cultivating a superficial appearance of elegance and beauty, yet here was somebody doing the opposite. John's girlfriend Janet, who was allowed to see him on Day 34, describes in a contemporaneous note below that he was so ugly that she even felt sorry for him. Even now as I write this paragraph, it goes against my grain to point out that he was ugly. And yet it was highly relevant. He invested himself with his brute appearance, making it part of his persona. He lived by his ugliness. Let what remains of his reputation die by his ugliness.

I must point out that at the time when Swanepoel confronted me I had become far less resolute than I had been when being questioned by the Cape Town interrogators. You do not get stronger with each detention. In addition, I had heard the story of how the dead body of one of my comrades in the underground, Looksmart Solwandle Ngudle, had been found covered in bruises. I had also learnt about clients of mine who had been made to stand and kept awake for five days until they finally collapsed, their resistance totally broken. I was wondering what would now happen to me.

As it turned out, I was not forced to stand on a brick but was allowed to sit down. With Swanepoel giving the lead, their technique was to shout and bang the table for ten minutes. This would be followed by twenty minutes of total silence. Noise. Silence. Noise. Silence. I realized that they were working in teams. When food was given to me, there was something in their looks of satisfaction as I ate that made me feel that some drug that would weaken my resistance had been mixed into the meal. At one stage, when I politely asked if I might stand, the interrogators spontaneously burst out laughing, and said yes, I could. As we went through the day, the evening, the night, I could feel my will becoming totally dead. I started thinking about managing my collapse as well as I could. I recalled my comrades who had held out for five days and had then been totally destroyed.

Eventually, well after daylight on the second day, I toppled off the chair onto the ground, with a sense of utter exhaustion and a total longing just to curl up and sleep – with a huge feeling of total relief, lying like a baby on the floor.

There were energetic movements all around me. I could see their polished shiny black and brown shoes and was aware that this was the moment they had been waiting for. Instead of there being just two pairs of shoes, suddenly there were about six, and water was pouring down on me, hands were under my arms, I was being lifted up onto the chair. I felt Swanepoel's thumbs and forefingers prising my eyes open. I sat there for a while, and then collapsed onto the floor again. I do not know how many times this was repeated. In the end I sat like a dummy, feeling utterly leaden and will-less, and somehow it became clear that I was going to respond to their questions. But I decided I would start my answers with at least a smidgeon of defiance, by opening with a statement about the circumstances in which I was doing so.

At the beginning of what I considered to be a 'managed breakdown' on my part, I sought to retain a tiny bit of dignity by telling Swanepoel to record that I was making the statement under duress. I then described in some detail the circumstance of my induced collapse. He was writing it down, writing and writing, and I felt just a small half-flicker of self-esteem being preserved in getting him to record the details. But later I noticed with dismay, and through my extreme fatigue, that he was shuffling the papers around; and when I realized that the opening portion of my statement was being eliminated and the pages renumbered, I felt doubly defeated. He had outwitted me. Not one physical trace of my duress and defiance would remain. He kept on writing as he asked further questions, and I remember him saying to me, not as a bully but as one rational person to another, 'What's the point of having code names in the underground when everybody knows who the people are?' I did not want to tell him that it was part of our culture, part of the mental conditioning we underwent. Then he said, 'Why is it that the only people you mention are people who are dead or have already left the country? Well, we'll come back to that.' The fact was that my second detention occurred two years after my first, since when I had not been active in the resistance, and so all my knowledge in that sense was rather stale. There was nothing in my statement that they could use against anybody there and then. But they did have the triumph of succeeding where the Cape Town interrogators had failed: they had compelled me to start answering their questions. I felt crushed. And I knew that they were far from finished with me.

As things turned out, however, fortune was to be on my side, not Swanepoel's. Another detainee, an architect named Bernard Gosschalk, who had been subjected to similar treatment (Gosschalk 2017) – possibly they had had two teams going at the same time in different parts of the building, with Swanepoel moving from one to the other – had been allowed after his interrogation to see his wife, and had whispered to her that he was being subjected to torture by sleep deprivation. Shocked by these words and by his appearance, she contacted a lawyer who then went to court and got an immediate order interdicting the police from following through with further interrogations of that kind. After my own interrogation was over, my conditions were relaxed and I was allowed to receive newspapers, so I read about Bernard's application with a surge of excitement. Then, using the cap of a thermos flask as a container, I managed to smuggle out of my cell the smallest legal document I have ever written: a square inch of paper saying that I too had been subjected to sleep deprivation. It turned out that the order granted to Bernard was wide enough to protect me, and Swanepoel was never able to delve deeper into my statement as he had promised to do. It is good to be able at this stage to acknowledge that, in the darkest days when most of the judges were enthusiastically or blithely enforcing racist and oppressive laws, there were still a few judges who remained willing to look at the facts in a humane way and to use what little judicial manoeuvrability was available to them to uphold certain basic rights. By the time John was detained, the Terrorism Act had been in place for two years. It ended any residue of judicial discretion, and gave sole authority to the Security Police for the exercise of the law. Yet hats off to Michael Corbett, John Didcott, Johann Kriegler, Laurie Ackermann, Richard Goldstone and a few more judges who then and later proved that, in even the most dire circumstances, people can make choices to diminish the amount of evil all around them.[4]

Beating Spears into Pruning Hooks

Two decades after my experience of sleep deprivation at the hands of Swanepoel, I found myself directly confronted with the following question: Was it permissible for a liberation movement fighting for freedom to use torture against captured enemy agents? What if they had been sent by the ruthless apartheid regime to destroy our organization? What if they had vital information about plans to kill our leaders? After my second detention I had gone into exile, living first in England for a number of years and then moving to newly independent Mozambique. Oliver Tambo, the president of the ANC, had invited me to fly to Lusaka to discuss what he called a 'problem' that had arisen inside the organization. He told me that they had captured a number of enemy agents sent by Pretoria to destroy the ANC, and he added that there was nothing in the ANC constitution that said anything about how to deal with captured enemy agents. I told him that there were international legal instruments that forbade the use of cruel, inhuman or degrading punishment or treatment, and that expressly forbade torture. He replied, 'We use torture.' His face was bleak as he told me this.

He then asked me to help to prepare a Code of Conduct for the ANC in exile. Of all the legal documents that I have worked on – and I include drafts for the constitution of South Africa and judgments I wrote as a Justice of the Constitutional Court – this was probably the most important. It was in effect a bill of rights for a liberation movement living in scattered groups in exile. We were mainly in Africa but were also located on other continents. It created a form of internal legality for any ANC members who might be facing charges of having violated the norms of the organization. What institutions and procedures should be created to deal with people believed to have stolen money from the organization; or to have engaged in sexual assaults; or to have driven its vehicles while drunk? And how should people be treated, charged with the particularly serious offence of working with Pretoria to destroy the organization? Should it be permissible in emergency situations to use what was referred to as 'enhanced methods of interrogation' to get crucial information from them?

I was asked to put a proposed draft of the Code of Conduct for discussion and adoption by delegates at an ANC conference in the small Zambian town of Kabwe. I remember standing on a high platform to introduce the draft. I stated that the code expressly forbade the use of torture, but asked the delegates whether, in special circumstances, intense methods of interrogation could be used to deal with captured enemy agents. We wanted the issue to be fully discussed. The first person to climb up the steps onto the platform was a young soldier from Umkhonto we Sizwe (MK), the armed wing of the ANC. He said most emphatically that there must be no exceptions to our draft Code of Conduct. He said that 'if you give the slightest leeway to our own security staff, they never stop there'. I had been wondering how the delegates would respond. Would they see me as just another middle-class lawyer spouting what they might call bourgeois ideas about justice, when their people were being subjected on a daily basis to every kind of physical violence? He was followed by another young soldier from MK. He went to the microphone and said: 'We are fighting for life. How can we be against life?' I was intensely moved by his observation. For me, it captured everything. We could not take our morality from the enemy. The source of our strength lay precisely in our conviction that the achievement of human dignity was at the core of everything we did. If we became torturers, we would not only be brutalizing the people we were holding captive, but we would be brutalizing ourselves and thereby undermining our whole project (Sachs 2018).

A few years later, at a time when I was a member of the Constitutional Committee of the ANC set up by Oliver Tambo to prepare constitutional guidelines for a new democratic South Africa, I was about to get into my car to go to the beach when everything went suddenly and catastrophically dark. I knew that something terrible was happening to me. And some time afterwards, while still in darkness, I heard a voice saying, 'Albie, this is Ivo Garrido speaking. You are in the Maputo Central Hospital. Your arm is in lamentable condition. You must face the future with courage' (Ivo Garrido was then a physician at Maputo Central Hospital. He went on to become Mozambique's Health Minister and then President of the World Health Assembly). I said into the darkness, 'What happened?' and a woman's voice answered, 'It was a car bomb.' I fainted back into the darkness, but with a sense of joy. It was that moment that every freedom fighter is waiting for – will they come for me? Will I be brave? And they had come for me, and I had survived! Somehow the bomb that blew away my arm also blew away the deep sadness that had lodged inside me since my experiences of solitary confinement and of being subjected to sleep deprivation at the hands of Swanepoel.

Weeks later, having been flown to a hospital in London so as to prevent the South African security forces finishing their job by poisoning my food, I received a note saying, 'Don't worry Comrade Albie, we will avenge you.' Avenge me? I asked myself. Do we want a country in which people lose an arm and the sight in one eye (as had happened to me)? If we get freedom and democracy, social justice and the rule of law, I answered myself, that will be my soft vengeance … roses and lilies will grow out of my arm.

Afterwards, when it was all over and we were telling our stories, the publishers and press in London and New York picked up on and identified with what we had to say – in ways they would not do with black people who had suffered far more grievous treatment. My *Jail Diary* was dramatized for the Royal Shakespeare Company and broadcast in a television adaptation by the BBC. I was thrilled that my experience was assisting the anti-apartheid movement, but saddened by the knowledge that the much more interesting and meaningful stories of the thousands of our black comrades in the struggle were not being published. It was as though a curtain of oblivion hung over the black experience. Happily, our great musicians, Miriam Makeba, Abdullah Ibrahim and Hugh Masekela, were able to penetrate the curtain of black invisibilization with their music. Finally and wonderfully, the story of Nelson Mandela's long walk to freedom ultimately became the best-known story in the world in the late twentieth century (Mandela 1994).

John speaks movingly of the nightly singing he used to hear from nearby cells while he was in Pretoria Prison, and of his slow realization that these songs, which had been bringing him some consolation in his solitude, were in fact coming from men awaiting their execution. The very first case heard by the eleven of us serving as Justices of the Constitutional Court created by our new democratic constitution, was whether the death penalty was consistent with the values of the constitution. There were more than four hundred people on Death Row. They had been sentenced to death in the apartheid era, and a stay had been put on any executions pending our court's decision. For three days we heard intense oral argument for and against the abolition of capital punishment. President Mandela sent Adv. George Bizos, who had defended him when he himself had been on trial for his life, to argue for abolition. The court adjourned. The issues were deep and emotional. We workshopped several times. In the end, the head of our court, Arthur Chaskalson, wrote what was called a magisterial judgment setting out reasons for declaring capital punishment to be unconstitutional. Each of the ten remaining members of the court wrote separate judgments explaining why we agreed with his decision.

Apartheid South Africa had led the world in terms of the number of judicial executions carried out – about one hundred every year. A gallows with seven nooses was used to save time and money. As Justice Ismail Mahomed, deputy head of our court, wrote, our constitution represented a radical rupture with a cruel, divisive past and its replacement with a society to be based on caring and concern. Some of us used the African concept of ubuntu as foundational to our thinking (Tutu 1999). Ubuntu underlines the interdependence of all human beings and the significance of our shared humanity. We declared that the question concerned not only what capital punishment inflicted upon the person who was executed, but what it did to our society. It tainted the whole community; it made everyone complicit in the deliberate, cold-blooded extinction of a human being. Some of my colleagues pointed to the way that race and class inevitably introduced arbitrary elements into the imposition of an especially drastic and irreversible sentence. I referred to the fact that great traditional leaders in South Africa, like Hintsa, Moshoeshoe and Montshiwa, had opposed the use of capital punishment. For various reasons we all felt that the very idea of the state cold-bloodedly killing its citizens was constitutionally repugnant. We accordingly decided – unanimously – that in the new democratic South Africa, capital punishment would be unconstitutional, because it denied respect for life and human dignity, and violated the prohibition of cruel punishments which our constitution demanded.

In the struggle days we did not focus extensively on the issue of what personal freedom would mean. Our gaze was fixed primarily on national liberation, on changing the system. As long as apartheid existed you could not get meaningfully to the issue of securing the rights of individuals. The very nature of the freedom struggle had encouraged us to denounce individualism as something egotistic and self-serving. At the purely technical legal level, we were worried that giant companies and conglomerates would claim for themselves the freedoms and rights of individuals to prevent any form of public economic intervention to secure greater equity in society. So, it was only when we started drafting a Bill of Rights for the constitution that we began to engage seriously with the question of personal freedom. It had certainly been in the back of our minds. We had lived, worked, studied and been trained in countries all over the world. We had seen at first hand how authoritarian rule and the arbitrary exercise of power in all the continents could destroy the spirit of individuals and give rise to great injustice. We had observed how power could be abused in our own liberation organizations. But overwhelmingly, we were influenced by the ghastly experiences of generations of South Africans under authoritarian racist rule. Our motto was to say: Never again! Never again should people be picked up from their place of study, as happened to John, and thrown into solitary confinement without access to lawyers or their families, without the right to be brought before a court within a reasonable period. Never again should detainees be made to stand on a brick for almost a week, and deprived of sleep, to make them talk, let alone be compelled to break their silence and make self-incriminating statements. Our constitution today is absolutely clear on all these questions. These are no longer just provisions in a law dealing with criminal procedure that could be amended or repealed by parliament at any time. They are entrenched as fundamental rights of the constitution. They are beyond the reach of parliament, save for possible limitations in a law that a court would find to be reasonable and justifiable in an open and democratic society, based on human dignity, equality and freedom. Never again.

For decades in our country we had rule *by* law, not rule *of* law. The text of the Terrorism Act could not have been more emphatic. The bitter paradox was that the law itself had been used expressly to grant to the Security Police a power to deal with their captives outside the realm of ordinary legal control. Detention without trial signified more than simply their right to hold people indefinitely without bringing them to court: it gave the Security Police the time and space to ill-treat captives without fear of exposure. The records show that scores of people died in South African prisons and police stations at the hands of the interrogators during that period. Tens of thousands of us will bear for the rest of our lives the physical, emotional and psychological scars inflicted by our interrogators.[5] So when a draft on the right to freedom was presented to me for my comment early on in negotiations at CODESA (Convention for a Democratic South Africa), I immediately and instinctively insisted on including a clause that expressly said, 'There shall be no detention without trial.'

The very intensity of our experiences in prison, in exile and in the underground had shown the extent to which the political was personal. Yes, the system had to be changed; but yes, as well, every individual counted. Personal integrity had to be inviolate. Protection was needed not only against abuse by the state of those in captivity, but also to reduce the amount of terror in society as a whole. Indeed, the theme of coupling freedom from fear with securing inviolability of the human body is central to the way constitutional protection was envisaged. It extended the sphere of the anti-violence principle from purely state violence to include violence in the home. In this context, the personal was not only political, it was constitutional. It related not only to physical security but to equality and moral citizenship in society. In this way, protections originally designed to save political activists from state terror in prison, were broadened out to come to the aid of those being systemically subjected to terror in the home (Sachs 2009, 2016).

Yet it is an unfortunate fact that the gap between the dignified existence for all as promised by the constitution, and life as actually lived by millions of our people, remains huge. We have very serious problems in our country: gender-based violence, inequality, racism, unemployment, crime, corruption and more. But when dealing with them, the point of departure now is completely different from what it was when John and I went to jail. No longer do we live under a system based on principles of racial supremacy. No longer does parliament have unlimited power to pass whatever laws it likes in pursuance of the will of whoever happens to be heading government at any particular time. We now inhabit a country with one of the most advanced constitutions in the world. It expressly protects the pillars of our democracy, and it establishes a number of carefully spelt out fundamental rights that parliament cannot override.

We are a nation of storytellers. Our constitution is perhaps our greatest story of all. It has become the most efficacious mechanism devised by our people to beat the pain of the oppression of the past and to provide hope for upliftment in the future. Our constitution has frequently been called a bridge between the past and the future. John's account is just one of the hundreds of thousands of stories about people still alive who have experienced the repression of the past in all sorts of different ways. They are now living through the changes that have come for the better, after the many disappointments that caused so much dismay and anger.

As the Ghanaian writer Ayi Kwei Armah said: 'The Beautyful Ones are not yet born' (Armah 1968). Meanwhile, we can only hope that more people will come forward and tell their stories with the vividness and candour that John has displayed. Let these tales be in all the languages of the country, recorded through oral tradition, on cell phones, in books and on film and radio. Let the grandparents share these stories in schools and libraries. And let those of the group we once called 'the enemy' also come forward with candid and reflective tales from their side – not to defend, glorify or excuse things that are indefensible, but to convey what it was like to be on their side and to show how they came in their own special ways to accept, at least, the broad sweep of the constitution.

Recovery from trauma is almost impossible in a setting where torture is ubiquitous and is known to be employed rather than denounced by those in power. Conversely, in an environment where torture is regarded as abominable, the chances of recovery are much greater. In the context of group-storytelling and interaction, early green shoots of trust can begin to reveal themselves. The universe of the spirit becomes less bleak and threatening. The right and wrong of your internal experiences come to be in accord with the right and wrong of the society in which you live. The healing can begin.

When, a decade or so ago, I was asked to give a lecture for the British National Archives, I decided to visit the South African National Archives to see if I could retrieve some documents relating to my own detention. It was distressing to find that there was nothing about me left in the files of the Security Police. Presumably all of the huge amount of documentation they must have collected in South Africa, the UK, Mozambique and the USA had been shredded. My whole negative biography, the notorious 'me', painstakingly put together over the decades, had been cut into tiny pieces. But when I looked in the files of the Ministry of Justice, I did discover a meaningful thin pink carbon copy of a statement I had made to a visiting magistrate. It recorded my experience of sleep deprivation. When I saw it, I felt exultation and joy; it did not matter to anybody in the world except to me that a physical trace of my detention actually existed, but I felt triumphant. Yet the general absence of the records that were shredded has made the telling of stories by survivors all the more valuable. And when the survivor has the calm, the recall, and the ability to focus on and capture significant detail that John enjoys, then the story becomes more than just a factual record of cruelty. It becomes a testimonial not only to what happened, but to what it was like to undergo that experience. In this sense John's story, entering our archives, represents a supreme example of the good that comes out of bad. The lack of an 'objective' recorded testimony has given rise to the creation of profoundly remembered subjective experience – a hard and brilliant gemstone of pain and hope that survives the wash of time.

John does not use the language of 'soft vengeance', as I did; but he, too, involved himself in a project of reparation. It was a form of reparation to be accomplished not in terms of money paid out as compensation for pain inflicted, nor even of solace offered for suffering endured, but through the establishment of human connections and the regeneration of optimism in those who had been severely bruised in spirit and rendered deeply sad in soul. It had a collective dimension for society as a whole, and an individual dimension as well; each and every grieving person on Earth was entitled to achieve restoration of dignity, hope and pride.

Who would have thought that a book centred on an unimaginably horrendous experience of endless standing on a brick, of sleep deprivation, of solitary confinement coupled with hearing the agonized last songs of people on their way to the gallows dawn after dawn, could end up as a story of hope? And it is not a forced hope, an imposed hope; it is a hope that emerged from the transformation of John's own life, his achievements. It comes from the extent to which his experiences enabled him to share professionally and personally with other people who had been through similar experiences. It is a hope that springs from creative healing, that comes from the collective interaction, from the group.

John's mode of achieving reparation has, accordingly, been very different from mine. It does not articulate itself in the form of a constitution for the nation, or in the matrix of a legal judgment declaring the rights of people. It works at the intimate, personal level. Its strength comes from the capacity of people to 'penetrate the heart of stone that holds the secrets of inner injury', to use John's own words (Schlapobersky 2016a: 146). I think it is fair to say that our uncertain, stressful world needs both. It needs public virtue, it needs public fidelity to principles, it needs public deliberation, thoughtfulness and rationality, and it needs true public belief in the fundamental right of equality for everybody. But it also needs an acknowledgement of subjectivity, and an awareness of intimate pain. It needs responses that touch on the unconscious, on the imagined, and that engage with the irrationality that is such a strong element of life, both public and private.

Through his own experience and that of others, John learnt just how torture isolates, even as solitary confinement lends added weight to the isolation. In my case, I came away from the two periods of detention with a sense of the liberation movement around me, close to me in so many different ways. My stigmata were visible. The *New York Times* carried a long piece entitled 'Broken but Unbroken'. The Young Vic Theatre in London put on a special performance of the *Jail Diary of Albie Sachs* with the participation of four well-known actors who had played me at different times. By contrast, John kept his history in communion with himself. He came out of prison into a strange and alien world – he had no home to go back to, and no movement to embrace him. His healing came first through the publication in a British newspaper of a report about what he had been through in detention, in defence of those then on trial. But the journalist who used his story gave it the headline 'How Vorster's Jailers "Broke" Me', which felt like a betrayal of his experience, and he shunned further publicity. It was through the healing therapy he underwent, and then, most profoundly, through the years of therapeutic work with fellow survivors, that he achieved his own form of reparation, enacting through his daily practice the Biblical injunction 'and they shall beat their swords into ploughshares, and their spears into pruning hooks'. He was able to turn the terrible negative energy associated with his interrogation into positivity connected with healing. He became a psychologist and psychotherapist and he has gone on to become a world leader in developing forms of group psychotherapy.

Furthermore, as he became a distinguished practitioner and original thinker in the field of group psychotherapy, he dedicated decades of his working life to the development of therapeutic resources for survivors of organized violence, especially torture. He became a close collaborator of Helen Bamber, whose work in exposing and denouncing torture, as well as in assisting those who had experienced it, achieved international renown. John has said of this work, '[I]n the forum of the group people can be most alive to the real, the lost and the unacquainted in one another and can harvest gifts of adversity from the most unlikely sources' (Schlapobersky 2016a: 459). *When They Came for Me* is such a gift, harvested from his own past – a great story by a born storyteller.

Albie Sachs was formerly a barrister at the Bar in Cape Town. He was instrumental in drafting South Africa's post-apartheid constitution and served as a Justice of the Constitutional Court for fifteen years. His *Jail Diary of Albie Sachs* was dramatized for the Royal Shakespeare Company by David Edgar and broadcast by the BBC. He was awarded the Alan Paton Award for two of his books, *The Soft Vengeance of the Freedom Fighter* (University of California Press, 1990) and *The Strange Alchemy of Life and Law* (OUP, 2009). His latest books are *We the People: Insights of an Activist Judge* (Witwatersrand University Press, 2016) and *Oliver Tambo's Dream* (African Lives, 2018).

Notes

1. The 2014 edition of *The Soft Vengeance of a Freedom Fighter* (Sachs 1990) contains an epilogue with a 'Timeline of Major Events in the Life of Albie Sachs' (p. 250) and an account of 'Persons Mentioned in the Narrative', including those who had been assassinated or tortured to death by the authorities (p. 255).
2. A full account of Krige's profound contribution to South African literature in English and Afrikaans is given in Jack Cope's fine study *The Adversary Within* (1982).
3. Hilda Bernstein's *Rift: The Exile Experience of South Africans* contains interviews with more than 330 people in exile who report on their experience of imprisonment and the brutality of the apartheid government's security forces. It concludes with a Chronology of Events in the history of apartheid, and the struggle against it, which gives a record of the police atrocities against members of the liberation movements (Bernstein 1994: 510–16). Further sources on apartheid's brutal history can be found: in Antjie Krog's *The Shadow of My Skull* (1999) and on the websites of the Truth and Reconciliation Commission, South Africa at: https//www.justice.gov.za/trc; and its successor body, the Institute for Justice and Reconciliation at: https//www.jmr.org.za/. Three recent publications give new weight to long-standing claims against the apartheid government over its human rights abuses for the duration of its tenure, and especially in its concluding years: *A Crime Against Humanity: Analysing the Repression of the Apartheid State* (Coleman 1998); *The Terrorist Album: Apartheid's Insurgents, Collaborators and the Security Police* (Dlamini 2020); and *Undeniable: Memoir of a Covert War* (Garson 2020).
4. The appointment of judges to South Africa's Constitutional Court in 1994, including some of those named here, is described in https://www.sahistory.org.za/article/appointment-judges.
5. See author's Prologue, notes 3, 4, 5 and 6.

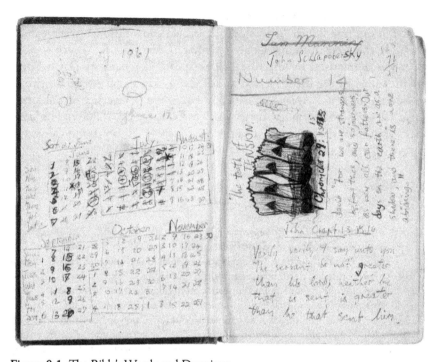

Figure 0.1 The Bible's Words and Drawings.

© Jewish Museum London. Photograph by Ian Lillicrapp.

PROLOGUE

Apollo 8
Three men flew to the moon last night
and a little child died without ever having seen it.
And enteritis killed her, they all say.
Just 100 of their billion-dollar-a-mile trip
would have let her see the moon.
And enteritis killed her, they all say.

—Poetry fragment, John Schlapobersky, January 1969

When Apollo 8 flew round the moon in December 1968, I was a university student in Johannesburg and wrote these lines of poetry in memory of a little girl who died at two. She was the daughter of Julie Nkosi, the domestic servant in the home where I had lodgings. I supported her mother's struggle to find funds for her treatment, and then saw her grieve when the antibiotics came too late. Apollo 8 rounded the moon soon after she died, and by the time Apollo 11 landed on the moon six months later, I was in a cell in Pretoria Prison and knew nothing about it. The warden who took me for exercise the next morning told me of it, and I decided to look for the moon that night. After they turned the lights out, I hoisted myself up to the barred window in the cell wall on the prison's second floor. Hanging there in the darkness I could see nothing outside except prison roofs in the glare of the lights, and silhouettes of jacaranda trees in the distance. The half-moon was on the other side of the building. I was in solitary confinement under the Terrorism Act and had good reason to believe that the people who had me detained, the Security Police, put my life at risk. On weekdays in the early mornings, people were hanged on the prison gallows nearby. The night before execution, their singing would rise from the condemned cells below and only stopped at dawn, when silence fell. I thought that, like them, I might never see the moon again.

Nearly fifty years later I visited the NASA Space Center in Houston, where they have a fine visitors' programme. The tramcar taking people round the site brought us to Historic Mission Control, from where the Apollo landings were directed. Above the controller's panel was the speaker that broadcast the memorable statements from Apollo 11 on 20 July 1969: 'Houston, Tranquility Base here. The Eagle has landed'; and then later, 'That's one small step for man, one giant leap for mankind.' I was very moved when I saw the speaker that I could not hear as it spoke to the world. Memories of my time in prison came flooding back and cut me off from the other visitors.

They were all difficult days, but 20 July 1969 – which corresponds to Day 38 of this memoir – was a turning point towards survival. Now I was presenting my recent book, *From the Couch to the Circle: Group-Analytic Psychotherapy in Practice* (Schlapobersky 2016a), at a professional conference in Houston, which happened to take place over my seventieth birthday. It calls on decades of work as a psychotherapist, mostly in London, with troubled people from different countries. The book has been warmly received and there are speaking engagements in many parts of the world. It describes my work in private practice, in the National Health Service and in pioneering the development of group methods for refugees and survivors of organized violence. I have trained generations of psychotherapists and seen to the development of a range of agencies and institutions to do this kind of work (Schlapobersky 1996, 2001, 2015a, 2015b, 2016a, 2017; Schlapobersky and Bamber 1988; Schlapobersky and Pines 2000). I am accustomed to what we call 'hearing thunder', getting close to people who have suffered nightmares at others' hands (Akhmatova 1988),[1] and I have had the benefit of therapy for myself. But these emotions at the space centre took me by surprise. Why so much feeling now? When I came to the Houston conference – as a leader in my field – I was in recovery from a back complaint that caused a level of pain that I had not known since my interrogation. So, already vulnerable, I could be ambushed by my history in an unguarded encounter with my past. The back complaint is behind me, but I am now on the threshold of another stage of life, and have set out to write this memoir and bring light to a dark chapter that still casts shadows. By unpacking it and putting it between the covers of this book, I look to memorialize our struggle and contribute to the liberty of others. Apartheid had its own coordinates of time and place, but threats to human rights are perennial. The memoir describes how even the rule of law was used as a vehicle for tyranny – and this continues today in many places. South Africa's new constitution and Bill of Rights, discussed by Albie Sachs (one of its authors) in his Foreword to this volume and set out in Appendix 2, provides safeguards of one kind. This memoir is intended as another. I believe one person's story can make a difference. Writing it has been difficult, but it is already strengthening me, and it is giving me more peace of mind. I will be pleased if 'the writing on the wall' – a man's name, Knox Masi, and his unfinished fate left on a cell wall in Pretoria to prophesy the doom of apartheid – can bring light to the dark places of human cruelty. I tried to do this at the time with the poem I wrote on Day 7 in 'Solitary Confinement' below.

Sitting in London and going halfway back in time to the events described here, we witnessed Nelson Mandela elected to office as South Africa's president in 1994 and saw the country's parliament sworn in as a new representative democracy. Amongst the Members of Parliament taking their places in the country's first generation of black MPs was one of my friends who had also been arrested at the time this story begins, Mongane Wally Serote. When elected he was already distinguished as one of the country's leading poets and is now South Africa's poet laureate. Our sense of pride was overwhelming, and we could only imagine how much more so was the pride of his own family. The country was transformed, its national anthem 'Nkosi Sikelel' iAfrika' [God Save Africa] is a song of freedom known worldwide as the African anthem. Much else had changed for the better. The new constitution now has a Bill of Rights supported by a Constitutional Court served by judges like Justice Albie Sachs, an earlier survivor of the kind of ordeal I underwent. He also survived a murder attempt by the Security Police, which he describes in his Foreword; and, carrying injuries that might have stopped anyone else in their tracks, he went on to play a leading role in shaping the country's constitution, helping to establish the Truth and Reconciliation Commission, serving as a Justice in the Constitutional Court and giving testimony to our history through his writing. All this pointed towards a future more radically changed than anything we could have imagined. So why these emotions now?

While in solitary confinement I had a daily visit to the bathroom where I used to say to the reflection of myself in the mirror, 'So, you're still here!' Beyond all probability I am still here. The regime is a thing of the past and its chief inquisitors are long dead. History was being made in Houston while I struggled through a different history in Pretoria inside four walls of obscurity in the valley of the shadow of death. At the NASA Space Center I could see where Neil Armstrong's voice had come from, and it has spurred me on to bring my own history out of the shadows and give it a voice. In my cell I would often think of Pastor Niemöller's lines that give expression to views for which the Nazis put him in a concentration camp, 'First They Came for the Communists', and though I could not remember all the words, I was worried that, when they came for me, there would be no one left speaking for me (Niemöller 2000).[2] Little did I know what activity was taking place on my behalf outside. Now this book will speak for me about a history that has shaped my life and that of my family. Today few amongst my colleagues know more than the outline, and it is now time for me to speak about myself.

I came through the ordeal with integrity, and made a life that was not defined by captivity. I am the eldest of four, and have two brothers, Colin and David, and a sister, Marian, the youngest. Like me, my family has survived and

flourished. We lost our parents to natural events, but our generations following are doing well, despite a catalogue of family problems, some of which were
set in train by my detention and deportation. I came to the UK via Israel as a
refugee, and was joined here by my siblings and later by my mother. We now
all have spouses and children, and some of us have grandchildren. My daughter
and stepson are thriving, as are our grandchildren, and good things are happening too in the lives and families of my brothers and sister. I was deeply moved
when everyone who could, joined me for a family meal in August 2019 to celebrate the fiftieth anniversary of my release. They know something about my
past, but I am shy to talk about it – as they are about asking me – so they are
waiting to read this book. We honoured the occasion by going on to a Prom-
enade concert at the Royal Albert Hall, in which my granddaughter Maia sang
Mozart's Requiem in a choir – a fine time of synchrony. I want this memoir to
stand as another marker – to the past, yes, but also to our concerns with the
present. My children are making valuable contributions in their own fields –
family therapy and documentary film-making – and my grandchildren are
training and studying towards promising careers. Common ingredients in our
lives and those of the next generation of our family, are careers that involve
creativity, teaching, medicine, psychology, psychotherapy, justice, film-making,
civic life and the environment. I am very proud of what we are all doing. My
grandson Leo told me recently of his wish to study earth sciences in order to
make a contribution to the environment. When I showed him how impressed
I was, he said, 'Well you did something when you could, now it's our turn to
step up to the mark.'

Those moments in Houston were the catalyst for a long-dormant writing
plan. I wrote the first and only documented day-by-day account of my detention for a pamphlet called 'Trial by Torture – The Case of the 22' (International Defence and Aid Fund 1970). When I came to the UK that year, the
organization was mounting publicity for the others who had been arrested
with me (ibid.). As the defendants were brought to trial for a second time, my
account was published in *The Observer* on 23 August 1970, with an introduction by the paper's editor containing allegations that both the accused and the
state witnesses had been tortured. My description confirmed this. *The Observer*
recorded how 'their case has provoked protests by lawyers, debates in parliament and criticism even from pro-government newspapers'. The judiciary were
not yet fully in the inquisition's hands and, thanks to the endeavours of many of
us, those who survived months and years in solitary confinement were eventually released and the cases against them set aside. They had been prosecuted on
grounds for which there was no evidence, and the courts came to this conclusion twice over. But, as the conflict sharpened in the years that were to come,
things got very much worse (Krog 1999; Gobodo Madikizela 2003).

Although my account was referenced in the South African press, the Terrorism Act prevented its publication there. Days afterwards, the head of the South

African Security Police, Brigadier P.J. 'Tiny' Venter, issued his own press statement, reported in the *Rand Daily Mail* on 29 August 1970, in which he attacked my account as 'emphatic lies', insisting that 'we did not harm him'. The newspaper was not allowed to publish the content of my allegations, but it described how I had 'given interviews on the BBC's regional Sussex Radio . . . and their Africa World Service. In addition, a number of weekly periodicals including the *Church Times* and the left-wing *Tribune* have approached him for contributions'. All copies of *The Observer* coming into Southern Africa had my story excised, and the South African newspapers – and my family in Swaziland – were warned not to provide any further publicity about me. The nature of the threat held over them is described below in the Afterword where 'What the Press Said' includes Venter's press releases. Two weeks later, on 15 September, the *Rand Daily Mail* described how 'it is just three weeks since the startling account by John Schlapobersky of his detention by the South African Security Police burst on the British public. It caused a considerable stir when the influential British Sunday newspaper, *The Observer*, published it and since then other journals, the radio and television have taken it up'. Sources for these and other press statements of the time are set out in 'What the Press Said'.

Readers will judge the authenticity of this memoir for themselves. It is made up of a number of original testimonial sources built on through careful, daily reconstruction. My concern with authenticity stands in contrast to records available in the South African History Archive. Despite extensive help from the coordinator of their Freedom of Information Programme, Nobukhosi N. Zulu, the documents so far secured from the government's agencies – police, judiciary and security – confirm my arrest, detention and release, but say little more. The statement I was forced to sign as a condition for my release has disappeared and, beyond my case number, 69/2713, nothing else survives to give detail to my interrogation or detention. Some of these documents are quoted from in 'What the Press Said', but the truth of what was done to us has been erased by apartheid's administrators. In Albie Sachs's Foreword he describes his own parallel discovery that archive sources that should have contained the state's record against him have been emptied. Marianne Thamm, writing in the South African newspaper the *Daily Maverick*, reported on 25 June 2020 that 'the apartheid state incinerated 44 tons of evidence in industrial furnaces in the lead-up to SA's first democratic elections in 1994', quoting from Jacob Dlamini's *The Terrorist Album: Apartheid's Insurgents, Collaborators and the Security Police* (Dlamini 2020).[3]

This gives added urgency to this memoir and its testimony. As a witness to history, I write to name the chief perpetrators in the Veiligheidspolisie, translated as 'Security Police', whom we called the SB – the Special Branch. Majors Theunis Swanepoel and Johan Coetzee had direct charge of me, and both later rose to the highest offices in the land. They were members of a small unit of security officers who had been trained in the use of torture and counter-insurgency in France and Algeria in the early 1960s (O'Brien 2011).[4] Swanepoel, already notorious for many deaths in detention, went on to become the Police Colonel responsible for the police shootings in the Soweto Uprising of 1976.[5] Coetzee became a general, rising from Director of the Security Police to Chief Commissioner of Police.

> The definitive 1998 Human Rights Commission publication, *A Crime Against Humanity: Analysing the Repression of the Apartheid*, edited by Max Coleman, found that between 1948 and 1994, 21,000 people died in political violence in South Africa and Namibia. The six-year transition ... between 1990 and 1994 ... documented in ... Philippa Garson's ... *Undeniable: Memoir of a Covert War* ... [shows that] at least 14,000 people died in the horrific spasm of violence ... stoked in part and in secret by Military Intelligence and other covert apartheid hit squads and third forces, [but] ... the collection of illusive evidence prevented the flushing out of the powerful vested political interests. (Thamm 2020)

Coetzee is believed to have devised and managed the assassinations and bombings that killed Ruth First, Jeanette Schoon (née Curtis) and her daughter Katryn, and maimed Albie Sachs, despite disclaimers recorded during the Truth and Reconciliation Commission where he later sought amnesty.[6] He must have been implicated in the development of Vlakplaas, a state-funded agency in counterinsurgency run by a team of mass murderers under the government's authority. Its commander, Eugene de Kock, was known by the press as 'Prime Evil' when he was later convicted of murder and crimes against humanity and sentenced to 212 years in prison (Gobodo-Madikizela 2003). The full extent of Coetzee's macabre career in which he oversaw developments like these, standing knee deep in the blood of many but with clean hands in public, does not emerge fully in the proceedings of the commission. As indicated above, most police records have been destroyed. The word 'apartheid' describes itself – it tore people's lives apart, even the lives of its chief agents, and it penetrated Coetzee's own family. Perhaps his son, who hanged himself in a psychiatric clinic, and his wife, who shot herself, knew more about him than they could bear (see 'Apartheid General's Wife Commits Suicide').[7] This was the man who goaded me repeatedly during interrogation with questions described on Day 39, 'Why are you left-wing people all so maladjusted?'

The five police officers named in my account include majors Swanepoel and Coetzee and their lieutenants, who interrogated me in two teams. Swanepoel's team was comprised of himself and Lieutenant J.B. (Gawie) Richter working as a pair; Lieutenant Trevor Baker and a colleague whose name I cannot recall, working as another pair; and a third pair whose names are also lost to memory. Richter and Baker reached the rank of lieutenant colonel before retiring.

This interrogation team kept me awake and on my feet on a brick for much of the time. Coetzee's team included Lieutenant J.H.L. (Jorrie) Jordaan and Coetzee himself. Jordaan was the man who – they would later brag to me – had arrested John Blacking, the professor of anthropology at Witwatersrand University, some six months previously. Jordaan was a police spy who passed as a student at Witwatersrand University and was present in the lecture theatre where I was detained. He assisted Coetzee in the review of my interrogation notes and in the manufacture of what they called 'my statement'. They were all known to my parents and my partner by name at the time, and Swanepoel and Coetzee are named by Major Unna, the Israeli Consul General, in his account later in this memoir.[8] They were also present on the day of my departure from Jan Smuts Airport, where they were seen and named by my brother David, though my sister can only remember Swanepoel. Their identities and later rank and status have been further confirmed by Paul Erasmus, formerly a detective warrant officer, who joined the service in 1976, went on to become a deputy commander in their Stratcom Unit, and was discharged on medical grounds. He gave evidence to the Truth and Reconciliation Commission at inquiries into the deaths of Ahmed Timol and Neil Aggett, who perished in police custody. He was introduced to me by Frank Dutton, the Chief Investigator of the Goldstone Commission who specializes in war crimes and crimes against humanity (See 'Frank Dutton', https://en.wikipedia.org/wiki/Frank_Dutton). Paul Erasmus has authorized the inclusion of his own name and credentials in this account, together with his confirmation of the names, identities, ranks and statuses of these five named Security Police officers under whom he later served. He informed me further that Jordaan also reached the rank of lieutenant colonel before retirement. Jordaan's name has been further verified by viewing – thanks to the help of Zureena Desai herself and the historian Susanne Klausen – archive copy of the *Rand Daily Mail*, the liberal Johannesburg newspaper that reported on Blacking and Desai's arrest and trial (*Rand Daily Mail*, 28 March 1969), where Jordaan and Coetzee are named as the Security Police officers in charge of the case.[9] There were other police officers involved in my case whose names I have not been able to retrieve – the three detectives who made my arrest at Witwatersrand University, and a further three interrogation staff who made up the team of six who dragged me through the sleep deprivation.

Sleep deprivation and solitary confinement leave no physical scars. During proceedings in the Truth and Reconciliation Commission against the men described here, I chose not to stand up alongside those who had lost loved ones, limbs or physical health. What I would have reported was that they kept me without sleep for five nights and six days, forced me to stand on a brick for much of it and then put me in solitary confinement in the Hanging Jail to listen to the condemned singing before their execution, finally subjecting me to deportation as the only way out. At the end they threatened us as a family against any public disclosures. And what would the perpetrators have had to say in their own defence – that I should be grateful that they did not kill me? I believe it was in their planning and their power. I could have been one more amongst the many others killed in detention. This too is a story worth telling. Albie Sachs's Foreword and the work we have done together on this book have been deeply enabling. The stones are only now being lifted off some of the sites of state-sponsored terror where they have hidden police murder and judicial complicity for decades.

Sadly, my parents are no longer alive to celebrate the publication of this memoir. At the time they instructed the best lawyer they could find to act on my behalf. Raymond Tucker's human and legal advice in the endeavour that led to my release is recorded in the Acknowledgements. However, he advised my parents that I was beyond the reach of the law – the Terrorism Act was the law. It gave the police sole authority to determine detention without limit of time. I was denied right of access to any outside parties, and no one was allowed to furnish information for or about me. My parents were encouraged to take what action they could, and in their battle for access to me they put themselves seriously at risk. They secured influence from unexpected quarters, and my release was negotiated with the condition that I left the country immediately.

My then girlfriend, who became my first wife, our beloved daughter, who came to us four years later, my brothers and sister, my stepson and a circle of close friends who lived the ordeal with me, then and afterwards, stood by me and have played their own part in what follows. Of the many others detained at the time, a small group was prosecuted, another group was used to testify against them as state witnesses, a third group was released months or years later, a fourth group disappeared forever, a fifth group died in detention or immediately after their release, and a sixth group was 'turned' to become agents or informers of the system – another kind of death. We read about some of these when they gave state evidence at the trial. During preparation for the first trial, Joel Carlson, the lawyer representing the twenty-two accused, reported to the Johannesburg *Sunday Times* on 2 November 1969 that, 'under existing laws [The Suppression of Communism Act], it was impossible to know for sure how many had been arrested, how many had been released, who were to be witnesses and if these were to be the only charges or whether there would be further trials'. Carlson's pursuit of justice for detainees is described in Days 24–32 of this memoir. After their second acquittal, he and his family were subjected to death threats, attempted letter bombs and many other forms of police-based intimidation that eventually drove them out of the country (Carlson 1973).

This is a difficult story to tell, and it may not be easy to read. Music is a guide and consolation. One of the songs from the years of struggle, 'Senzenina', means in isiZulu, isiXhosa and siSwati 'What have we done (that we must suffer so)?'[10] It emerged in the 1950s in the church halls and restricted gatherings permitted at the time. Over the years it swelled into the tide that overwhelmed apartheid's pernicious laws. In the decade before Mandela's release, we would watch from London and see televised documentaries and news broadcasts of battles in the townships in which police in armoured cars (called Casspirs) fired live ammunition on children and families, whose only defence was their number. As crowds grew in strength and size through the years, this song gained in power. People would hold their hands high above their heads and sing its single, opening line in spontaneous and repeated harmonies, with a bottomless sorrow. It is now sung by choral groups worldwide, some of which may be unaware of its origins. People are drawn to the song's appeal as a worldwide anthem against injustice, and they rise in stature as they sing it. Twenty years ago, my daughter, living in Devon, England, rang to tell me with pride that her women's choral group was singing it for a local performance. I recently learnt that it was in the repertoire of the choir of a close friend, Jenny Zobel in Harlech, North Wales. It is a song of grace in defiance. Like many of the other songs of the struggle, it defied the weaponry of the police, who lost more and more control as they meddled with the temper of crowds inspired by these songs. So many were buried to its chords that 'Senzenina' became one of the songs of leave-taking at funerals. Its later verses were changed to sing of meeting in heaven with the lost. I cannot hear it without weeping, and used to think of it as the voice of others' hurt; but in writing this memoir, I have found it is also about my own. It says to me, not only 'What have we done?' but 'What did they do to us?' It defies perpetrators and consoles the injured. I have written my account in this spirit – to defy the perpetrators of my past, to call on others to join me in defying today's perpetrators, and to invite public concern for the well-being of refugees and survivors. In my day we were almost invisible, but we have a high profile today. I was one amongst many tens of thousands, and I tell this story on behalf of us all. May the words match up to their task.

In South Africa, celebration replaces sorrow as people's lives are lived out in freedom, which is reflected in the country's music. 'Asimbonanga Mandela' is a popular song composed in the 1980s about the country's leader, who at the time was still imprisoned on Robben Island.[11] It was one of the many songs that appealed for his release, and it says: 'We have not seen Mandela' and sings out the names of some who perished in police custody – Steve Biko, Victoria Mxenge, Neil Aggett – saying: 'We have not seen our brother or sister in the place where they died. And you, and you, and you, when will we arrive at our destination?' Johnny Clegg and Savuka, the band who gave it birth, sang it at a famous open-air concert in Paris in 1999. As it appeals for sight of the man who had already been president for some years, Mandela himself appeared from the darkness backstage, without warning and completely by surprise, dancing hand in hand with the lead vocalist, Mandisa Dlanga. Mandela had attended the concert unannounced during a state visit to France. They danced to the front of the stage as she called out Mandela's praises, and they took the crowd by storm. Watching, you see caution on Mandela's face open to joy as he comes to the front, and his delight is radiant.

Some of the places in which I encountered horror are still there. I used to listen to the condemned singing their comrades through their last night alive, and they would fall into silence before the dawn executions. The prison is still there and the gallows stand as a museum and memorial, but there have been no hangings since 1990. Albie Sachs reports in his Foreword how, in the first sitting of the country's new Constitutional Court in 1995, they chose to make their first judicial ruling a decision about the death penalty – and they repealed it. The fear that those gallows cast throughout the country was lifted, and my memoir is dedicated to those who perished there. For many, including me, Albie Sachs's account is the first description we have read of how the Constitutional Court went about its work. I am honoured to have my memoir opened with his account of those historic events. Compol Building ('Compol' stands for Commissioner of Police) in Pretoria is now a police museum; and in Johannesburg 'The Fort', the jail that stood at the top of Hospital Hill, has been demolished and replaced with the Constitutional Court. This jail once held Gandhi, and Nelson and Winnie Mandela. In the Introduction I describe how our gardener, Paul Moesethle, and countless others, were brutalized there. Constitution Hill now stands as a beacon for justice and a landmark of transformation. Some of the key textbooks recommended by Albie Sachs that describe the workings of constitutional law in South Africa, and the constitution's Bill of Rights, are listed in the Bibliography (Currie and de Waal 2005; de Vos and Freedman 2014; Brand and Gevers 2015).

The Introduction describes some of my childhood in Johannesburg and Swaziland in the 1950s and 1960s. The central portion of this book, 'The Days', describes fifty-five winter days in 1969, from my arrest on Friday 13 June to my release on Wednesday 6 August. It follows a daily narrative interrupted in places to furnish readers with explanations about the story and its context. The interruptions are clearly marked out. The police took me to the airport from prison, allowed me half an hour to say goodbye to my family, and saw me onto a plane to Israel. I could not return freely for the next twenty-five years. The Epilogue describes the contribution I have made to therapeutic work with other survivors over the decades that followed. The memoir is concluded with an Afterword offering reflections on the differences between memory and testimony, source material from the literature of imprisonment and resistance, my correspondence with the South Africa History Archive and an inventory of articles from the papers of the day, called 'What the Press Said'. This is followed by 'Acknowledgements' and three appendices. The first appendix contains my Arrest Warrant, which I saw for the first time when it was secured from the National Archives in 2019. The second appendix contains the text of Section 6 of the Terrorism Act of 1967 under which I was held, 'The Sword', and this is contrasted with the text of the new constitution's Bill of Rights, 'The Ploughshare'; and Albie Sachs, one of its authors, provides a commentary. The third appendix contains a report on psychotherapy with survivors that I wrote to guide our practice when we established the Medical Foundation for the Care of Victims of Torture (now Freedom from Torture) in London in 1985 and in the years following. The memoir is illustrated with photographs of entries written into my prison diary.

Those of my records that formed the basis of my original article are called on here. I managed to hide a police pen on me when taken from interrogation to solitary confinement, and I kept a secret diary on toilet paper. I had no idea just how many others in similar circumstances had recourse to this driving determination to record what was happening to us. Some of the others are cited in the Afterword. Under conditions of close observation, I could only keep the toilet paper diary secret for a limited time, and have described how it was stolen from my cell on Day 20. Although later assured of its return, I never saw the toilet paper again. The warders did not take my pen and so I just kept writing. Later the police even allowed me ordinary notepaper to write on. I was allowed to take a Bible with me to prison so kept another record here and a calendar on its flyleaf, which is reproduced at the front of this Prologue. I used coded annotation to keep track of what was happening. Other entries in the Bible include poetry, coded notes and transcriptions of Biblical text, some of which are also included. Other documents, including entries from some of the surviving paper and toilet paper diaries, are reproduced in 'The Days'. These include notes and letters to my family; correspondence from my mother, who wrote to the country's (then) prime minister on my behalf; and a note by Janet Beattie, my partner at the time. She was allowed a visit on Day 30, and the note she made describes my condition at the time. Following the police rebuttal of my *Observer* article in 1970, my mother gave the *Rand Daily Mail* an account of the desperate state in which she found me during her prison visits, but the newspaper chose not to publish this because of police threats. That material is now written into the 'The Days'. Detail about the later and continuing threats are documented in the Afterword, along with the newspaper sources.

In the year after my release I found amongst the papers sent on to me in London, writing fragments left behind by Mongane Wally Serote after he stayed with us in June 1969. He was arrested just before me, soon after he left our home. He had written these lines as a tribute to another one of his friends who had already been arrested. He was not to know that his own arrest would soon follow, any more than I could foresee mine. He wrote to wish his friend strength through interrogation and detention. Of apartheid and its agents, he wrote: 'Time and the truth are not on their side.' I write now to honour his words. With the publication of this memoir, we will celebrate the eventual upshot of this and the many other stories, together with our children and grand-children. And we will join with the unnumbered others whose loved ones were driven alone into the darkness.

Notes

1. For the passage in Akhmatova's poem 'Almost in an Album', from which these lines are taken, see Appendix 3.
2. Niemöller's prose poem about public complicity in the persecution of others can be found at the following website: https://en.wikipedia.org/wiki/First_they_came_... It is reviewed in: *And the Witnesses Were Silent: The Confessing Church And The Jews* (Gerlach 2000: 47). It gives the context of his own early complicity with the Nazis, and then his human rights stand on behalf of the Jews and the persecuted others, which led to his own imprisonment.
3. 'Author and scholar Jacob Dlamini writes that in this purge of its misdeeds, this "paper Auschwitz", (was) a conscious effort by the apartheid state to "deliberately and systematically destroy a huge body of state records and documentation in an attempt to remove incriminating evidence and thereby sanitise the history of oppressive rule."' See Thamm (2020). Retrieved 26 June 2020 from: https://www.dailymaverick.co.za/article/2020-06-25-alleged-apartheid-era-criminals-must-account-and-there-are-many-in-happy-retirement/.
4. The Truth and Reconciliation Commission (TRC) reports that:
   > It was widely believed by many political activists of the time that, in the early 1960s, a special squad of security policemen received special training in torture techniques in France and Algeria and that this accounted for a sudden and dramatic increase in torture. The Commission established that the following officers received training in France at some point during the first half of the 1960s: Hendrik van den Bergh (then head of the Security Branch), TJ 'Rooi Rus' Swanepoel, DK Genis, Lieutenant Daantjie 'Kardoesbroek' Rossouw, G Klindt, a Major Brits (from the Railway Police), a Lieutenant van der Merwe and one Coetzee . . .
   > Following the general failure of the Security Branch to conclude investigations into sabotage cases in the early 1960s, a tougher approach was adopted, and a group of police was drawn in from outside the ranks of the Security Branch to constitute a special 'sabotage squad' . . . part of a more extensive restructuring of legal provisions . . . introduced by the new Minister of Justice, Police and Prisons, BJ Vorster . . . Officers associated with this squad include: Major TJ 'Rooi Rus' Swanepoel, Major George Klindt, a Major Coetzee, Major Britz, Lieutenant DK Genis, 'Kardoesbroek' Rossouw and a Captain or Major JJ van der Merwe. Others who appeared to form part of this team, or who worked closely with them, include Warrant Officer 'Spyker' van Wyk, Captain JJ Viktor, Lieutenant Petrus Ferreira, Lieutenant Erasmus, Lieutenant and/or Captain van Rensberg and Sergeant Greeff. (See 'The Use of Torture in Detention', which is an extract from the TRC's final report.)
5. 'The TRC (Truth and Reconciliation Commission) found that Colonel Theuns "Rooi Rus" Swanepoel of the SA Police Riot Unit – a notorious thug – adopted a "shoot to kill" policy. The police action ignited the fury of the young marchers. By midday rioting had broken out across Soweto. See 'Remembering and Learning from the Past:

The 1976 Uprising and the African Working Class'; and Tutu et al 1998, Truth and Reconciliation Commission Final Report, Vol. 3, Chapter 6, Sub-section 20, page 568, paragraphs 153–70. 'The Commission finds that Captain Swanepoel (and others) . . . were responsible for the excessive use of force which led to the death of 575 students. 2,380 people were wounded, more than 2,000 arrests took place, and 11 died in custody. The number of incidents of torture escalated and the State, Minister of Police and Commissioner of Police were directly responsible for gross human rights violations.' Retrieved from: 'https://sabctrc.saha.org.za/reportpage.php?id=13472&t=%2Bswan epoel+&tab=report'.

6. See 'Coetzee's "Fairy Tales" – The Mail & Guardian 11/09/1998': Retrieved 1 December 2020. https://mg.co.za/article/1998-09-11-coetzees-fairy-tales/\.

7. See 'Apartheid General's Wife Commits Suicide', 2013.

8. Itzhak Unna was known to us at the time only by his military rank, which is also how the police referred to him. I saw how he took up a position alongside South Africa's Security police majors, as their ranking equivalent. On his later appointment as Israel's ambassador, he must have set this rank aside in his public profile. See 'Itzhak Unna Appointed Ambassador to SA'. Retrieved October 2020 from http://www.jta .org/1974/03/11/archive/israel-names-full-ambassador-to-south-africa.

9. I am grateful to Zureena Desai herself for the information she recently shared about those events 51 years ago, and for introducing me to the historian Susanne Klausen whose further confirmation led me to these newspaper reports in the *Rand Daily Mail*. Klausen's forthcoming book about South Africa's Immorality Act will be published in 2022. A preliminary publication of hers on the subject is referenced below (Klausen 2021).

10. See '"Senzenina" by Cape Town Youth Choir', 2010 (formerly Pro Cantu Youth Choir) 2010. youtube.com. Retrieved May 2020 from https://www.youtube.com/ watch?v=5fDU1PYWT8A.

11. See 'Asimbonanga by Johnny Clegg (With Nelson Mandela)', 1999. youtube.com. Retrieved May 2020 from https://www.youtube.com/watch?v=BGS7SpI7obY.

INTRODUCTION
The Years Before

I was supposed to be a man by the time I turned 21, by anyone's reckoning. By the apartheid regime's reckoning, I was also old enough to be tortured. Looking back, I can recognize the boy I was. The eldest of my grandchildren is now approaching this age, and I would never want to see her or the others – or indeed anyone else – having to face any such ordeal. At the time my home was in Johannesburg, only some thirty miles from Pretoria, where I was thrown into a world that few would believe existed, populated by creatures from the darkest places, creatures of the night, some in uniform. I was there for fifty-five days, and never went home again. This Introduction has been written with the support and participation of my brothers and sister. We had an eventful and curious childhood, which was capped by my detention. We were all affected by the events described below, and our bonds continue to see us through.

I start with my father's father Harry, our grandfather whom we knew as Oupa. His stories went back to his youth in Lithuania, nearly as far back in his life as the story of imprisonment reaches in mine. We loved his stories. They were recounted in a Yiddish accent in a deep, slow voice, and were given in great deliberation with big hand gestures for emphasis. On the margins of memory, and confirmed by family photographs that remain a delight, was the experience of my brother Colin and me being scooped up by him, and each of us put on one of his big knees. At a crucial moment, to make his point or to let us hear exactly how Red Riding Hood or The Three Bears or The Three Little Pigs made calls on their own grandparents, or were called on by the wolf, he would break into Yiddish. The wolf would say, '*Kinderlekh, kinderlekh, loz mir arayn*' [Little children, little children, let me come in]. These were the only Yiddish words some of us knew. Oupa told of the ice and snow of Lithuania. We had never seen ice or snow. He told of losing one of his galoshes in a deep snow fall. We wanted to know what galoshes really looked like – they sounded like such strange foot garments. And we wanted to know what a wolf sounded like. He would lift his head up and howl like a wolf was supposed to do, and we would copy him. They would send flour from their mill in their hometown of Keidan to the nearby city of Kovno, and to keep the wolves at bay in winter, they would put a strong man on the back of the sled with a stick. We would want to know how big the stick was, and he would show us with outstretched arms. We were accustomed to the story's repetition, and would stretch out our own arms, anticipating his gestures. There was another favourite story about a place he called the Belgian Congo. A certain Mr McDougal went there to see the gorillas and pygmies in a big truck with very high wheels. We heard the story so often that we would raise our hands as he came to the account of just how big the wheels were. He would pause and ask us to show him how big the wheels were, how big the gorillas were and how small the pygmies were.

Immigration controllers today would call our Oupa an 'unaccompanied minor'. Aged fifteen and alone, he sailed from the Baltic coast via England and arrived in Cape Town in 1901 after three weeks at sea, surviving on rye bread and pickled cucumbers, and arriving with only one shilling and sixpence in his pocket. As he was getting off the ship, the cannon at the harbour fort sounded noon, the daily time signal. Alarmed that the Boer War had come to Cape Town, he turned around to get back on board. But his uncle was waiting on the quayside, and he called out to reassure him. He had family who had already settled there, so he had a place in their home and went to school in District Six, where he learnt English. He later moved up to Johannesburg with them, where he founded a business selling paraffin to the claim hunters on the mines. When he died sixty-four years later, he left a widow, five children, thirteen grandchildren, and a thriving oil company. Four more grandchildren were born in the years that followed. Three have passed away, and the remaining fourteen of us are living in Canada, South Africa, the UK and the USA; and in the next generation we have cousins who have moved to Australia and Israel.

I come from a long line of storytellers – at least, I am in the third generation of storytellers known to us. The stories of those who lived before our grandparents' generation lie in the silence of unmarked graves. They perished in 1941, almost to a person. I have visited these killing fields outside Lithuania's towns and villages where the Jewish population – three-quarters of a million people – were gunned down by the *Einsatzgruppen*, the killing arm of the Nazi SS, assisted by Lithuanian collaborators. Our Oupa lost his entire family there, with the exception of one sister who survived, and one baby who was a hidden child. We do not even know how to calculate their numbers (Oshry 1995; Lerer-Cohen and Issroff 2002; Levinsonas 2006). My four grandparents were only 'spared' because they or their parents had taken the adventurous option of emigration two generations earlier, when threats against Jews in the Russian Empire sparked a mass migration. So, in the eyes of those left behind early in the twentieth century, our grandparents went to a remote place called 'The

Cape' situated in the South Atlantic at the bottom of Africa. After the Boer War there was extensive settlement on the goldfields, and Johannesburg and the other Reef towns grew on the proceeds. My parents were born there, as I was, and my three siblings.

The stories are passed on to this day by our Uncle Ivan, Oupa's youngest child, who is now in his eighties. Along with our father and other uncles – Uncle Issie, my father's older brother, and Uncle Charles, husband of my father's younger sister – they are in the second generation of storytellers. Ivan's own stock of stories took a turn in the direction of modernity, along with his interest in jazz and architecture. One of his greatest was about 'Jack and the Pulsating Chicken Liver Orchards', but its title is all I can recall. Our father's stories had his own unique humour, and his greatest tale was about Fifi Matzpanis (Fifi Marzipan) from Vladivostock. We loved the sounds of the words, the French and Yiddish in one great name, and a place so far away that it was on the wrong side of the world where everything was back to front. Fifi would emerge as a figure in his many accounts of impossible events and strange people. My sister even had a doll with her name, which her children – now adults – know all about.

I was named after my mother's father, John Romm. He died in a farm accident three years before I was born. He was still driving himself around his farm in a horse and cart at the age of 77, but by then he was deaf and he did not hear an approaching train on the line that went nearby. His startled horse bolted and overturned the cart, and he did not survive. He came from Rokishik, another Lithuanian town, and moved to the Cape after first settling in Baltimore, Maryland, where the rest of his family had made their home. We never learnt why he left them there but we grew up knowing that, as the youngest of twelve, he had a large family in the USA, and we continue our connection with this family association.[1] He trained as a bookkeeper in Baltimore and must have done well enough in the Cape to buy a highveld farm at Syferbult, just outside Krugersdorp, during the last years of the Transvaal republic. He was a Bundist, the follower of an association of Jewish socialists in Eastern Europe and Russia. His life was informed by these values, and they were passed on to us by my mother. During the Anglo-Boer War he hid his farm horses in their living room to show empty stables to the 'Khakies', the British soldiers, who would have requisitioned them for military use. He made them available instead to the Boers, the underdogs in the conflict, whom he supported, but when the Union of South Africa was declared in 1910, he joined the protest against the restriction of citizenship to whites only.

His first wife and child both died in childbirth. Later, during a reclusive life on his farm, he and my grandmother, Annie Adelson who we later called Babela, befriended each other when he brought milking cows into town to the kosher dairy that she ran with her family in Krugersdorp. They had originally been family acquaintances in Lithuania. On marrying, they settled on his farm, and their only child, my mother, was born there. They were known as *Afrikaanse Jode*, Jewish Afrikaners, and they spoke Yiddish in the home and Afrikaans on the farm, which was named after my mother in her honour. Ruthville became a visiting place for friends and family from Johannesburg, many of whom had radical views. My mother was given her name because she was born on the Jewish festival of Shavuot (The Giving of the Law), when we read the Book of Ruth in synagogue. Decades later, when I visited the farm with my mother and her cousin to track our history, we found elderly staff who recognized her and still remembered my grandfather. They called him *'Die Baie Ou Jood'* (the very old Jew), and said he looked after everyone, black and white, English and Afrikaans. When Colin and I were little, my parents took us there for weekends, and on arriving, we would jump out of the car and run into the arms of his widow, my grandmother, who lived alone. She would scoop us up and embrace us with love and warmth, calling us 'Babela, babela, babela' – 'little baby' in Yiddish. She became known to us as 'Babela', and we still refer to her that way. When the farm was sold, she came to live with us and brought Yiddish and her exuberant love into our Johannesburg home. She was very present in our lives, but my mother was jealous of her mother's exuberance and sometimes there was trouble. When we later moved to Swaziland, we left her in a residential hotel in Orange Grove. Despite having devoted family nearby, she did not get over our departure, and died one year later.

Fifty years ago, the world of my childhood was in the northern suburbs of Johannesburg where most of the Jewish population lived. The year was filled with family occasions and religious festivals when we gathered in one another's homes or on the verandas of our gardens. Most other children knew no one from outside these circles except for the people called 'servants' who lived in outhouses behind our homes. We were unusual because my mother came from a farming world beyond; and my father had been to the war 'up North', where he had learnt Italian. He also spoke Afrikaans and isiZulu. They had an adventurous spirit and a moral concern that set us apart from many of the other families we knew; and they took a genuine interest in the welfare of our domestic servants whose bounty we lived on, though we knew little about them as human beings.

The suburban gardens were full of exotic trees – jacaranda, oak, pin oak, liquid amber, flame trees, camphor, syringa and blue gum – in full leaf through the summer when afternoon storms filled the sky with black clouds. Today these suburban gardens are the continent's largest human-made forest, planted with indigenous and unfamiliar trees that provide homes to birds drawn from far and wide – it even has its own microclimate. Thunder and lightning accompanied the downpours that filled the air with the smell of rain on dry earth. In winter the trees were bare, and everything was scorched brown by drought and cold. Winter skies on the highveld are a bright cobalt blue that I have found nowhere else. They bleed into sunsets coloured crimson by the mine dust. I was told that when I was little, if we were out driving beyond our suburban sanctuary and saw a mine dump – mine dumps used to be everywhere, mountains of pale orange sand along with slag heaps and pitheads, and one of them had a drive-in cinema on its flat top – I would get upset if someone in the car said 'there's a mine dump' and I would challenge them. No, I would say, 'it's *my* dump'. Over the years these mine dumps disappeared in stages as they were consumed by more advanced refining techniques that extracted further gold from even the spent ore.

We had no idea what mines were. We never heard the hooters sending people to work at dawn or signalling 'tjaila' (Time out!) in the evenings. We knew nothing about the hundreds of thousands of men coming by train and railway bus from all over Southern Africa to work underground on contracts that allowed them home for just a few weeks a year. Their destinations were the gold mines of the East and West Rand and the coal mines of the eastern Transvaal that run from Witbank to Breyton. We did not feel the tremors of the underground explosions as they blasted ore out of the rock and, as children, we knew nothing of miners' phthisis and tuberculosis. We did not know that from the equator south, our city was known amongst black people as 'Egoli', the Place of Gold. The region was responsible for more than half the world's gold at the time, and, more recently, for coal, uranium and platinum. Miners lived in hostels as virtual prisoners and worked in shifts that ran round the clock. Their proprietors traded shares on the Johannesburg Stock Exchange during the day, and in the evenings they went home to their families in the northern suburbs (Van Onselen 1982; Mandy 1984; Wheatcroft 1986; Sampson 1987).

Our suburban world ended where our father's parents, Oupa Harry and Granny Janie, lived above the ridge in Yeoville, near the synagogue that we called 'shul'. We were at their home on Friday nights and went to shul on Saturday mornings. Following our move to Swaziland, I went to live with them for a year to prepare for my bar mitzvah and returned to the primary school that I had previously left. Their home in Regent Street was a family landmark – important and mysterious. You could hide beneath the hydrangeas in the front garden, climb the jacaranda tree in the side garden where you could pick soft fruit, and in the back garden the fig tree produced a crop that fed everyone, even the birds. It is still there, but is now in the grounds of a block of flats. Back then, the toilet did not flush easily, the fridge made very strange noises, and every internal and outside door had to be locked every night and then unlocked by my grandfather in the morning. My school was nearby and, as well as the secular curriculum, I had regular lessons in Hebrew, Torah, Scriptures and Liturgy. As the bar mitzvah came closer, I had private lessons to learn how to read the Torah in shul for the occasion, and when the event came I was ready for it and was proud to do honour to my parents and family. My grandparents were gentle and loving, but remote, and, as the only child in their home, I had a lonely year and missed my Swaziland family. Their big dog Ben adopted me in the absence of his missing master, my Uncle Ivan, and we were inseparable. Friday night was the week's highpoint. I enjoyed a place of honour participating with my grandmother in the ritual lighting of the candles at sunset. There was serenity in her reverence for the prayers, and she was calm and gracious when we walked to shul. As we approached, we could hear the choir begin to sing the psalms that open the service, followed by a beautiful melody for the song that welcomes the Sabbath as a bride. My grandmother's faith was deep, grounding and beautiful, and was passed to me without any open sign of conveyance – I can feel it to this day.

Sometimes my father's older brother Israel, whom we knew as Uncle Issie, would attend with us for Friday night services, and then I would have a seating companion in the men's area, and he would guide me through the prayers. It was always a comfort, and this bond with him was to become a safeguard in the years to come when relations between my parents and my uncle broke down. We had opposing political views, but the catalyst for the break had to do with the inheritance due to us as a family on the death of our grandfather. Issie was the executor of our grandfather's will, but despite us living through serious financial strain, he stood in the way of its distribution for some five years. He became mayor of Johannesburg the year before my detention, but by then our families were not on speaking terms and the divide between us became a chasm on my arrest. Years later he did try to reach out to me across the divide, and on the rare and occasional visits that I could make to Johannesburg after deportation, he would make a point of taking me to the synagogue of his and my father's childhood, the old Jeppe Shul, which he would open for occasional services with fellow congregants. Whenever he visited London with his wife, our Auntie Phyllis, they would make a point of taking me out. In these later years the bond between him and my father was restored, and Uncle Issie, Auntie Phyllis and their daughters Elaine, Sandra and Jill showed my father a lot of kindness, befriending him and his partner Thelma. In these later years Issie's conduct with each of us – me and my siblings – was as might be expected of a benevolent uncle. The original enterprise that Oupa had established and run with his two sons, Issie and my father, was called the Pacific Oil Company. Thanks to Issie, Oupa's desk from Pacific Oil was passed on to my father during his latter years in Joburg. It became Thelma's desk during her lifetime and, now with me, is the desk on which I have written this book.

Going back to those early years, the whole extended family would arrive for the Friday night meal – aunts, uncles and especially cousins. My father was the middle of five children, with an older and younger brother and an older and younger sister, and in those years we were close as a family. I had the room that belonged to my Uncle Ivan, the youngest of them, who was away in Israel. After everyone else left, the Friday night candles, the 'Shabbes lights', would burn themselves out through the night in a quiet corner and I would go and sit by them on my own, which I found to be a hallowed time.

Years earlier, on the way up Munro Drive, we could look back from the car going up Houghton Ridge to see the suburbs spread out for miles towards Pretoria. At the viewing point we would sometimes be taken out of the car to look back – our parents took delight in introducing us to what we could see. From here the suburban lights twinkled into the distance in winter, and in summer the houses and their tree-filled gardens stretched as far as we could see. At the top of Munro Drive was the ridge of white water, the Witwatersrand, where gold was discovered in 1886. It sparked one of the world's great gold rushes and, like other such events of the time, it brought immigrants from far and wide. This one had a character of its own based on the extraordinary underground reserves and the ruthless ingenuity of Britain's colonial policies that turned indigenous populations into mining and industrial labour. Jews from a small locality in Lithuania came in numbers, some in flight from persecution and others as economic migrants, and they settled in the cities and country towns. The original population of white settlers, the Afrikaners, were subjected to two wars of conquest by the British Empire and were then turned into the Union's policemen. When their National Party won the election in 1948, they took matters into their own hands and created the apartheid government. Going south beyond Yeoville, through Hillbrow and into town, the street names tell of the opening phases of the gold rush: Twist, Quartz, Claim, Banket, Nugget and End streets. Its British overlords were known as the Randlords in their day, and many of the other streets, suburbs and districts of the city were named accordingly – Empire Road, Harrow Road, Houghton, Oxford Road, Munro Drive, Rosebank and Yeoville (Thompson 2000).[2]

South-western townships – hence 'Soweto' – stands on the periphery of Johannesburg, providing homes to a black population once as large as the rest of the city areas combined. Closer to our home, on the edge of the northern suburbs, was Alexandra township, housing a black population who serviced the white homes and industries of the area. We only saw it from a distance – it was known then as the Dark City because it had no public lighting. Its streets then were untarred and rutted, and only some of its houses had basic utilities – water, electricity and sewerage. It had its own shanty town on the Far East Bank where people made homes of corrugated iron and plywood boards, some of which would tumble into the river valley in heavy rain. Its layout, like nearby Tembisa and other such townships, shows how apartheid's planners – the inheritors of Britain's original policies – gave a squared-off place to labour. They are defined rectangles with industries and houses for whites outside all their margins. Today the street names are different, and reflect the new spirit of our times – Lenin Drive, Thoko Ngoma, Aldo Magano. 'Alex' was reached by travelling north along Louis Botha Avenue, beyond our dentist and the Doll's House – a roadside eating house and one of our favourite places – and then to the Pretoria main road, the M11, which still stands as the township's western boundary. I travelled on this road in the back of a police car on the day of my arrest as we went to Pretoria.

As the first-born generation of local whites, my parents lived in compliance with the order of the many apartheid practices they inherited, but they stood in opposition to the principles and policies on which they were based. The combination of high principle and emotional neglect on which we were raised created confusion, especially as the principles – including family loyalty – were contradicted by their neglect. They could be remote and absent, and neither of them found children's need easy. We had better and more loving relations with them when we were older and needed them less. As children we were reliant on family, friends and neighbours and, following the death of our maternal grandmother Babela in 1960, we were especially reliant on our domestics. Boarding school later provided our parents with a way out of the problems they faced over the care they could not give us, and there I became a parental child looking out for my younger brothers. I had already left for university by the time my sister arrived at the boarding school. Our first farm was sold in 1967, and for several years our family home was relocated to Johannesburg. Our parents then re-established themselves on a new farm in Swaziland where my mother remained, long after all the children had left.

Our parents were married in 1947, the year after my father returned from service in the Italian campaign in the Second World War. They spent the first year of their marriage in a political campaign against the impending government of the newly formed National Party – an alliance of fascists and Afrikaans nationalists who won the election just three months after my birth. Despite this setback, for the rest of their lives my parents remained in opposition through different kinds of activity. Before marrying, my mother played the piano at meetings of the Congress movement, organized by the Communist Party. At unguarded moments she could break into song and 'The Internationale' would emerge. She had a network of associations kept 'under cover' during my childhood, some of whom emerged as open-hearted new friends when I arrived in London as a refugee aged twenty-one. My parents contributed to feeding schemes for black people, and my mother became a member of the Black Sash, a non-violent movement of white women that was organized to resist apartheid. I would see her going out to attend street demonstrations wearing her black sash. I was unaware of all she did, but later learnt that they had brought cases of injustice to the attention of their MPs and kept vigils outside Parliament and government offices. Like other members, she was vilified by some in our Jewish community. Over dinner I would hear her telling my father about the catcalls and verbal abuse, such as 'kafferboeties' and 'nigger-lovers', with which they were attacked in public by apartheid's supporters.

There are links between my arrest and my parents' and grandparents' grounded sense of humanity. They were not colour-conscious like others of their generations. My parents spoke their minds and eventually acted on their principles and got away from apartheid by moving out of Johannesburg just before my eleventh birthday. I spent the following years in Swaziland, which was then a small British protectorate on South Africa's border, where my parents went farming.

Our move took us out of the world of privilege and prestige in which the rest of our Joburg family lived, and from then on our lives were troubled by emotional and financial insecurity. We were cherished by the place itself – our farm – and we have many good memories of its beauty, simplicity and fertility. It was called Mawawa, the siSwati name for the hadeda ibis that nested on both dams and by the river. The call of these birds as they came and went at sunset and dawn still evokes the daily passage of time. The farm was bordered on one side by a mountain and on another by the Great Usuthu River, which we could hear at night from our house. Despite its modesty, our home was a loving oasis two miles off the main road, the last homestead on a challenging dirt track, surrounded by trees – fruiting mulberry and flowering bauhinia – that brought an abundance of birdlife. We had no electricity, and the phone shared a party line with others. All the amenities were basic, but the sense of home was vivid and welcoming. We all have memories of lighting the mantles of the gas lamps in the evenings as the birdcalls outside grew silent, and it darkened to the night sounds of frogs and insects. The bookshelf on one side of the living room took up the whole wall, and on the other side of the same room, separated by our dining-room table, was the piano where we would gather to sing while my father played. As adults all four of us have created homely environments in our living spaces that bear some correspondence to our Mawawa home, especially in our gardens and in our love for the natural world. The Persian carpet we played on as children is still with me, and so is the dining-room table.

Following agricultural plans laid out by government research, my father and his team of workers planted ten thousand orange trees based on an irrigation system that fed the farming valley of Malkerns. The research was flawed, however, as the climatic conditions did not produce export-quality fruit and we had to fall back on cash crops. The Swazi people we lived amongst were kind and genial. Some lived in tribal areas over the river and came to work on a daily or weekly basis, and others had longer-stay homes in what was known as 'the compound'. Its facilities and living conditions were a grave indictment of my parents' liberal values. My father suffered from two serious lapses in his health, which added to the strain, and while I was away in the USA the farm was sold. I returned to find my mother back in Johannesburg and living in a rented flat with my siblings, who were attending local schools. My father worked to re-establish himself in Swaziland and in time he was successful with a new enterprise, a new and more modest farm and a new and inviting home. The strain between my parents was always worrying, however, and their marriage broke up in the year after my detention, at which point my father returned to life in Johannesburg and my mother remained in Swaziland. She was to live there for most of the next two decades.

Within a year of Janet and me arriving in the UK, David and Marian came to live with me in Brighton, where I had made a home while studying at Sussex University. Colin joined us a little later. As a family of uprooted siblings, we made our way as best we could. Life was never easy in those years, but I had already been 'trained' as a parental child and, though not always successful, I did what I could to look after my siblings – and, in the case of Marian at least, see to their education. David later returned to South Africa, where he has a flourishing life and, with his partner Felicity, a distinguished ceramic studio in Swellendam with an international reputation. Colin and Marian have also made their way in the UK on admirable terms. Colin works with his wife Simone in a London-based company restoring old stone and wood, and refurbishing homes. He has two grown-up daughters and three grandchildren. Marian is an educational psychologist with a PhD, and a distinguished career in local authority services and private practice; she lives in Norwich with her husband Peter, who is a consultant surgeon in the NHS. They have three grown-up children: one son and two daughters. She served as the president of the Norwich Hebrew Congregation and is currently the city's sheriff.

In the 1970s, my father returned to Johannesburg, where he established a settled life with a new partner, Rose Kay, and their relationship lasted nearly two decades. He worked first in business, and then he joined the much-loved partner of his later years, Thelma Carson, in a landscape and gardening company that she renamed Archie's Plants. On his death, the Johannesburg evening paper, *The Star*, published an obituary to him in their gardening section. My mother, who remained single for the rest of her life, went into agricultural business in Swaziland until her health failed, and she then retired to join us in the UK. In her first business, Swazifresh, she worked with the government to provide agencies for Swazi farmers just coming out of subsistence agriculture to help to market their produce. It did not fare well while she had a health crisis, but she started again in a second enterprise to provide food for the newly liberated country of Mozambique after the Frelimo government had taken charge in 1974. From a small office in Swaziland – now an intermediary country on the border of free Africa – she created a company that imported fresh produce from the Johannesburg food markets and exported it to Maputo, the newly named capital of Mozambique. She called on her background familiarity with the highveld farmers of the Transvaal – ultra-white, ultra-right and mostly Afrikaans – to convince them she could secure new markets for their produce in black Africa. She drew on political credentials, through my own story, to convince the new Frelimo government – black revolutionaries who had won a colonial war against the Portuguese – of her good faith. As an intermediary marketing agent who could be trusted by both warring parties of a major conflict, she brought South African meat and potatoes through Swaziland to feed people in the southern part of Mozambique, and we remain very proud of her legacy.

As different as my parents were, they shared deep-rooted interests in poetry, classical music and the natural world to which they introduced us, and they both looked towards a future for justice in South Africa. When my mother passed away in 2003, we placed an inscription on her tombstone in the Western Cemetery in Cheshunt, outside London, taken from the opening and closing verses of a poem she would often recite, even while living in the UK during her later years:

> Cast the window wider, sonny;
> Let me see the veld
> Rolling grandly to the sunset
> Where the mountains melt,
> With the sharp horizon round it,
> Like a silver belt.
> . . .
> There's a spot I know of, sonny,
> Yonder by the stream;
> Bushes handy for the fire,
> Water for the team.
> By the old home outspan, sonny,
> Let me lie and dream.
> —'The Veld' (P. Gibbon, in Crouch [1908] 2018: 65–66)[3]

My father died five years earlier and is buried amongst the rest of our family in Westpark Cemetery Johannesburg, where his tombstone has an inscription from Wordsworth:

> Therefore am I still
> A lover of the meadows and the woods,
> And mountains; and of all that we behold
> From this green earth . . .
> —'Lines Composed a Few Miles above Tintern Abbey' (Wordsworth 2006: 243)

It also has a poetry inscription from his partner Thelma – twenty years later she was buried nearby – with lines from a verse we were unable to source at the time. These lines were finally traced by Berghahn Books' editorial assistant Mykelin Higham to Oscar Hijuelos's *The Mambo Kings Play Songs of Love*, and we extend our grateful thanks to her.

Love is the sunlight of the soul
Water for the flowers of the heart
And the sweet-scented wind
Of the morning of life.
(Hijuelos 1989)

Going back to Johannesburg in the 1950s, the domestic servants of my childhood years are remembered for their special qualities, but most regrettably I cannot recall all their family names or places of origin. Paul Moesethle, Frieda, Martha and Rosie were like family members as they contributed to our lives in vital ways, but we knew little about theirs. There were others too – Augusta in the earlier years and Sergeant later on. I would have been about four when our father and Paul, our gardener, laid a concrete driveway at our house in Greenside. I slipped and cut my knee while playing in the rubble. It must have been a serious injury for I still have the scar. While recovering I had a recurring dream, and it still colours the landscape of childhood. The Johannesburg zoo was nearby, and we could hear the lions roar at night. In my dream a lion was on the loose. My father was standing guard inside the front door of the house with the pistol from his bedside cabinet, with Paul standing guard inside the back door with an assegai, a sharp-tipped spear. My mother and my baby brother Colin were protected in the inside bedroom, but I was stuck outside on one of the concrete strips, where my sore knee was stopping me from moving and I could not get back to safety. The lion was getting closer and I could hear it roar. There was a glare on the concrete, and everything was the stark grim yellow of rocks at Westpark Cemetery on the road going west – the same khaki yellow as the police uniforms.

There were always bad dreams. I would often go to my parents' bedroom in the night to tell them I had had a bad dream, and they would put me in bed between them. Sometimes in a dream the 'machayanis' and the 'tokoloshes' would come. Machayanis lived down the plug hole of the bath. Our nanny Frieda could only get us out of the bath by pulling the plug and waiting for the gurgling sound of the water running out to create enough fear to get us to jump into her arms. If we did not get out quickly enough, the machayanis would jump out of the plug hole and get us. The tokoloshes – evil spirits who threatened our servants in their bare concrete rooms in the backyard – were even more dangerous. They were always lurking, so the servants had to put their beds high up on bricks. When we were allowed to visit them in their rooms, they had to help us to jump to safety on their beds before the tokoloshes underneath could get us.

As children we were safe in the embrace of our families and servants, but nothing could protect us from the sense of threat that these servants faced every day. The lions on the loose wore khaki uniforms with gold buckles that said: SAP – South African Police. I knew their threat, both through our servants' fear and our parents' sometimes hopeless attempts to protect them. These 'lions on the loose' were Afrikaners with brown leather belts around their waists and over their shoulders. Each one had a gun in his holster. Their caps came low over their faces, and their arrival in police vans spelt trouble. We would see the vans on the road and they often had prisoners in open cages on the back. The crest worn on police caps and lapels had a lion above a shield supported by a springbok and a gemsbok which was also emblazoned on the country's passports and drivers' licences. Our later move to Swaziland allowed us to get British passports and Swaziland licences, and to refuse any use of the apartheid government's insignia. I never carried a South African identity card or passport, and to this day its detail, like the republic's original flag, 'Die Driekleur' (the tricolour), has the same nauseating effect on me as a swastika.

Paul first came to work for us in the garden before my memory begins. He must have been in his late teens when he arrived. Frieda, who worked in the kitchen and looked after the children, was older and took a motherly interest in him. In the yard they would chat to each other in their own language, Setswana, but when in the house they talked to each other only in English. That must have been the protocol. Sometimes when Frieda was unavailable to do the cooking, Paul would come inside to work in the kitchen, and later she would tease him for doing women's work. I do not know what became of Frieda, but Paul was with us for the next ten years. He even moved out with us when we left Johannesburg for Swaziland. He became our father's 'right handyman', as he called him, on the farm we moved to in what was still a British protectorate. He wore a hat like our father and, like him, smoked a pipe. Once we were settled in Swaziland he did not stay long. Our beloved dog Tigger was killed in a car accident on the drive outside the farmhouse soon after Paul returned to Joburg. My siblings remember the immediate days after Paul's going as a major loss. I was away at boarding school at the time, and returned for a weekend to find Paul gone and Tigger dead. Paul told us he wanted to go back to his own people so we 'passed him on' to our good friends who lived in Joburg, as white families did with their servants. He worked for them for much of the rest of his life, and I would sometimes see him when visiting them 'in town', which is what we called Joburg. There was always a bond between us. It was upsetting to see him get older at double the rate of the people he worked for. Age took its toll on the lives of our servants in very physical terms. I would often wonder if he knew what had become of me in the years that followed, especially while I was in prison.

Paul was a vital person with a laughing, mischievous way. He was always industriously working on one thing or another. When I was five, we moved from our first house in Greenside to a larger one in Oaklands; it had a big garden that our parents filled with flowers, so Paul had a lot of work to do! He introduced me to Setswana names for the birds and insects in our garden and

I learnt to tell the difference between those shongololos – millipedes – that were inquisitive and those he called stupid: inquisitive ones wriggled when you picked them up, and stupid ones just lay there doing nothing. In our garden we were visited occasionally by a hamerkop – a large ground-feeding bird that scoured the flowerbeds for grubs and insects, and especially for shongololos. Its Afrikaans name means 'hammerhead', and Paul would have called it 'mma-masiloanokê' in Setswana. Zulu and Swazi people call it 'thekwane' or 'impun-dulu', which translates as 'the lightning bird' in English. Mythology about it has generated a whole literature.[4] The large crest on the back of its neck gives it a unique appearance, and although it is now widely found in Joburg, along with many other species not previously found there, it was rare at the time. Paul told me the bird could bring lightning and so we had to be careful not to upset it. I would watch it foraging and wonder how it changed the weather, but heeded his advice and never dared to approach it. Paul knew little English when he came to work for us but he learnt quickly and was soon teaching me long words like 'inquisitive'.

He became an expert in everything, even in the kitchen, where I would watch him making mint or parsley sauce by chopping up the leaves that he had collected from our vegetable garden and simmering them in a pan. Some-times I would go outside with him and Frieda while they had their lunch, and I would also sit with them in their own kitchen, which was a little room in the backyard between their bedrooms. It was served by a cast-iron stove for which they chopped the wood in the yard. After preparing our greens in our kitchen, they would sit down in theirs to a meal of bare slices of white bread and sweet tea. When I asked my parents why they had bread with nothing on, I was told that that was what they preferred. Our parents were liberal employers, unlike the parents of many of my friends. In one grand house on Houghton Ridge the servants had to save the used tea bags of their 'master' and 'madam', as they were only permitted to use second-hand bags for themselves. Their 'master' was an engineer who designed some of Joburg's tallest buildings and their 'madam' had a regal presence in Jewish affairs and university life – they wanted for nothing. Second-hand tea bags were amongst the many details of the servants' daily lives that kept them in an abject position, as bare slices of bread did to ours.

Aged about five, I dislodged a brick that must have been loose, in the porch wall. The span of this memoir is marked out between this first story of a brick and the later story about a brick I was forced to stand on during interrogation. Paul was standing below the first brick, and it fell directly onto his forehead – an alarming accident. He was hurt and, looking up at me in anger, he held the brick up at me and said he would report me to my mother. I could see the bump bleeding – it came up like an egg on his shiny black forehead. I ran away to hide behind my mother's dressing table in their bedroom which is where she found me. With blazing eyes and a flare of rage, she beat me with my father's ties and belts that she pulled at random from the cupboard. I do not remember the physical injuries, but her blazing eyes and uncontrollable rage were dreadful. The nightmare of those blazing eyes would return to haunt me when I was in prison years later, and I had nightmares that my mother was peering in rage through the 'eye in the door', the peephole through which the guards scanned us when doing their inspections. At the time I injured him, Paul was the one who consoled me when I later went to join him in the garden. He was raking up leaves on the lawn and had put a record on my little black gramophone, and together we sang with the chorus, 'We'll catch a fox and put him in a box, and then we'll let him go.' Soon after that, together with a group of other little boys, I climbed up the trellis that now stood over the concrete strips of the driveway. I was the youngest, and when the time came to end our game and go in for dinner, I was the only one who could not get down. The others disappeared, and I was left alone and crying. Frieda found me and, looking up at me from below, she called my mother. Eventually Paul was sent for, and he climbed up quickly. Standing on the trellis frame, he picked me up and, with one arm firmly around my waist, he climbed down and put me into my mother's arms.

One day Paul was missing. I must have been seven. My parents explained that he had been to Warmbaths north of Pretoria. We visited there regularly with my maternal grandmother, Babela. There was a resort hotel built close to a series of natural hot springs. Paul's family lived there in a township in the veld and I knew that he visited them, but this time he did not return. After some days a letter arrived that upset my parents. He had written to them from jail. I had seen black people handcuffed to black policemen dragged down the street to jail. I imagined jail was even worse than the machayanis. My parents went into Paul's room with Frieda to search for his pass, and when they found it one of them drove off to collect him from the jail in town called The Fort. It was built into the side of a small mountain on the Rand, close to Hospital Hill – a dreadful place that we would try to look into as we drove past. The whole area is now the site of the country's new Constitutional Court. It took them a whole day to get him out, and seeing them return was one of the first great shocks of my life. Paul's face was so bruised that he could hardly open his eyes. My mother and Frieda took care of him and put gentian violet on his many lacerations. Frieda started wailing as soon as she saw him, and covered her face with her apron. Then, while tending to him, she made many loud exclamations in Setswana. Our GP, Doctor Willie, came by to do a house call and I heard him tell my mother that there appeared to be no damage to Paul's skull, but without an X-ray he could not be sure. I thought a skull was a ghostly thing, like the machayanis – I only saw skulls on the pirate flags of the ghost train at the funfair. Skulls had crossed bones beneath, and I was alarmed to be told that Paul had a skull inside his head. It was just as troubling to then be told that I also had a skull inside my head. I tried to find where it was but all I could feel was my head and face. Years later when I was in Pretoria Local Prison – 'The Hanging Jail' – and realized that the comforting songs in the evenings were coming from condemned men before their execution, I could only half allow myself to consider what it meant to have your head pulled off your spine by a noose.

Paul made a full recovery and then resumed his normal working routines. But he was subdued and quiet, and did not play much. When I could muster the courage, I asked him what had happened. He told me that he had forgotten to take his pass with him when he visited his family in Warmbaths. He had left it in his room at our home. There was a police search at the station when he got off the returning bus. They called on everyone disembarking to produce their passes, and arrested him when they found he did not have one. I asked him what it meant to be arrested and he showed me his wrists and the bleeding bruises that the handcuffs had made. When I was arrested fourteen years later there were no handcuffs and there was only moderate physical violence, but they had other methods for whites. When the police took Paul to the jail, he tried to talk to the chief policeman to say that he did have a pass but had accidentally left it at the house where he worked. He tried to tell them our phone number or get permission to make a call. The policeman got angry when he repeated the number, and he told me with a chuckle that he behaved like an 'inquisitive one' and would not keep still. They beat him, but still he would not stop asking for a phone call – so they beat him again. They were going to send him to another jail on a farm a long way off where he would have to dig potatoes for a month and then go back to his 'tribal' home near Warmbaths. He managed to get a paper and pen from one of the other prisoners, wrote a note to my parents and gave it to another prisoner who was about to be released. He posted it to us, and that was how they came to bail him out (Carlson 1973, Johnstone 1976).

I asked Paul what a pass was, and he showed me – a little brown book with writing in it. He showed me his name and the name of the place where he was born, near Warmbaths, where he was allowed to live freely, without a pass. Then he showed me where it said 'Influx Control', and explained that it said he could work in Johannesburg at our address, which was written into the pass – 9 Meyer Street, Oaklands, Johannesburg. My parents later told me that all black people had to have passes to live in Johannesburg. They were against the government that made this law, and thought it was terrible. They took a case against the police for Paul's injuries, but the police claimed that other prisoners had done this to him. Much of this was beyond me at the time but I did understand Paul's account of how the country's prime minister – the man he called 'The Big Boss', J.G. Strijdom – had a car that did not need an engine because there was a team of black people in harnesses who had to pull it along, like oxen. At that time, we were still travelling west to my grandmother Babela's farm in the Magaliesberg, where we would see the ox wagon pulled by many pairs of oxen. It made a grinding noise as it went down the road, groaning under a heavy load of mielies – maize cobs. Paul told me that a policeman with a big whip walked beside the team of people who pulled the prime minister. I had seen the man with the long whip beside the ox wagon. When I later asked my parents about this, they told me the prime minister was indeed a terrible man, but his car did have an engine and black people did not have to pull it. They reassured me that no one, not even the police, could whip black people – but Paul told me they did, and said I should keep it a secret.

Our holidays were spent on Cape beaches, celebrated worldwide for their beauty. When I was eight, we were near the end of our summer stay at a resort called Hermanus where friends in a beach party near our own – they came from the same Johannesburg suburb – passed on news that our home had been burgled. We had no phone in our rented accommodation so were otherwise out of touch. I was not sure what a burglary was. In a confusion between buglers and burglars, I wondered why strangers had come to play bugles in our home while we were away. In Johannesburg one road into town took us past a boys' secondary school – it was my Uncle Ivan's – and at certain times of the day you could see a cadet band marching up and down the playground to the tunes of their buglers. My mother told me in the years that followed that, when even younger, I would call them 'the tootle-toos' and would wonder if that was where the war was. At three or four I had thought my father had been to war across the school playground from which you could hear bugles and see target practice with rifles.

My parents' irritability towards my questions on the beach that day – about buglers and burglars – left me at a loss. We returned immediately and, after the long two-day drive home, we found the place ransacked. I accompanied my father to the local police station where he filed the incident report. Standing beside him at the public enquiry desk where he was speaking to a big white policeman, I could look under the fold-up, fold-down counter and saw a black urchin in rags lying on his back on the floor under the feet of another, much younger white policeman, who wore big boots. The sight was hidden to an adult's view, so my father had no knowledge of what I was seeing until the child began to scream. He howled in pain and terror as the big man trampled up and down on his little body. My father was speaking in Afrikaans to the older policeman at the desk, which I did not understand at the time. He had come in vexed by the burglary, but I saw him startled by the sounds of the child's distress. There was more conversation and then I saw the little boy being bundled out of the area and taken to some nameless place in the anterooms of the police station while he made the most dreadful cries. When we later came out and I asked my father what had been going on, he told me they had caught someone like the burglars who had stolen from our house. But I could not understand why the policeman had walked on him! My father explained that this policeman's boss, the older one he had been talking to, had told the younger officer to stop hurting the little boy and take him to the police cells. Years later he revealed the truth: the station commander had instructed his young colleague in Afrikaans to make sure he had '*die kaffertjie*' (the little kaffir) out of sight and sound before he 'questioned' him further.

My abhorrence for these people associated the image of a child under the feet of his tormentor with the colour of the policemen's uniform and the sound of Afrikaans. Events like these, of which I later learnt there were many, informed my parents' decision to leave the country, and we emigrated to Swaziland soon after. The price we paid for living on a farm was a boarding school in the capital Mbabane, twenty-seven miles from the farming valley we lived in. The school had been established by the Church of England but was now in government hands and was attended by the children of Swaziland's civil servants, British expatriates and local farmers. We were all white. It had an august religious name, St Mark's, and a motto, Nisi Dominus, 'except the Lord', the words that introduce Psalm 127, 'Except the Lord build the house, they labour in vain that build it'. Life in the boys' dormitories was more like *Lord of the Flies* than anything inspired by the better values of the Bible. The boys lived out their parents' colonial regimentation and brutality. We had to line up for everything, and shoes and clothes, hair and hands were all closely scrutinized by teams of prefects, supervised in turn by the masters. Meals were preceded by grace, 'For what we are about to receive may the Lord make us truly grateful', and then we would sit down to steal one another's bread, butter and jam, and go outside afterwards to settle scores with our fists. With a few cherished exceptions – people I have gratitude and regard for to this day – my teachers were the rejects of old educational orders in South Africa, the UK and its toppling colonies who washed up here. They did little to attend to children's pastoral needs. Cruel sport was made of the vulnerable, the odd ones out, or even those who just did not like sport. With my two younger brothers we were the only Jews in the school, and the only Jews many of the children had ever met. They did not know what to make of our identity or our name, which was distorted into many humiliating variants. There was a serious bully at work amongst a gang of others, and sometimes we would find the label off a bottle of HP Sauce plastered onto our places before meals. It was some time before we discovered what this was intended to mean – 'Hebrew Pig'. I learnt to fight and box, and gave as good as I got, but the battles left many scars, some of which are still with me. I did my best to protect my brothers, but we were all exposed to this abuse and there was not much we could do about any of it.

Swaziland (known now as Eswatini) was Britain's last African colony. The year 1968, in the dying days of empire, saw the Union flag come down for almost the last time in Africa at the Somhlolo Stadium beneath the beautiful Mdzimba mountains, and we were there to celebrate. By now David and Mar-

ian were enrolled at Waterford Kamhlaba School, the first multiracial estab-
lishment in Southern Africa, and they participated in the school choir that won
the award to sing for broadcast the new national anthem, *Nkulunkulu Mnikati
wetibusiso temaSwati.*[5] Its music and its lyrics are full of beautiful promise –
they thank God for bestowing blessings on the Swazi and their country. Today,
tragically, the country has the highest HIV rate in the world, with an epidemic
compounded by TB. Dual testing and retroviral programmes are making head-
way, and the advancing mortality rate has recently been stabilized.

We had a flagpole at my own school where, just three years before independence, I had been responsible for playing the Last Post on a bugle when
we took the Union flag down in the evenings. The strange irony that put this
responsibility in the hands of one of the school's only Jews was not lost on the
other boys, some of whom continued to refer to us with scorn as 'Jewboys'. The
insults continued to hurt us and we still talk about it. But momentous events
were under way. The colonial order still held sway in the mind-sets of people
living inside its fabric throughout Southern Africa, strained as it was. My immediate family was different and, like other people of conscience, they were
ahead of their time by generations. Those of us with outlooks like ours lived
isolated and sometimes ostracized lives. But the Freedom Charter was shaped
during the mid-1950s, and then in February 1960 the visiting British prime
minister, Harold Macmillan, delivered his famous 'wind of change' speech to
the South African Parliament. He made clear that South Africa's policy of
apartheid would not enjoy Britain's further support and, within a month, popular movements representing the non-white population brought matters to a
head in campaigns calling for the defiance of unjust laws, focused on the pass
laws. In March, the police opened fire on a crowd of unarmed protesters in
Sharpeville. The massacre was a defining watershed. The government declared
a State of Emergency, banned the African National Congress (ANC) and Pan
Africanist Congress (PAC), and arrested their leaders.

Later in the year the ANC president, Albert Luthuli, was awarded the Nobel
Peace Prize, but he was only allowed out to receive it one year later. By the time
he did so in 1961, South Africa had declared itself a republic, and the ANC
initiated the armed struggle on 16 December, a date sacred to Afrikaners, on
which they annually commemorated their 'covenant' with God. Elsewhere in
the world that year, the UN General Assembly condemned apartheid, the trial
of Adolf Eichmann took place in Israel, and the cosmonaut Yuri Gagarin was
the first to orbit the earth. In 1962 Mandela was arrested, the Rivonia Trial
began in 1963 and Martin Luther King's 'I Have a Dream' speech was delivered
in 1964. The Beatles' career was just beginning and Bob Dylan's epic song, 'The
Times They Are a-Changin'', was released on an album in 1964 to 'soon shake
your windows and rattle your walls'. The cultural fixtures and values of the

world order were under radical change, but the South African regime, standing firm at one of its focal points, resisted progress of any kind.

There was a corresponding catalyst on our own domestic front in the mid-1960s. It followed historical events in Lithuania during the Holocaust. Yehuda Ronder was the sole survivor of the Jewish community of Keidan – a population of nearly four thousand men, women and children – who perished in 1941. He passed on a report about my grandfather's youngest brother Tzodik, the leader of this community, who died as a hero when he killed at least two of their murderers before they killed him. The story's outline reached our community in 1949 with the Johannesburg visit of Rabbi Ephraim Oshry, one of the few rabbinic survivors of the genocide. My brother Colin was born soon after Oshry's visit, and was named in Tzodik's honour. Oshry later published a Yiddish account of the genocide, now translated into English (Oshry 1995), in which Ronder's testimony describing the massacre gives a vivid account of Tzodik's stand (Chrust [1977] 2018: 234). During the most alarming days of my detention, when I thought they would kill me in the cell, I was sustained by Tzodik's story and I have described this in Days 24–32. I have visited these killing fields in Lithuania and have given talks and published papers about what befell our family during this first phase of the Holocaust, before the development of gas chambers (Schlapobersky 2002, 2017).

Our Oupa helped Rachel, the youngest of his siblings and the only one in Lithuania to survive the Holocaust, to come and visit us in South Africa in 1963–64. Before the war she had married and left the family home in Keidan to settle with her husband in Kovna (Kaunas). When the Nazis arrived early in July 1941, they were impounded in the ghetto, along with her older brother Eliahu, and his wife and their baby Rivka, who was just one year old. Rachel smuggled herself out of the ghetto and took Rivka with her in an empty potato sack to place her with a Lithuanian family before she herself was later reimpounded. The Lithuanians raised Rivka for the next two years as a hidden child and then abandoned her to a local orphanage (Shlapobersky-Strichman 2011: 231–40). Rivka's parents and Rachel's husband perished but Rivka and Rachel survived. In 1945, Rachel was liberated by the Russians from Stutthof, a concentration camp north of Berlin. She made her way back to find all her family dead except for Rivka. Her account of these appalling events is given in *The Keidan Memorial Book* (Chrust [1977] 2018: 236). They were killed in numbers we can only guess at – thirty, sixty, eighty? She found Rivka in the orphanage, adopted her and raised her as her own. She remarried with a survivor from Vilna, and they settled in Israel in 1958. Rivka was by then a well-educated student and attended the Technion in Haifa where she graduated as an engineer, going on to become a leading member of her profession. They have remained in Haifa where her husband is a distinguished business executive and they now have three children and five grandchildren.

Rachel's visit to us in South Africa was an epic event. Our parents went to Johannesburg to meet her and participate in a series of family gatherings arranged in her honour. I met her myself, briefly – a dignified, solemn woman with an appearance and bearing much like Oupa. I cherish the photograph that Ivan gave us of his father and Rachel together. At one of these gatherings Rachel recounted these events of the 1940s. Oupa went into shock on hearing the full account, and was to live for only one more year. My father reported on how, at some point during the course of Rachel's visit, he had turned to his siblings and appealed to them – in the light of what they had heard from her – to consider their own positions under apartheid. He took no satisfaction in describing how his sister's husband, a barrister at the Johannesburg bar, had said: 'Archie, how can you compare the Jews with the *schwarzes* (blacks)?' My father replied: 'You know, during the action we saw in Italy during the war, we were stuck on the Gothic Line in the Apennines in the winter of 1944 and heard news about the liberation of Auschwitz on the BBC. We were taking many German prisoners as the line was crumbling and, with my Yiddish fluency, I served as our unit's translator. The prisoners thought I was a British soldier who spoke a strange German. I would say, "We've heard about Auschwitz and know that you've been doing similar things elsewhere. We've interviewed many Italian Jews whose families you've sent to concentration camps. How could you do such things?" And their reply? Just like yours! "How can you compare Jews with human beings?"' For once the QC was stumped for an argument (Shimoni 2003).[6]

Did this make them question their values? Probably, but it was only with my own arrest six years later that our Johannesburg family took real account of how unsafe everyone is in a police state. My uncle the barrister later provided my parents with undercover legal guidance when they were struggling to get me out of prison. I understand that in the later years of the struggle another of my uncles provided shelter for ANC members in hiding. Between my deportation in 1969 and the country's first democratic government in 1994, life in exile over the decades meant that I had no exposure to changes in the value positions of my many younger relatives. But it has been heartening to discover that my own contribution to the struggle is as acknowledged and honoured amongst the younger generations of our family in South Africa as it is amongst those raised in the UK.

During my last year at boarding school in 1965, I came into a deserted dormitory one evening, when the other boys were still away in the dining hall, to find movement inside and was startled to see a little Swazi boy, who was just as startled. He jumped out of the window and I realized as he fled that a team of children had been pilfering our things. I gave chase, shouting as I went. He ran up the hill into the path of other schoolboys coming down. When I called out, they also gave chase, so he ran in another direction. Eventually I brought him down with a rugby tackle that tore our clothes – his and mine – as we tumbled down the dirt road.

When I seized him, I was disconcerted by his trembling body and, still under an adrenaline rush, I held him to me tightly as he tried to break away. Then I realized how hard his heart was beating and how much terror he suffered at being held. Others had by then caught up with us. No one wanted to hurt him, but not knowing what to do we took him to the schoolmaster's house. By then one of the other pilfering children had been brought in too. The master packed us into his car and drove us down to the police station in Mbabane. We – the white children who had caught these blacks – were vocal in our indignation and called for them to be charged.

The station commander – a big black man – spoke to them in siSwati in a stern but kindly manner. I could understand some of the exchange and was startled by his geniality and his shift in perspective from a law enforcer to someone concerned for its transgressors. He pointed out to us that they were dressed in rags. 'These children are very poor,' he said, 'they are homeless and have no adults in their lives to care for them. They are probably also hungry.' They were trembling and responded to his questions in monosyllables and with averted eyes. Although they looked eight or nine years old we were surprised to learn that they were in fact teenagers, so only a little younger than ourselves but half our size. When the commander wanted to know what they had stolen we went back to the dormitory with our schoolmaster to do an inventory and returned to report that nothing was missing. So, at this point they had nothing in their possession, nothing was found missing and nothing was found on their pathway of flight. The commander said they could be prosecuted for trespass but not for theft, though he preferred to put them in the care of a social worker. We had no idea what a social worker was or would do. I was to become a social worker myself, years later. But, at that time, we were indignant that they would not receive their due punishment – by contrast, our schoolmasters would have given us six cuts with a cane for a much lesser trespass. We returned, the children remained with the commander, and we heard nothing further.

This was the last incident to separate me from the white supremacy of my upbringing. Although I had few internal resources to appreciate what had happened, the moment of capture – feeling this child's frightened, beating heart – shifted me from the position of being a white bringing force to bear against black delinquency, to having an identification with these lost and frightened children.

I left school with a scholarship to study medicine at the University of Cape Town, where I began in 1966. I had grown up fascinated by the biological sciences and was inspired by my mother's first cousin, Alec Folb, to become a doctor like him. At UCT I was befriended by student leaders who were bringing people together to oppose apartheid, but I gave priority to my studies, got absorbed in my subjects and struggled to survive the rough culture of College House, the men's dormitory in which I had the misfortune to be placed. News soon arrived of another scholarship awarded by the American Field Service – a student exchange programme – to go to the USA. After completing the first half of the year at UCT, I left to spend the next year in Scarsdale, Westchester County, New York. I lived with a local family and attended a state school with standards above those of my university's first year. The country was bitterly divided, and racial and political conflict would soon set it ablaze. The Vietnam War was raging, and the civil rights movement was breaking new ground in the Deep South. Boys in my school year were being drafted for military service, and the bombing of Hanoi had just begun. The year turned into more of a political education than an academic one, and exposure to an outstanding teacher gave me the confidence to begin writing.

I returned to university in Cape Town where I led a double life – reimmersed in basic sciences at medical school and, at the same time, uplifted by the student movement that was enrolling young people all over the world. I soon fell foul of the right-wing culture of people in my hall of residence, who turned on me violently, especially as I had previously played a part in inviting Robert Kennedy to deliver the annual Day of Affirmation lecture in 1966. I describe these violent events in Day 4. I got depressed, found it hard to study, withdrew from the course and moved up to Johannesburg to enrol for a degree in psychology at the University of Witwatersrand the following year. I had a successful first year studying psychology, literature and especially philosophy, in which I became deeply immersed. In the second year my curriculum included history and isiZulu, and I was halfway through this when I was arrested and deported.

In January 1968 at the beginning of my second year at 'Wits', I wrote a poem to both honour and question the launch of Apollo 8. I contrasted this triumph with the recent death of a baby girl whose mother worked as a maid for the family I was in lodgings with. Julie Nkosi looked after the kitchen and did the cleaning and laundry. She lived in one of the poky backrooms in their yard, like most black domestics, but her real home was in Alexandra township where her mother and sister looked after her two-year-old baby, along with other children in their family. Her husband was working elsewhere on a contract that kept him away from the family for most of the year. She had hidden the fact that she was a mother to protect her terms of employment. The pass laws only allowed those coming from Alexandra to work in white areas if they had no family responsibilities. Having grown up in Swaziland I had some command of siSwati, the country's language, closely related to isiZulu in which we would often chat when they were out. I was studying isiZulu at university and she would help me with the language. She also knew that I had friends in the township and trusted me with worry about her baby who lived there with her mother. She needed money to meet the cost of antibiotics and, when I succeeded in persuading her to disclose this to the family, they refused to help with the treatment cost, as they said she was not even supposed to have a baby. I raised funds on a loan from friends, but it was too late, and the baby died.

For some days Julie did not turn up for work, and then very early one morning when she did return, she found she was locked out. She woke me in the dark by tapping on my window from the outside to have me let her in. She was grieving, and her head was covered in a blanket. I woke the family to appeal for their help, but they refused to assist with the funeral expenses and, once more, I secured what I could on a loan from family friends. Later I drove into Alex on my motor scooter to Julie's family home, where I found them all sitting around in mourning, and I put the funds in the hands of Julie's parents. She was sitting in a corner hooded by a blanket. They had not yet been able to get news to her husband, the baby's father, who was working on a contract somewhere far away. I left my lodgings, and later wrote a poem to the dead child and the moon, a fragment of which opens this memoir. Julie had no such option. She needed the job, so she stayed on and I never saw her again. I hope she had other children, that she raised her family in Alexandra and that they saw deliverance from the terms of apartheid.

During my short spell at Wits I joined the South African Volunteer Service (SAVS), a student organization that raised money and recruited suitably qualified students to build schools in rural areas during university vacations. My first assignment involved leading a work camp to build a school in a remote part of Swaziland, which was something like going home. By then I had been befriended by a number of black students whom I invited to join us. We recruited some twenty white university students – men and women – and were joined by other volunteers on the site, most of whom came through the Quaker movement. We were housed in thatched huts in the village, dug an open latrine for ourselves and bathed in a nearby stream – men at one site and women at another. The villagers brought us clean water daily, and we cooked over an open fire. It was a cold winter in the mountains and it sometimes frosted overnight. We had several engineering students on the site who took charge of the build, following a pre-planned layout ordered and paid for in advance. People rotated through membership of the different teams – digging, cooking, offloading steel girders and breeze blocks, and later mixing and casting concrete and supporting the bricklayers who were laying breeze blocks. We had some wonderful singers and guitar players in the project, and evenings round the fire at night were musical and convivial. Our build was successful in the three weeks available and, lying in the mountains north-west of Mbabane, the school is still standing in the village of Makwana.

I had come across two of the blacks who joined us on the project, Ezekiel Mokone and Milner Moroke, when they visited the university common rooms. I was introduced to the third, Mongane Wally Serote, by Bill Ainslie, an art teacher who, with his wife, opened their home to writers and artists. Wally was an aspiring writer who, without any university education, was better read in literature than anyone else I knew. By then I was a committed participant in a writers' workshop with Lionel Abrahams, one of the country's leading writers, and I would often present my poetry there. When Lionel passed away in 2004, I sent an epitaph to his widow in which I described how he had taught me to read and write for a second time. I introduced Wally to this group, and we would arrive on my motor scooter and later leave under their inspiration to go away and work on our respective writing projects. I saw Wally fashion poems that have become landmarks in the new South African literature. Our bond was both a friendship and a writers' alliance. We hid some of his work, and mine, in a wardrobe in my home, together with a stock of his political literature for which I provided safekeeping, at a time when police raids in Alexandra township had created new threats. When I was arrested and the police raided my own home, its secrets were not discovered. Like our friendship, they were safeguarded through our respective interrogations. The poetry in his voice, like his central role in the struggle, has inspired generations. I have watched with pride and respect as schools and universities build their teaching curriculum in South Africa on new foundations laid by his own poetry and novels, and by the literature of many others (Serote 1978a and 1978b).

I conclude this Introduction with a poem by Serote that he wrote while on a Fulbright Scholarship at Columbia University in New York in 1975, five years after enduring nine months of solitary confinement. He published it in his 1978 anthology, *Behold Mama, Flowers*.

When Lights Go Out
Mongane Wally Serote
(for some who are in South African jails)[7]

1
it is with the shadows of night
when the sun comes and goes
the moon comes and goes
that we ask, in weary voices, which fall into
                              the depth of the gulf:
how does it feel to be you
to be watching and waiting
to feel the heavy weight of every minute come
                              followed by another

and nothing
even everything written in blood
says nothing about how we could wake up tomorrow
                              and build a day

2
your eyelids shut, if they ever do,
and the memories of those you knew, flood behind
                              the darkness of closed eyelids
spiralling into patterns of pain
and you alone know
that once there were hopes
that once the footsteps of the people sounded on the
                                          horizon
and now
silence strides across the sky
where the sun sets, proclaiming a wish to rest

3
can we tell you
the children of a long hour a long day a long
                                    night
that hope never befriends fools
yes
time, in absolute eloquence, can erase our faces
remember Sharpeville?
in those days, violence and disaster were articulate
and now
today you watch and wait

4
so one day hope begins to walk again
it whispers
about the twisted corpses that we saw
sprawled across the streets on this knowledgeable earth
the tears
the blood
the memory
and the knowledge, which was born by every heavy
                              minute that we carried
across a wilderness, where there were no paths
where screams echoed, as if never to stop
it is when there is no hope, that hope begins to walk
                                          again
yet
like we said
hope never befriends fools

5
since we have eyes to see
ears

and fingers to touch
only if we know how, can we harness time –
can you hear the footsteps
New York 1975 (Serote 1978a: 69–70)

Notes

1. The B'nai Avraham and Yehuda Laib Family Association (BAYL) publishes an annual newsletter in Baltimore called *The Bulletin*, which records the life of this now extended family association. BAYL is due to celebrate the 120th anniversary of its foundation in May 2021. Retrieved May 2020 from https://bayl.org/wp-content/uploads/2020/09/BAYL-Bulletin-Vol.-74-Sept.-2020.pdf.
2. Sources for the many historical references in this book will be found in Thompson 2000.
3. Lionel Abrahams helped me to track this poem down and find its provenance and publication (see Gibbon 2008) by introducing me to Malcolm Hacksley, the then director of the National English Literary Museum in South Africa. My grateful thanks to both of them.
4. Retrieved May 2020 from https://en.wikipedia.org/wiki/Lightning_bird.
5. Swazi National Anthem. Retrieved May 2020 from https://youtu.be/iR3B4bYmpBI..
6. Gideon Shimoni provides the most comprehensive and authoritative study of the Jewish community in South Africa, its relationship with the Afrikaner government and its opposition to and complicity with apartheid.
7. A range of Serote's publications in poetry and prose is given in the references. He is the recipient of a number of literary awards including the Ingrid Jonker Poetry Prize in South Africa for his first anthology, *Yakhal'Inkomo: The Cry of Cattle at the Slaughter: Poetry*, in 1973; the Noma Award for Publishing in Africa in 1993; and the Pablo Neruda Award from the Chilean Government in 2004. His Fulbright Award took him to Columbia University New York in 1975, and he remained in exile working for the African National Congress until 1990, when legislation banning the liberation movements was repealed. As a Member of Parliament he served as Chair of the parliamentary select committee for arts and culture and then as Chief Executive Officer of Freedom Park, a national heritage site in Pretoria, opened in 2007. Retrieved May 2020 from: https://en.wikipedia.org/wiki/Mongane_Wally_Serote.

THE DAYS

ARREST
University of the Witwatersrand

Day 1: Friday 13 June

On the morning of Friday 13 June 1969, I walked to the university with my partner, Janet. We had been living in a shared home in Joburg for five months. I had recently turned 21 and was in the second year of a degree course at the University of the Witwatersrand, where Janet was a librarian. We would normally go there on my motor scooter, but it was out on loan to a friend, Mongane Wally Serote, who lived in Alexandra township. He had come to spend the night with us two days before, when he described the worry about the many arrests in the black community that he came from. They included Mrs Winnie Mandela, wife of Nelson Mandela, Joyce Sikakane, a prominent black journalist in Johannesburg, and many others. There were regular press reports about these detentions, and our student community had been to prayer services convened by the university's Anglican chaplain in support of the detainees. I encouraged Wally to go and stay with my family, who lived in Swaziland; he had spent time with us there before, and I thought it might get him out of the way. But he was determined to go home, and so had used my scooter to get back to Alex – but he was arrested the day after, which I knew nothing about.

On our walk, Janet told me her menstrual period was irregular and she was concerned she might be pregnant. Uncertainty about this remained with me for the weeks in prison that followed. Pregnancy had not been one of our plans up to then. I left her at the library and went on to the morning's first lecture on Comparative African Government and Law, in which we tried to make sense of Ian Smith's new Rhodesian constitution.

One of the students who would always sit nearby was, I later discovered, a police spy whose real name was Jorrie Jordaan, who was to later take an active part in my interrogation. What I did not know then was that to protect me, my friends in detention had disclosed to the police only a previous address for me – my mother's unoccupied flat. The night before my detention, Janet's mother, who was a neighbour, had heard the door being broken open and had reported it to the police, but she had no idea that the police themselves were responsible. She did not think to phone and warn us, and it never occurred to me that I might be their target.

———

The police came for me at the university just as the lecture was starting. An administrator came in – someone we did not know – and asked for me to identify myself. We could see he was agitated in front of this large hall of students. When I put my hand up, he said someone outside was waiting to see me. In the days following, I would often think back to those moments and wonder what else I might have done instead of wave my hand in the air and rush out. My mother had been on her way from Swaziland to Joburg by car that morning, and so my first thought was that perhaps something had happened on the road. Only the administrator knew what was going on, but he gave nothing away, left the scene as I came out and alerted no one, so I simply disappeared.

Three men in suits were waiting. The one in charge was familiar. He knew exactly who I was and held up a police card to identify himself saying: 'Mr Schlapobersky, I see. We meet again.' He gave his name and, introducing himself as a detective from the Security Police, he said: 'I am arresting you under Section 6 of the Terrorism Act. Come with us.' The composure in his manner was dreadful – both threatening and polite. I went cold and icy and remained so. I did not say a word – there was nothing for me to say – and went along with them in a dream state removed from what was happening. They maintained quiet, severe control for some hours until they had me in Pretoria, where they all turned into monsters. For now, the three of them made a kind of scrum with me in the middle, and we walked quietly off the campus. Going through the university grounds I saw a friend, Derek Momberg, in an alleyway doing some work on his car. I called out to him, 'Please tell Janet', which was as much as I thought I could get away with. I thought what was happening would be obvious. He stared at us walking past and, saying 'Sure', he returned to his job. Did he know what was happening and choose to look away? Was he simply perplexed? At the time no alarm was given, and I never heard from him or saw him again. He is now a celebrated lawyer in Johannesburg, specializing in intellectual property.

I got into the back seat of the waiting car and we went off in convoy, as another similar car followed with two other policemen. The detective driving – the one who had arrested me – asked me to take them to where I lived. I had no idea they did not know where this was. During solitary confinement I would think back again on these moments of capture. What if I had taken them to my mother's apartment where I had been living until just six months before? I did not know that they had already been there and, getting no reply, they had broken in to satisfy themselves it was unoccupied.

My home was at 11 Queens Road, Parktown – a condemned property in what had been a fine old house near the university. It had been the university's Anglican rectory but, as it was due for demolition soon, it had been rented to university students like us. We shared it with others and turned the outhouse garage into a 'hostel' for the street children we would find begging at the university entrance. Other students joined us in the project, and we had donations of bedding and food. Some eight or ten black children set up home in the garage, from which they came and went. We provided them porridge in the morning and hot soup at night and, for the rest of the day, we got on with our lives as they did with theirs. We knew each other by name and could communicate in broken English and isiZulu. Some of the children were subdued and quiet, but others had jaunty personalities with survival skills like Gavroche in *Les Misérables*.

When the police brought me to our home, their convoy of vehicles came up the back drive, and when it stopped outside the children's garage, the children emerged cautiously. They looked puzzled at finding five strange men arriving in two cars, but relaxed when they saw me and approached us. I panicked for their safety, and so shouted out in isiZulu: '*Baleka bafana. Baleka! Baleka! Lawa ngamaphoyisa. Banayo wangibamba futhi bazokubamba nawe. Baleka! Baleka!*' [Run, boys. Run! Run! These are the police. They've caught me, and they'll catch you too. Run! Run!] Their shock turned to flight as I shouted, and the picture of these children scattering in every direction, jumping over hedges and fences, and diving through garden undergrowth, was one of my last memories before prison. The police turned to ask me what I had said, and made no comment when I explained.

They came into the house and were greeted with affection by our dog Mehavya, whom they treated kindly. It made me sick to see their hands showing him affection. They spent some three hours taking the house apart and searching in every book for information they thought relevant. They opened our bedding, opened every box and drawer, and made a pile of seized property in the middle of the living room. It included books, typewriters and papers, and was all loaded into the second of their cars. I fed and watered the dog, shut him in the kitchen and, after being denied the right to leave a note for Janet, I was loaded into the first of their cars and we left for Pretoria in a convoy.

The memory of sitting in shock with my arms around the dog as I watched the police take the house apart for those three hours has always been with me. Certain items had to be checked with me in a great 'pose' of police responsibility. Janet had a set of precious coins in a hidden place in our wardrobe, and they wanted to be sure that I saw them open the case and close it again without removing anything. I was even more on edge in the bedroom search as the wardrobe had a false bottom in which – together with Wally – we had hidden political magazines including a set of back copies of *Sechaba*, the official organ of the ANC, a magazine that had been banned for years. It takes its title from the word for 'nation' (*setjhaba*) in the Sotho languages. Wally stored them in Alexandra and, to keep them safer, I had agreed to hide them here. The wardrobe also held a lot of our poetry –Wally and I were both active writers, as was Janet. The police never thought to take the top off the base of the wardrobe, and so the material, some of which would have been grounds for conviction and a prison sentence, was kept secret throughout. There is more about what happened to our political hoard on Day 33. Throughout the search they looked for photographs they believed I had taken of them.

During a street demonstration outside the university some months before, these very police had brought cameras to photograph us. To retaliate, I had borrowed a camera from the university newspaper's office which, though it had no film in it, put the detectives on the run when I aimed it at them, as they did not want to be identified.

Now they were getting their own back but were puzzled not to find any of the pictures they thought I had taken. They came across odd scraps of paper with people's names and addresses, and took these very seriously. Everything was numbered and catalogued, and when it came to diaries and address books they took everything they could find. I understood from all this that they must have thought me a key figure in an underground intrigue, and so I could not wait to get to Pretoria where – they assured me – I would be able to see a lawyer. Then I would be able to tell them the truth and come home again. I convinced myself that I would be away for only a few hours. By noon they had assembled a car full of items, including Janet's typewriter and my father's old Remington typewriter – on loan to me – that he had brought back from his wartime service in Italy.

When one of them found my old high school Bible on my bookshelf, he took it down and put it in my hand. He need never have bothered, and at the time I wondered why he was giving it to me, but it proved to be a life-saving gift, an unexpected act of improbable kindness. In response to my puzzlement he said simply and quietly, 'Where you're going, you may need something to read. Keep it close to you and look after it.' I have often wondered what his name was and where he might be living now. He was within my age range and is possibly still alive. Perhaps he will be one of those who reads this memoir?

The Bible was to become my source of reading, my lexicon and my calendar. It is now on permanent loan to the Jewish Museum in London. This memoir is illustrated with photographs of entries I made in the Bible. I drew a calendar

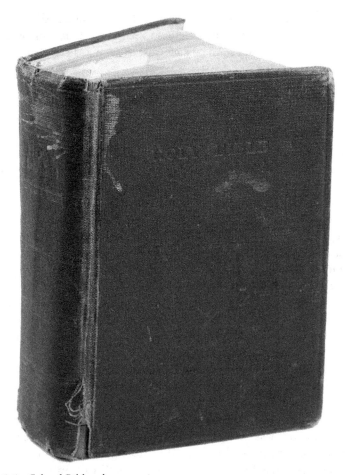

Figure 1.1 School Bible taken to prison.
© Jewish Museum London. Photograph by Ian Lillicrapp.

on its flyleaf on Day 9, Midwinter's Day, which is reproduced as Figure 1.2. On Day 24 I wrote into it Biblical passages of special meaning (Figure 1.4) and wrote a poem onto another of its pages (Figure 1.3); and on Day 25 I drew a warning signal on another flyleaf – 'The teeth of tension' – by which to obscure potentially incriminating notes I had entered earlier (Figure 1.5).

I shut our dog Mehavya in his familiar space in the kitchen after giving him food and water, and I never saw him again. I was under such scrutiny and in so much shock that I could not think of what to do to alert Janet when she got back. While searching the house the police had monitored my every move, and had even stood outside listening when I went to the toilet. Later I would wonder repeatedly what else I might have done to leave a trail. I had taken them at their word – that there would be a chance to see a lawyer as soon as we got to Pretoria. I thought I would soon be back, just as soon as I could give a reasonable account of myself.

I was loaded into the first car again, and we set off in convoy once more. The journey to 'the lawyer' in Pretoria took us on a familiar route close to our original home in Oaklands and past the Doll's House, a roadhouse restaurant that was still in business until quite recently. These landmarks seemed strange in the company in which I found myself. I imagined getting out and having a milkshake as we drove past, and wondered what the detectives would order. Would they have chocolate malted or green lime? No, I thought, I would do this later in the day when I came back from the lawyer in Pretoria.

Once we had left town and got onto the open road to Pretoria, the empty winter landscape and scorched brown earth were forbidding. I realized I was trembling and very cold. Halfway to Pretoria the car was held up by some roadworks where I saw prison labourers at work shovelling gravel in unison. One sang, and the rest joined with a response as they dug their shovels into the earth together. They paused for the next verse and then in song they tossed their shovel loads into the gulley they were filling. The dust rose above the falling earth and they began again. The dust rose as the earth fell again, and the singing continued. I watched it happening as if in a dream, and then we were on our way. Soon I would be listening to the falling and scraping sound of shovels at work in the darkness of the prison, as early morning labourers stoked the furnace. The picture of dust rising from falling earth captured my attention then as it does now – and the rhythmical sound of shovels working.

Pretoria Prison was a landmark building in Potgieter Street on the south-western boundary of Pretoria. We knew it as 'The Hanging Jail'. We pulled up and, still in a dream, I got out with my police escort on either side as we went towards the huge doors set in a forbidding stone arch. One of them rang a bell, a hatch opened in one of the doors and a face appeared. There was an exchange, and a smaller door was opened through which I was escorted into jail. The front Control Room was full of white prison officers in khaki uniforms. I asked someone who seemed to be in charge if I could see a lawyer. The detectives surrounding me winked at him and he replied in Afrikaans that this would soon be arranged and they all started laughing. A warder approached me roughly and told me to empty my pockets. While I was doing this the detectives left, still smirking and joking with one another. After emptying all my possessions into a sack, I had to take off my belt and shoelaces, and sign for everything. Then I was escorted by another warder through a series of barred grill doors, each of which had a black prisoner standing on the other side to unlock it and then lock it again behind us. We went up two flights on a wrought iron staircase and then through further sets of grill doors that had to be opened on one side and closed on the other by someone permanently stationed there. Finally, we arrived at a corridor that seemed to stretch for ever.

On one side there was a row of high-set windows, and on the other an end-less row of closed cell doors. I had never been in a prison before and it was all overwhelming. The warder brought a set of keys up from a chain at his waist, opened cell number 1 and, speaking in Afrikaans, he told me to get undressed. I professed not to understand, and he started stripping clothes off me, so I got the idea and took everything off. I was lightly dressed in only those things that I had worn to university that morning – a casual shirt and trousers – and had not been allowed to take any further clothing with me from the house. I was unprepared for the sense of cold in the prison that was to become a permanent feature. It was very exposing, and I shivered standing in front of the warder. He was in no hurry – he examined each garment and flung things into the cell, item by item, taking his time as he went. Then, as I was standing there naked, he pushed me in after my clothes and as I rushed to start putting things back on, he slammed the door shut. I had to kneel at the slops pail to urinate and had barely sat down on the blanket when the door was opened again, and the warder called me out to accompany him. On his instruction I left the Bible behind on the blanket. We reversed our route and I found the same two detectives waiting in the Control Room. They explained that I was wanted immediately at 'Compol'. The Afrikaners call it Kompol – with a 'K' – it was originally Paul Kruger's bank and was now the headquarters of the commissioner of the South African Security Police.

When Janet came back from the university at the end of the day, she found the house in some disorder but not enough to indicate a burglary. There was no sign of me, and the children were nowhere to be seen. When the winter day began to close in without any news, she contacted my mother, who had driven up to Johannesburg from Swaziland just that day. Their developing unease that I might have been arrested was confirmed when my motor scooter – still out on loan to my friend Wally in Alexandra township – was returned by his friend who reported that he had been detained. However, the police denied any knowledge of me, and advised my family to approach the hospitals and mortuary in case there had been an accident. There was no trace of me through these painful enquiries. Meanwhile, I was under interrogation in Compol Building. Police denial continued until some hours later, by which time it was completely dark. Then Janet heard a tap on the window at 11 Queens Road, and she found the children from our hostel outside. They had returned in the safety of darkness to tell her of what they had seen. Armed with this certain knowledge, my family roused the British ambassador in Pretoria with the help of our lawyer, and overnight he made representations to the minister of justice and in turn to the Security Police.

INTERROGATION I
Swanepoel in Compol Building

Day 1: Friday 13 June

I could smell food being distributed as I came through the prison corridors, so it must have been about lunchtime on Friday when I got back into the police car outside. We drove into Pretoria, went down Pretorius Street and stopped at an intersection at Church Square where I had been just one year earlier.

In 1968 I was part of a peaceful student demonstration from Witwatersrand University, organized in a convoy of cars that drove to Pretoria. Our delegation was held up on our way to deliver a petition to the prime minister's office at the Union Buildings, signed by many thousands of students. We were demonstrating against the termination of teaching contracts for black staff at white universities. I was in one of the rear vehicles in the convoy. We had come out in sympathy with a student sit-in at the University of Cape Town over the rescinding of a teaching contract with Archie Mafeje, a black anthropologist who was formally appointed but prohibited from taking up his contract by apartheid legislation.[1] We never reached our destination as our convoy was broken up by Afrikaans students from Pretoria University who beat up many of us, and tarred and feathered those at the front.

Now we drove past the corner where this had happened. It still had a sinister aura, but the centre of town was busy and looked quite normal. There were people on the streets, and none of them knew what was happening to me. Outside the car it all looked so ordinary. We pulled up in the front yard of Compol, and I was escorted up an imposing flight of stairs and into a big stone building. I was cold and trembling again but would not let them see my body's panic. We turned away from the Police Museum into a different section of the building, past a series of offices and along a corridor that led to a large open space with small cell-like rooms leading off it. These looked like military offices I had seen in films, and I was more curious than appalled. It gave some relief after the Hanging Jail, for I was still to discover that this was the corridor to hell. The policemen on either side kept me moving, but I assured myself that they had taken me out of prison because they had discovered their mistake. I told myself that I would be allowed to see a lawyer now and could answer their questions and then go home. In my mind I was preparing my opening statement to a lawyer. Denial can keep you on your feet in the most frightening places.

I was to get to know this corridor well as it was the route to the toilet and went past the office of Major Swanepoel – the policeman who was to be in charge of my case.

As we came into a large open space, some men were standing next to a big table where I saw the typewriters of my father and Janet. Also there were our books, notebooks, papers, files, diaries and address books – all spread out and under examination. There was a man in charge looking on and talking to the others, who replied from their occupied positions. What were they doing to our things! Now I was indignant, but they all turned to look at us as we came in and started shouting. The two in my escort dropped their guard and turned on me. I was surrounded by an enraged mob shouting scorn and derision that stuck to me like spit. Swanepoel was already notorious, but his notoriety had passed me by in the press, so when I addressed him I had no idea who he was. They were demanding things of me that I was determined not to understand. When I asked if I could please see a lawyer, he shouted like a gun going off. Swanepoel's rage was overwhelming. I spoke to him as politely as I could, saying, 'Excuse me sir, but if you want me to answer your questions would you please speak to me in English – I don't understand anything you're saying.' The rage that followed was another explosion. It was threatening just to look at him. He was shorter than me but twice my weight – stocky and bull-necked with a bloated florid face and close-cropped ginger hair on a head shaped like a bullet. He had an oval face that was puffed up and red, and he had swollen freckled hands with thick fingers. The skin on his face was sallow and mottled, and his eyes were bloodshot and angry. He attacked me in a withering rage for being a South African who did not even know his own country's language – *'Die Taal'*, the language, *'Ons Taal'*, our language.

We had to study Afrikaans at school, and it was our mother's first language, so I did in fact understand. I found enough self-possession in the moment to say I did not – it was my first and only defence. Although the claim caused more immediate injury, they went on to use English with me, and in the days following they came to talk freely in Afrikaans amongst themselves, so I knew something of what they were looking for, which gave me a marginal advantage. This margin, hidden throughout, was all I had to keep them at bay.

Swanepoel did respond in English but on doing so he scowled: 'So, you're an angry one, are you! I like them when they're angry, sonny boy. Oh, I like them! We'll have some fun with you and your anger!' And he led the team to crowd me into one of the small interrogation rooms. He gave focus to the fury as they crowded me into the vault where the other savage one, Richter, slammed shut the steel window, cutting off access to the street outside as he and the others baited and beat me while others came crowding in from the back, shouting as they came. I thought I was going to die. From somewhere within, I summoned up and pictured the face of Janet. Her imagined presence was to see me through – she became my guardian angel in the days and weeks that followed. For about half an hour I stood facing them with my back to the wall as they shouted, threatened and taunted. They made sordid jokes about my personal life and Jewish nose, and frightening threats about how much they would enjoy working me over. Then Richter produced a brick. He held it up in front of me, right in my face. I can still remember its detail – it was so close I could see its granular surface and I thought it so abrasive that it would score my face when he hit me with it. But he put it calmly down on the floor in front of me and told me to stand on it. His instructions were so bizarre that I did not move and simply stared, which produced more rage. There were fists in my face, and they tore at my beard and long hair. To this day I am reluctant to allow anyone to touch my face. There were so many of them. The violence was at its most intense as they drove me onto the brick at my feet. Looking up at the jeering mob at the door, I realized that events of this kind must have been regular, as more and more police officers seemed to come from elsewhere to lend their voices to the general rage. I thought, well, that seems easy enough, at least he is not beating me with it – and so I stood on it. What a strange thing, I thought, balancing on this brick in front of a raging mob of Special Branch.

After some time, the rage subsided and the mob thinned out as Swanepoel and Richter, his interrogation partner, sat down at the big desk that I stood before, balanced on a brick under a bright light. There was a washbasin in one corner of the room and nothing else. Like the rage they had used to overwhelm me at the beginning, this phase had no clear focus either. What they said was that I was here to talk. I would stand on the brick until I told them what I knew they wanted to hear. They did not like silence, and now that they were interrogating me in English but speaking to one another in Afrikaans, I could monitor their approach. From time to time others appeared at the doorway and stood looking on. One of them became a familiar onlooker who put an appearance in each day but said very little. He turned out to be Major Johan Coetzee, who later took charge of my 'statement'. These other observers were there for sport and curiosity, but I had no idea that it was different in Coetzee's case – he was studying me. Swanepoel's interrogation partner, Richter, was many years his junior and liked to show his superior just how aggressive and 'persuasive' he could be. He was talkative about the process and made regular comments about me. They had decided I was a cheeky little Jewboy who would have to learn his lesson on the brick. I was still holding everything back, Richter said to Swanepoel: '*Dis 'n vurige* bastard, *hy dink hy's slim. Die Joodjie sal sy les op die baksteen leer*' [This is a cheeky bastard, he thinks he's clever. This Jewboy will learn his lesson on the brick].

The proportions of a brick vary. The brick I was standing on was a red South African face-brick 8¾ inches long, 4 inches wide and 3 inches deep. It had been laid across the direction I was facing, and I was standing on it just three inches above the ground. I found a stable way of standing by fitting the width of the brick – the 4 inches – inside the arch of my feet, so the heels of my shoes wedged against its rim. That way I could keep my balance, but it hurt after a while, so I would nudge backwards on the brick to stand on it with the balls of my feet. They would shout at me for fidgeting and tell me to stand still. Then I would lose my balance and end up with one or both feet on the floor just behind the brick. Although I was standing just three inches above the ground, it felt as if I had fallen a hundred feet, as the floor was strictly prohibited. I was punished with rage and threats, and told that 'a fucking Jewboy like you has no right to stand on the floor. Your place is on the brick. So, get back up on your bloody brick.' So, this was mine, I said to myself – this brick was mine and I would stand on it, damn them, for as long as I had to. I made it manageable by just getting from one hour to the next and by moving my weight from one foot to the other, and by bending one knee and straightening it, and then bending the other. Relief came when I asked for the toilet and was taken back along the corridor that I had come down earlier. Sitting on the toilet eased the pressure on my feet and I stayed in the cubicle until they shouted from the outside to get me to come out.

I returned to the brick from the toilet and got up on it as if I was mounting a stage. Swanepoel and Richter went at me for some time, demanding answers to half-stated questions that gave nothing away. They demanded, simply, to be told whatever answers my anxiety would produce. Richter wrote and Swanepoel barked out threats. My confused and incoherent answers produced a paroxysm of rage and abuse, and more threats against me, my parents and my girlfriend. They decided I was being uncooperative and was withholding information. Whenever I asked what I was supposed to talk about, I had the same reply: 'You know bloody well, you communist Jew.' At one point they seemed to be winding up for the day, and I thought it was over. But they were then relieved by another team of two interrogators whom I will call X and Y. I knew their names at the time, but they are lost to memory now. I was allowed to sit down while the two pairs of interrogators changed shifts and discussed me. When the new pair were installed at the desk and one of them had settled down at the writing pad, they had me back on the brick and kept up the pressure – but they took up a quite different line of questioning. They wanted to know about my university courses and my reading and personal interests. X produced some of the books that had been seized from my home and explained that they were 'proscribed' – a long word, I thought – and they warned me that each of these books could earn me a prison sentence. They were curious as to how I had come by them and were even more so when I explained that I had been in the USA on an exchange programme for a year and had returned with these books. Y, the one who did the writing, was reticent and hardly engaged me. I thought his English was limited, but he wrote and wrote, and it was all in English. The other, X, who engaged me in conversation, was a big, jaunty man with a booming personality and a fluency in English, with barely an Afrikaans accent. He took some pride in explaining to me that he too was well travelled and had recently returned from an observation tour in India. They kept going at me for four hours, and were winding up somewhere near 4.00 p.m. I was increasingly exhausted and, still in a state of shock, I just wanted to sleep. Only then did I discover that there was now to be yet another change of shift – here was another handover!

Two gentle, softly spoken and urbane police officers, Baker and his colleague Z, came in. Baker was to later take a prominent role in my 'management' and, like Swanepoel's and Richter's, his name has an indelible place in my memory. His interrogation partner's name, however, is lost to memory. (I may yet discover the identity of the second of these two *'Durban manne'*, the two 'Durban guys', as they were described by their colleagues.) I was horrified. This was just going on and on. Once more I was allowed to sit at the desk while they took a briefing in Afrikaans from the other two, who then left, and then they reviewed the growing pad of interrogation notes. They too got me back up onto the brick and began to ask me about my family and personal history. As my biography unfolded, they explained how confident they were that once *'Die Majoor'* ('The Major') understood who I really was, he would be much kinder towards me. They engaged with me in a conversation about how threatening he was, and reassured me that they would encourage him to be kinder, once I started being cooperative with them. I would have to show much more cooperation for them to be able to get me off the brick, so I could stand on the floor. 'Don't you want to stand on the floor?' they would say; 'It would be much easier on your feet.' I was still on the brick when we reached 8.00 p.m. and, as they got ready to go, I thought it was finally over for the night. I just wanted to be able to sit down or, better still, lie down and sleep.

One of them took me to the toilet before they left, and when he brought me back I discovered that Swanepoel and Richter were reinstalled at the desk. They brought terror back into the room and the walls closed in for the next four hours. There was no peace in their presence. The shouting earlier was now replaced by penetrating questions on issues across the range of my recent history. Where did they find so much to question me about? It just went on and on. I understood from some of the information they had about me that Wally Serote was already in their hands. Our association was based on a shared interest in writing and in documenting the social ills of apartheid through poetry. There was nothing illegal about this, hostile as we were towards the state, and I thought I could be most protective by showing that I had nothing to hide. So, I was quite open about what we had been doing and hoped these disclosures would obscure just how political our consciousness was. This was not thought out in any way – I told them about the poetry they found in my desk and the readings I had given at Dorkay House, an African cultural centre in town, in order to call attention away from a much bigger compilation of writing we had hidden together in the wardrobe at my home. It included Wally's back copies of the ANC magazine *Sechaba*, which they never discovered. The level at which I answered their questions about him kept attention on our poetry, in which they took no interest. They were in search of much more 'political' information and, convinced that I had other associations with more incriminating people, they steadily lost interest in him.

Then at midnight it eased up again and, just when I thought I might sit or even lie down, X and Y came back and we returned to the topics they had identified as their own for the next four hours – my reading material and university life. Somewhere in the early hours of the morning, when my resources were at their lowest ebb, Baker and Z reappeared and seemed puzzled to find me still on the brick. By now, they told me, you should have been allowed to sit down during interrogation. Clearly, they said to me, you have not been cooperating with our colleagues. Now, will you tell us about what you have been doing so we can get permission from '*Die Majoor*', to allow you to sit down? These transparent efforts at manipulation were not frightening – they were too well dressed and well groomed, I thought, and their 'smart' attire seemed to go with their fluent English accents – but it was all dreadful. Through the misery and confusion of the night I was able to get the measure of their carefully orchestrated approach, and then, as they got ready to leave for a second time, I thought Saturday might soon be here and it would all be over.

Day 2: Saturday 14 June

When Swanepoel and Richter returned at 8 a.m. on Saturday, I thought this was the end of their interrogation, but, to my horror, I found that it was only just beginning. They had been on at me for eighteen hours and I was still on my brick. Swanepoel's rage now had a new focus – my passport. It emerged in the expletives he used about me with his colleagues as he and Richter sat down with the other two at the desk for a kind of progress review. Now I saw more of Swanepoel's physique. He had a deep chest, big shoulders, enormous forearms, and hands that looked swollen and bloated, which he fiddled with all the time. Whenever he was seated, he leant forward on the desk, occupying much of its surface, and, when enraged, he would beat it with clenched fists. But now they talked to each other in low voices, again in Afrikaans. Swanepoel explained that '*Hierdie blerrie Joodjie het 'n Britse paspoort*' [This bloody little Jewboy has a British passport], and '*Wat meer is, hulle sê hy was onlangs baie siek. Hy het geelsug gehad*' [What's more, they say he's been ill recently. He had a serious dose of jaundice].

Swanepoel told them he had directions from Brigadier Venter, his superior officer, to have me medically examined immediately because of the jaundice (they called it *geelsug*), and there were now complications with the British Embassy. And then, looking up at me on my brick and in a way very different to anything he had shown me before, he asked, in a way that showed the first signs of human recognition, where I had got a British passport from. Surely, I was born in South Africa like the rest of the Schlapobersky family? His anger was now focused on the passport. I explained that although I had been born in South Africa and had lived in Johannesburg, we had moved over the border to Swaziland, where I been naturalized as a British subject when I was eleven. I had never used a South African passport. He wanted to know about military service, and I explained that, living outside the country and holding a UK passport, I was not eligible for the army. And then he wanted to know where my ID card was and what its number was.

As a matter of principle, I carried no South African ID. I did not tell him that the insignia of the state that he 'protected' – the three-coloured flag of the Republic of South Africa and the crest they wore on their caps and lapels – had the same effect on us as Nazi swastikas.

Again, I explained that as we had settled in Swaziland while I was still a child, we had never been registered as South African citizens, and therefore I did not have an identity card.

I only learnt through what I now had to face that though he was a ruthless investigator – the leading one in the country – they had done no preparatory work to gain intelligence about me of any kind, and must have jumped to hasty conclusions as to who I was and what they might gain by my detention.

Next, he wanted to know when I had recovered from yellow jaundice, and so I gave him an account of the condition. By then it was clear that my parents were on the case and must have been trying to find grounds to mitigate what they knew would be harsh treatment.

I later found out that my parents had passed their concerns on to the British ambassador, who then got in touch with the minister of justice overnight, and he in turn had been in touch with Brigadier Venter.

I felt more relief when I saw the exasperation my UK passport was giving Swanepoel. He was more careful then, and explained that his colleague Dr Venter (a different Venter – I had no idea if he might be related to the Brigadier), a very good doctor he assured me, would be with us soon and would give me a careful examination and any treatment I required. Richter wanted to know what I wanted for breakfast. I was bemused and at a loss. They told me about the breakfast menu at the nearby restaurant and encouraged me to choose what I wanted. I could hardly believe this. When it arrived, they allowed me to sit down on the other side of the desk and I had a hearty meal. This was the first I had had to eat or drink for 24 hours – since breakfast the day before – but it was my feet that enjoyed the greatest relief.

When someone came in to report that the doctor had arrived, Swanepoel himself took me out to his office where I shook Dr Venter's hand as if we were colleagues in some strange meeting. His expression told me that he thought I stank. He had me on a sofa with Swanepoel watching and did a thorough physical examination, giving special attention to my liver. I had been seriously ill less than a year before. I panicked when he got a syringe out, but he explained that he was drawing blood, not injecting anything. On concluding, and before I had fully got my clothes on again, he turned to Swanepoel and commented under his breath, with the voice of a man whose time was being wasted: '*Daar is niks met hom verkeerd nie. Ry hom. Ry hom met geweld.*' [There is nothing wrong with him. Ride him. Ride him with force].

They went out together, talking, and I was returned to the interrogation room to sit at the desk and wait. Now what would happen? Did he really say what I thought he did? This was a doctor telling the police to 'ride me with force'. What would they do? Half an hour later Swanepoel came back in a dangerous state – as if he could bite. He shouted out, 'Get back up on your brick, Sonny Boy, we've had enough games from you and your family, and your bloody British Embassy.'

I later learnt that they had taken immediate legal advice that allowed them to challenge the British ambassador's appeal for access to me. I had been issued with a British passport but, being South African-born, I was formally someone with dual citizenship and their claim on me as a South African took precedence – they now had due legal authority to torture 'their own'.

So, I got up on the brick once more and the interrogation continued on terms that were even more ferocious than the night before. I found a way of making terms with the brick and, under my breath, I spoke to it as things continued. I learnt to say to it, 'If you don't hurt me, I promise to stand on you as gently as I can.' They must have reported my fitness to withstand torture to the brigadier, who must then have authorized continued and vigorous interrogation – but their approach did change. They saw to it that I had three meals daily, they put a jug of water on the desk so that I could drink when I needed to, they allowed me to go to the toilet when I needed it, and – most important – they never laid a hand on me again.

Swanepoel was specially focused on why injections frightened me. 'So, you think we have the truth drug here do you, sodium pentothal? We'll get what we want out of you, drugs or no drugs, so start talking now.' At a loss now and even more frightened, I got tongue-tied and must have spoken incoherently. His rage was inflamed again, and he challenged what he called 'all this exculpatory rubbish'. 'Where did your associations with these *kaffertjies* begin? And why is everything you say so exculpatory? You declare yourself responsible for nothing at all, and yet you've been breaking the law by having *kaffirs* in your home.' At that stage I had no clear idea that one of my black friends was already in their hands, or that they were already on track to bring in another. I just thought, what a long word for such an inflamed and angry man. 'Exculpatory,' I thought, 'exculpatory'.

They referred to blacks only as kaffirs. In South Africa today, you can go to jail for using the word 'kaffir'. They referred to my black friends as *kaffertjies*, a diminutive that corresponded to what they called me – *'die Joodjie'* – not diminutive as in affection, but as in derision. Their word use corresponded to their picture of blacks as subhuman. This was the nub of apartheid, and these were its high priests.

The pattern that emerged overnight was to continue for the days that followed. I stood on the brick around the clock, with breaks for meals and toilet, as a team of six men working in pairs settled down to interrogate me in four-hour shifts. I talked to them in an open voice, but in another inner voice I talked to the brick without revealing it, and the brick and I continued the ordeal together. The police each kept to defined roles in a programme that Swanepoel coordinated, and the brick 'stood up to my weight' over the days that followed. The brick and I became well acquainted, and I would talk to it under my breath, especially in the early hours when my reserves were at their lowest. Swanepoel and Richter were the 'bad cops' full of threats and hatred. The second team of two, X and Y, were the 'intellectuals' who took an interest in my studies and wanted to discuss politics and philosophy with me. One of them told me of the PhD he was working on, and said he would like to recruit me to teach his children 'the good English' I spoke. There were more sinister invitations that came later as we discussed 'the future of our country'. The third team of two, Baker and his colleague Z, were '*die Durban manne*' [the Durban guys] who spoke English like me and isiZulu like a Zulu. They were the 'good cops' who looked to befriend and protect me from '*Die Majoor*'. The interrogators had tea and coffee brought to them on a regular basis by orderlies, and '*Die Durban manne*' would sometimes engage with them in long conversations in isiZulu, some of which I could follow. They would let me sit down whilst they reviewed the material that others had been writing on the increasingly full pad of paper on the table, and they took a keen interest in my personal history and upbringing. In each team of two, one would ask questions or engage with me in direct conversation, while the other would keep a running record of everything I said. A cycle would come to an end after twelve hours and the original two would begin again, which I called 'Swanepoel's return'. It was marked by a sense of dread as he reviewed his colleagues' notes to take up issues with me that he wanted to focus on. He would trash everything I was recorded to have said, and then insist that I had better start talking. He would fling invective and credible threats in my face, all of which were sinister – and one, in particular, was appalling.

I was as frank and open as I thought I could be, not knowing how their picture of me was surrounded by layers of distortion. There were certain key things that I kept from them, some through a deliberate and conscious withholding and others that I hid from myself. I was only able to take a full inventory of my own disclosures and secrets once I was in solitary in the weeks that followed. When Swanepoel and Richter were back on duty for their evening shift, one of the men who had played a part in my own arrest came in with a sack of items that he emptied over the interrogation desk. Amongst these things were books that I knew. They belonged to a friend, Ezekiel Mokone, whom we knew as Moji, and some of them were books I had lent him. There was nothing political or suspect in any of them – they were just the possessions of a thinking young man from Soweto with aspirations to become a town planner. His plans were spilled over the desk, as mine had been the day before. There was his pass and the travel document he had used when he came to Swaziland with us. We had worked hard together at the work camp to build the school, and now he too was in here somewhere. When Swanepoel saw Alan Paton's novel '*Cry, the Beloved Country*' amongst Ezekiel's items, he turned on me with renewed scorn to disparage its author, formerly one of the leaders of the Liberal Party.

The Liberal Party had refused to comply with recent apartheid legislation that banned political parties from having mixed racial groupings in their membership and they rather chose to disband.[2] Paton had given an inspiring address at the Johannesburg disbandment, which I had gone to hear just months previously. He spoke of vision, pluck, courage and a shared determination to keep a liberal spirit alive across racial barriers. He encouraged us to maintain those bonds we could, and to do so outside organizational or institutional life, so we could defy the authorities by maintaining our own values without contravening the law. He concluded with a plea to keep hope alive for a future without apartheid.

Swanepoel knew the speech – they would have had their own people there – and he used this knowledge to pour scorn on Paton's ideas and on the novel that he said was only written to make the world feel sorry for the country's kaffirs (Paton [1949] 2002, 1968). I had no idea that I would soon be locked up close to where a central character in the novel was hanged for murder.

My emotional reaction to seeing my friend's possessions strewn across the desk gave me away. Swanepoel took careful note of this, and they questioned me closely about our relationship. They soon fell into further discussion with one another about other issues connected with his detention, and I lost track. Standing on the brick as they talked to each other, I found I was saying to myself, 'Cry, the beloved country, cry, cry, cry, cry, cry, cry, cry!' There were no tears, only dry rage and a wish to kill these men – an emotion that is still just beneath the surface when I think of them. By then the brick had become a kind of companion, a solace to this silent state of rage, and I talked to it in my mind about these terrible people sitting in front of me. In the end Ezekiel came out alright, and we later resumed our friendship in London, though I have no idea where he is today.

Day 3: Sunday 15 June

The conclusion to a night-time of interrogation should have seemed like a relief, but there was no daylight in the room and so the lights were on all the time. The markers for time through this interrogation period were provided by the arrival of meals. I was allowed to eat sitting on the opposite side of the interrogators' desk while they talked to one another and were visited on a regular basis by colleagues who were interrogating other people elsewhere. I could sometimes monitor what was happening elsewhere, but there was a lot going on and it was hard to keep track. I would look over my shoulder at the brick that had been left on its own while I was eating, and would reassure it that I would soon be back again. Breakfast might have been cheering but it was also the signal for Swanepoel's return at 8 a.m., when I was snapped to my feet once more and got on my mount as he began reading the night's interrogation notes. 'Swanepoel's return' would always culminate in a most sinister threat – to bring my girlfriend in if I did not disclose a name they wanted.

At that point I was still able to keep a record of time, so I knew it was Sunday – but I could also attribute to it the civilian clothes that Swanepoel was wearing, as on other days he would wear a uniform. The other detectives were always dressed in either suits or casual wear. He had no headgear, but he was in other respects always a police officer of seniority. His personality was at its most commanding this Sunday morning when he was visited by at least two junior police officers who I thought could be his relatives or, perhaps, were staff who were new to work of this kind. I got the impression they felt privileged to be able to pay him a visit. I stood on my brick like a scarecrow with my back to the wall while this small assembly sat down to talk together over coffee. If I got dozy and stumbled off the brick there would be a yell as one of them came and forced my head under the tap in the basin and then got me back on the brick again, so they could resume their conversation with one another.

They must have thought I was of so little consequence that they could discuss their work in my presence. Even if I had had no Afrikaans, their discussion could still have been followed, but they had no idea how much I was able to take in. Swanepoel liked an audience and, as these young officers had come to spend the morning with him instead of going to church with their families, he did not disappoint them. Their discussion ranged from accounts of his early years as a uniformed officer in the townships to his recent point of honour – the capture of Bram Fischer. The exchanges took place in gestures as well as words. At one point he was guiding them on the need for their own constant vigilance by recounting an experience in which he had been on patrol as a young man their age. '*Ek het op 'n verdagte kaffer afgekom*' [I came across a suspicious kaffir] in a township he named, and called on him to show his pass: '*Waar is jou pas, jong?*' [Where is your pass, boy?] The suspect put his hand into his pocket to give the appearance of compliance by reaching for his pass but, sensing something out of the ordinary, Swanepoel pounced on him, grabbed his hand, and, '*Kan jy dit glo, dit was 'n pistool!*' [Would you believe it, it was a pistol!] A pistol! He only just intercepted the trigger finger as the story came out in dramatic terms. It was accompanied by descriptive hand gestures, and was followed by advice about how to anticipate danger on the streets. He told them the biggest challenge of his life in the Veiligheidspolisie, the Security Police, was the capture of Bram Fischer. He reported just how many times Vorster, the prime minister, had said to him: '*Wanneer vang julle Bram Fischer? Wanneer vang julle Bram Fischer?*' [When will you catch Bram Fischer?] Without disclosing operational detail, he shared with them the glory that the capture had brought him and the team he worked with from the government, the police force and the country at large.

Fischer was an Afrikaner like them and, in Mandela's later appreciation in *Long Walk To Freedom*, he gives tribute to him 'as an Afrikaner whose conscience forced him to reject his own heritage and be ostracized by his own people, he showed a level of courage and sacrifice that was in a class by itself' (Mandela 1994: 389). He was an advocate, a senior lawyer who had held a position at the Johannesburg Bar and a leading member of the team of lawyers who defended Mandela and others, first at the Treason Trial in 1956 and then at the Rivonia Trial in 1964 when their lives were on the line. No one suspected that this prominent Afrikaans lawyer, grandson of the president of the Boer Orange River Colony and son of its judge president, was the secret head of the South African Communist Party. He was in due course identified and arrested, only to disappear during the course of his own trial while out on bail. He lived secretly in the country, directing the work of the underground until Swanepoel and his team caught him. I was still at school at the time, but it was reported in the press and we followed these events from our home in Swaziland.

I tried to take in as much as I could from the brick, feeling like a witness to history. My girlfriend Janet worked as a librarian together with Bram Fischer's daughter Ilse at the Witwatersrand University, so I was especially alert to anything relating to her father. He was still alive at the time and serving a life sentence in Pretoria Central, a more recently built prison that held political prisoners – whites in a secluded wing – and others serving long sentences. Some six years after conviction Fischer developed cancer in prison and had a fall that led to multiple fractures. The authorities' cruelty towards him had no limits. He had no appropriate care or treatment, and he was released to die at his brother's home only some weeks before his death. Today he is honoured in many ways, and one of the most notable is that the airport in his home town of Bloemfontein, the capital of the Free State province, was renamed after him (Clingman 1998).

———

Occasionally Swanepoel or Richter would look across at their man on the brick and send some special invective my way. I would respond by talking to the brick under my breath. The brick and I would discuss how they were abusing us again and I imagined the brick talking back to me saying, 'Don't worry, they'll pay for this!' Richter went on to tell his admiring audience of his work fighting against SWAPO (the South West Africa People's Organization) in what is now Namibia. SWAPO was engaged in a guerrilla war against the South African Defence Force, who were there to enforce an old League of Nations mandate. The control of the country they maintained, against the will of its people, had already been declared illegal by the United Nations. This was to be their 'bulwark' against free Africa. These Security Police were key to the counterinsurgency, and one of the prime objectives of the Terrorism Act under which they held me was the legitimation of torture in that conflict (Thornberry 2004). Our detentions were the first to widen the remit of this legislation 'for domestic use'. Richter told them he was in Windhoek more often than he was in Pretoria, and was getting used to the Boeing, which took less than three hours. He talked to them about the war against the guerrilla army and gave accounts of the capture and interrogation of their fighters, for whom he had only hatred. He was only sometimes in Windhoek – more frequently they needed him in the field. I concluded he was one of their leading torture specialists, and I still found it extraordinary that they had assigned my own case to such lethal men. He told them of his time on the Caprivi Strip, where there was regular illegal movement across the border. From my own vantage point on the brick, I contrasted his reviling hatred towards the SWAPO fighters with his strange regard for '*die Boesman*' – the 'Bushmen' or San people – whose home it was (Barnard 1992; Lee and DeVore 1995). He spoke to these colleagues with touching regard for their innocence, and it seemed to me bizarre that so sinister a man as he could also have a heart.

Day 4: Monday 16 June

During Swanepoel and Richter's morning shift I gained a new understanding of the seriousness of my position. Evidence could condemn me but lack of it could do me even more harm. They went through their colleagues' interrogation notes written the night before, focusing on my earlier university life. They had already mapped out everything I had been associated with in recent years at Witwatersrand University in Johannesburg. This past evening, they had gone through the detail of my earlier year at the University of Cape Town. I had played a minor part helping to arrange Robert Kennedy's visit to deliver a celebrated human rights lecture in 1966.[3] The police hated our students' union and were deeply suspicious of everything we did. Only one year had passed since the events of 1968 in Europe and North America, and they were determined to pre-empt any corresponding activity.

College House, the hall of residence I stayed in while at the University of Cape Town, was occupied by many reactionary white students who were angered by my close involvement with the National Union of South African Students, NUSAS. They also resented the scholarship I had earlier won to study for a year in the USA. One night they broke into my room, put a sack over my head so I could not identify them, took my clothes off, put a woman's nightie on me, and tied me up to the Rondebosch Fountain at an intersection near the university. Then they removed the sack and I stood exposed in women's clothing tied to a lamp post, and they made a large circle at a safe distance and sang, 'I like to be in America, everything's free in America ...', from *West Side Story*. When the police arrived, they arrested me. The students who were responsible later came to the police station to acknowledge what they had done, but the police still regarded me as the suspect. Although I was released without charge, a report was made, and I had to attend interviews with both the police and the university authorities. The experience shook me, left me profoundly depressed, helped to unsettle my stay and I did not complete the year there. Although this incident and the dreadful atmosphere in the hall of residence were not the only factors at work, they contributed to my decision to drop out of medical school in Cape Town and to re-enrol at Witwatersrand University in Johannesburg the following year.

This whole story came out during the overnight interrogation. On reviewing the interrogation notes, Swanepoel and Richter sent directions for their colleagues to phone the Security Police in Cape Town to find out what I had been doing there, but news came back during the day that I was not even known to them. They must have done a trawl through their intelligence service at the university and then at Cape Town's equivalent of Compol, based at the Roeland Street Jail. Swanepoel and Richter were on duty when the news came through and I followed the exchanges by which the investigators outside brought the interrogators inside up to date. At one point, Swanepoel turned to Richter and said, as if to reassure him that they had not arrested the wrong man: '*Die kommunis is nie in NUSAS nie. Hy sit agter die skerms en sy werk is onsigbaar*' [The communist is not in NUSAS. He sits behind the scenes and his work is invisible]; '*Ons het baie meer om te ontdek*' [We have got a lot more to discover].

Richter went on to challenge the way I always cast myself as 'innocent'. I was a student organizer, he said. Given how much Marxist literature they found in my home – which he now had the chance to have a look at – I was clearly an organizer and would lead people in the direction of what students had been doing in London, Paris and the USA. He was convinced we had been planning things sitting round the fireside at our work camp in Swaziland, and that was evidence enough. What is more, he said, I would do it invisibly and from behind, pretending to the world that I was doing nothing more than building schools. The absence of evidence only worked to underline my culpability.

During their evening shift, Swanepoel and Richter moved on to different areas of enquiry. They had given up their earlier strategy of a non-directed 'floating enquiry'. Now that I was so grossly affected by sleep deprivation, they were focused and wanted to know if I had ever met Winnie Mandela. I had been expecting this. In order to conceal the truth about my one, passing encounter with Mrs Mandela, I gave an open account that withheld its content and detail. What follows is the substance and truth of the encounter, followed by the different narrative I gave the police.

I explained that I had been visiting the United States Information Service in Central Johannesburg, USIS, to review entry requirements for my future postgraduate study at an American university. I met one of their information officers, a black man from Soweto named Mohale Mahanyele, and in the course of two or three visits there we befriended each other and I invited him to dinner at our home. Our mother was then living in Johannesburg, my younger brother David and my sister Marian were attending local day schools and I was in my first year at Witwatersrand University. Invitations of this kind across the colour bar did not happen in Johannesburg at that time, but our own values were different. We had recently had a black family from Swaziland to stay with us after they had driven up to collect their daughter when she returned after a one-year scholarship to the USA on the same programme that had sent me there two years earlier. So, a black guest coming from Soweto for dinner was not outside our own set of values.

I had set the arrangement up with my mother, and found, when the guest arrived at the door, that he was accompanied by Mrs Mandela. He presented her at the door and she then introduced herself. It took my breath away. I recognized her from newspaper photographs and was immediately aware that I was in the presence of a remarkable person – articulate, poised, dignified and beautiful. We set an extra place at the table and over dinner she had a warm, engaging presence and interacted with my mother and little brother and sister, and with her own companion. When the children were later sent to bed, we went to the living room for coffee together and talked politics. She knew I had been responsible for bringing young people from Alex and Soweto out to work camps to build schools in Swaziland, and was impressed. She went on to tell us that her husband Nelson was made to suffer seriously on 'The Island' (Robben Island, where he was imprisoned), along with the others. She explained that the strength of his presence there made him a leader amongst them, and that he would one day be the country's first black president. We could only express our shared hope that this would come about. My mother and I were concerned to know how her husband was coping, and how their daughters were. They were younger than my own siblings and she was especially interested to hear about my mother's plans to enrol David and Marian at Waterford Kamhlaba school in the coming year. This was to be the school her own children would later attend. The detail of our exchange is lost in the mists of time.

At the time I shared with our dinner guests a story of my own as we had coffee together, and I described how I had escorted our other guests – this black family from Swaziland – to the airport when they collected their daughter. They had then come back to stay with us overnight, but left well before dawn for the long drive home through 'enemy territory'. A family of blacks in their own car driving through the East Rand and highveld with Swaziland licence plates was a sitting target. They could have been subject to police violence and I wanted to help them get beyond the most hazardous part of the trip. Their car followed mine through the darkness on an easy route I picked out for them through the mines of the East Rand and onto the open road on the other side of the town of Springs. I left them there to continue the journey home. In the pre-dawn drive we passed columns of mine workers in their hundreds setting out for underground work from their hostels with their miners' lamps on. I described to Mrs Mandela and her colleague what I had seen, and thought it only a matter of time before those columns of people rose against their servitude. She said, 'We are waiting.' There was an implied invitation for me to join her in what they were waiting for, but I demurred. That was as far as our exchange had gone and they left soon after. I did not see her again and never visited the USIS again either. Days later I contracted jaundice and the illness laid me low for the remainder of the university term. In discussion with my mother later that night, we agreed on just how fortunate we had been to meet this remarkable person, though we concurred that further association would be unwise.

The account given here is not what I shared with the interrogators. I told them that we had kept the truth of Mrs Mandela's identity from my mother, and had just had an evening of talk about the United States Information Service, about cultural things and world politics, and about Waterford Kamhlaba School, where she was considering sending her daughters and where my brother and sister were enrolled to begin soon. I relied on the truth in this account to hide what I did not want the police to discover. The evening's events are returned to in Day 33, to illustrate how Mrs Mandela herself protected my mother and gave very little away in the account she provided to the police. Swanepoel and Richter were far from happy with my account. They were convinced that there was more to it than I had disclosed. But then they wanted to know about somebody else, a distinguished black journalist I knew in passing, Joyce Sikakane, who had been detained together with Winnie Mandela in the first of the arrests. I hardly knew her, but on one occasion I raised a question with her on behalf of a young musician who had befriended me.

This friend, Bethue Folie – we knew him as Pepe – played the jazz clarinet and wanted to get to Lusaka to join another close friend, Dumile Feni, a leading artist who had left South Africa to go and live there. I had come to know these artists and musicians through an interracial association based at the home of Bill Ainslie, director of the Johannesburg College of Art, whom I was just getting to know.[4] My friend Bethue the clarinettist was attached to people with whom he could feel secure, and was upset when his revered friend Dumile Feni left for Lusaka. I was at the time so naive that I had no idea 'Lusaka' was a coded reference for joining the African National Congress, which had its headquarters there. I later learnt that Dumile, the artist, had joined the liberation movement there. He went on to play a significant part in the struggle down the years, and one of his works now stands in a place of honour at the front of the country's Constitutional Court.[5] My picture of his young friend Bethue was of a vulnerable person who had lived in a highly dependent relationship with Dumile. He seemed to have transferred his attachment to me and, whenever we met up, he would ply me with requests to help him to get to Lusaka. I passed this query on to the journalist Joyce Sikakane when I met her in passing at the university. She could not help, and from then on she seemed to avoid me (Sikakane 1977). In the months following, Bethue found a way of booking his own rail fare to Lusaka. He then asked if I could help him to get his suitcase from Orlando – a part of Soweto – to Park Station, where he would catch his train. I only had a motor scooter but knew one friend who had a car, Derek Momberg, and we made the arrangements to collect Bethue and his suitcase in Soweto. Derek was a university friend with an Afrikaans background who had introduced me to Lionel Abrahams's poetry circle. Our plan was that Bethue would come to my home and, from there, direct us to his home in Orlando to collect his suitcase and possessions, and we would drive him to the station. We would not otherwise have been able to find our way to where he lived. We did this and saw him off. Some months later I again found Bethue at the gathering of another friend. He had been to Lusaka where he had found his friend Dumile, he told me, but he had been encouraged to continue with his musical career in Johannesburg.

These events had all taken place a year and more prior to my arrest. I could not understand why the police were so focused on them. What disappointed them most was the discovery that, in getting Bethue to Lusaka via Park Station, I was helped by this white friend Derek who had an Afrikaans name. We had done everything so openly, which, instead of allaying their suspicion, only heightened it. They discussed with each other in Afrikaans Derek's likely identity and made a careful note of his details, taking account also of a visit I had paid to his home in a part of the city in which wealthy Afrikaners lived. They were even more disquieted when the one who went out to make further enquiries came back to report that in the family to which my friend belonged, the father was indeed, as they thought, an influential figure in finance or mining – I cannot now recall what he did – and held a position of authority in the Afrikaans world. It seemed they knew him by his reputation. I had no doubt that they were at that point investigating Derek to see what they could find out about him. They were also infuriated with me that I had given them only Bethue's first name. I continued to insist that I had never known his surname.

They were increasingly frustrated that key leads of enquiry, which were evidently responsible for my detention, had led them into shallow water. I had no deeper political involvement in anything, but they were not yet satisfied that they had the whole story. Swanepoel and Richter continued with relentless aggression, and then began to threaten that unless I told them the rest of the story, they would bring in my partner Janet. This took on a new level of horror. I had so far given them only Bethue's first name, and I insisted that I did not know his surname and could not recall the address from which we had collected him in Orlando. At some point during the onslaught, Swanepoel said to his lieutenant, to quieten him down and temper his aggression, 'Hy's *nog nie gebreek nie. Môreoggend of miskien môreaand sal ons heeltemal uitvind'* [He's not yet broken. Tomorrow morning or perhaps in the evening, we'll find out everything].

Well, they never did, but later that night the exchange took an even worse turn. I was no longer on the brick as I could hardly stand. Now while X and Y were on their shift, I was seated at the desk facing them and, after the scorching I had had from the 'bad cops', it was a relief to exchange something with someone who talked to me like a human being. X was a thoughtful and educated man and was interested in the areas of my university curriculum I was most involved with currently – the philosophy of mind. He had already told me that he had recently done a lot of travelling in India doing work-related tours of enquiry, and he had made jokes about getting me to teach 'my good English' to his children. He was looking to foster an accord. In the previous year one of my history lecturers had shared with us his approach to historical methods of research that lay behind his books on the Portuguese voyages of discovery in the fifteenth and sixteenth centuries (Newitt 1995). At some point in the darkest hours of the night, as we talked about these subjects, X learnt that after I had recovered from jaundice the previous year I had been on holiday in Mozambique during the summer holiday.

I was interested in Ilha de Moçambique, the small island in the north that had given its name to the country. Vasco da Gama had set out for India from this island. I went to the country's capital – still known as Lourenco Marques at the time – just two hours' drive from my home in Swaziland and booked a berth through a shipping line on one of the boats that sailed north to the island – there was no other way to reach it. After making my booking, I got onto the boat in the evening, ready for a very early start the next morning, and settled in the cabin I had booked. Unexpectedly, I was taken off with the dramatic intervention of a police escort. Frelimo, the Mozambique Liberation Front, had succeeded in liberating large parts of the country's northern provinces where they were engaged in bitter fighting against the Portuguese army and its South African allies. Although this was a civilian boat, it was in military service on this voyage and so would not allow civilian passengers. The shipping line had seemingly acted in error, and I was directed to get off the boat and go back to the shipping line and reclaim my fare the next day.[6]

As X took up my interest in African affairs and history, he led me to talk about my own future. 'Well,' he said, 'you have a strong commitment to the country and its people. And, so do we. If you wanted to work with us, we could pay your way through the rest of your university course and we could send you to Ilha de Mozambique. You could do some very valuable work for us.' I was waiting for something like this but had no idea where it might come from or what it might look like when it did. I asked him if he was a Christian, and he laughed and said he was supposed to be the one asking the questions. 'Well,' I said, 'if you are a Christian then you would know that according to your own religion, the world is divided between good and evil and, according to your faith, the Devil is in charge of its evil. Why would I want to join those of you already in hell working for the Devil?' They did not like my reply and put me back on the brick, which is where Swanepoel and Richter found me in the morning. When I got back onto the brick, I sang silently to it, 'Hello darkness, my old friend / I've come to talk with you again.' The brick and I got even closer that night as I began to sing to it under my breath.

Simon and Garfunkel were my solace and support. I could not remember all the words at the time but the repetition of this opening to 'The Sounds of Silence' allowed me to feel I had secret companions, and to this day I still smile about it. The song has seen me through many dark nights since. My daughter Hannah used to sing it with me in the car on the long evening journeys back to her mother's home, and she will now read for the first time when this music, like 'Shenandoah' and 'The Song of the Volga Boatmen' that we used to sing together, became my music. I have put 'The Sound of Silence' to work in so many different ways. It opens a chapter in a previous book of mine devoted to silence and resilience in psychotherapy (Schlapobersky 2016a: Chapter 5). I call on it to encourage people in extremis to treat health threats as 'old friends' to whom they can sing these words. The return of a recurrent illness that someone may have hoped they were free of – from arthritis to cancer or depression – can be addressed with words like these and, though they cannot halt the course of a disease, these words can lift the spirit and help people to rise above it.

Day 5: Tuesday 17 June

This was a defining day. They were making sure I ate well, had food of my choice brought in three times daily and they even began to allow me to have a cup of whatever they were drinking – tea or coffee – to ensure my stamina was kept up to endure the standing ordeal and maximize the effects of sleep deprivation. I had not yet slept at all since the previous Thursday night at home. I was increasingly confused, which is what they wanted. My feet were now so painful they could hardly tolerate the brick that I had been put back on overnight, and a back pain had set in that would not go away. The interrogators were ferocious in their continuing engagement and I was still puzzled about why. Each of the three interrogation teams continued with the ardour of their own respective 'protocols' – Swanepoel and Richter with fire and brimstone; X and Y with intellectual jousting; and Baker and Z with a seemingly benevolent interest in the people I mixed with in Swaziland while at school, and in the USA during my year abroad.

Swanepoel was as enraged as ever when his 8 a.m. shift began. He claimed he had discovered a whole new set of facts that proved I had been involved in illegal activities. He worked himself up into an extraordinary rage as I stood mutely in front of him. Unless I 'talked' by that evening, my girlfriend would be arrested, he said. They hammered this point home throughout the day, but I could not fully take in what they were saying. I dozed off on my feet and walked into the wall, waking up when my face banged against it. There were roars of laughter from somewhere, but I could not get my eyes to focus and see who was laughing. It happened repeatedly and when I finally got some clarity, I saw that a whole mob of police had crowded into the room to watch me walk into walls. I smiled meekly, so pleased they were happy and not angry. And then I was somewhere else, and grotesque images unfolded in front of me. I was in the science laboratory back at high school, the bell was ringing, and it was time to go home. 'I'm going home now,' I said, 'the experiment has gone far enough.' There were more roars of laughter that seemed to come from a long way off.

I was allowed to sit down for a period and gained some composure on a chair, but there was more drama once office hours enabled Swanepoel and Richter to direct their staff to get in touch with the secret police in Mozambique. They thought they might find some sort of lead there, but when the news later came into the interrogation room that I was unknown there too, Richter finally discounted me, saying to Swanepoel: 'Hy's nie 'n kommunis nie, hy's mal' [He's not a communist, he's mad]. 'In die een geval na die ander volg ons 'n ondersoeklyn, net om uit te vind daar is niks daarin nie. Hy's rooi, heeltemal rooi, maar sy hande staan leeg en ons mors ons tyd' [In one case after another we pursue a line of enquiry only to find there is nothing in it. He is actually as red as you get, but he hasn't done anything and we're wasting our time].

He had much more to say about me along these lines, but this was the gist of it. By Tuesday evening my orientation in time and place had been destroyed. I did not know which stage of my life I was living in, or where I was. I finally got the picture of what they were looking for during Swanepoel and Richter's night shift. They were taking advantage of the effects of sleep deprivation – confusion and bewilderment – to get me engaged in wide-ranging conversations about one thing or another, and they would then come around with a snap focus – so what's the name of that man you sent to Lusaka! I would stand my ground and insist that I had not sent anyone to Lusaka. Then one of them would say, 'But you told us a few hours ago that you sent him to Lusaka, and you helped him with your friend who had a car.' 'Oh,' I would say, 'so you're talking about Bethue again.' 'Yes,' came the reply, 'and what's his surname, his full name.' And I would again insist that I did not know. We went around like this so many times. Swanepoel and Richter threatened that unless I told them the name, they would detain Janet. I was very worried, as it was possible that they might not be bluffing. Later I heard them talking to each other in Afrikaans about how, if necessary, on Wednesday morning one of them would collect Janet from the university library where she worked and bring her in without arresting her. They did not appear to have a strategy for her detention but I think they intended using her to frighten me into further disclosure. When they came around again to ask me for the full name, I gave it – Bethue Folie – I said. At first they did not accept the disclosure as it was given, and we went around in further circles of interrogation for some time. But then they moved on to other lines of enquiry and did not come back to further questions about Bethue, which indicated to me that they now had as much information as they needed, in order to find him.

Bethue was detained a day or two later and held for some months, and was then amongst the first contingent of black detainees to be released. At the time I felt I had betrayed him, as indeed I had. The burden has never left me and the acknowledgment of it in this memoir, given here so many years later, may help me to live with this a little better. I learnt from others I knew in the London world of South African music that he had survived the detention and had resumed a musical career in Johannesburg afterwards. One of his fellow musicians in London said to me that it was important I knew at first hand what they were going through all the time.

The 'soft-liners' were on duty from noon and through the afternoon. Their 'charity' and 'concessions' – sitting instead of standing, and coffee to drink when theirs was brought in – put me in a state of dependence as I had grown to rely on them for any residual sense of safety. But today they ended their 'conspiracy of kindness', withdrew their concessions and threw me into a state of further alarm. They became abusive and threatening, which caused acute confusion. By the time Swanepoel and Richter returned for their evening shift, I could only mutter nonsense in a high-pitched voice. I could not eat, became faint and dizzy and was increasingly bewildered. Sleep deprivation had made me psychotic – I saw and heard things that were not there. I was dreaming as I talked to these police, and I experienced the dream as if it were a hallucination –

something real happening in the room. I saw past assailants clustered around me only to wake fully in a startled state to realize I was facing a policeman. Then I imagined I was walking into the school laboratory and a wall woke me with a blow to the face as I recognized where I now stood. I believed I was at any one of a number of different places in Swaziland at different stages of my upbringing, and especially at school. Thinking I would go for a swim in a mountain pool outside the town in which the school was located, I would try to walk off but then bump into the wall, which woke me back to my real location. I would look up and find the two interrogators 'on duty', plus several others who had crowded in. As before, they were all laughing as they watched me walk into walls.

They allowed me to sit at the desk, but they still intended to continue with their routine. On asking for the toilet, I sat down for as long as I could on the toilet seat with Richter standing outside – a strategy I had been making increasing use of as a way of getting the weight off my feet. I was soon told to come out by an irritated and increasingly angry Richter. I looked down at my feet on either side of the toilet, but they did not seem to be mine. They were much bigger and looked like they belonged to a giant. My shoes had no laces and it looked like they were being split open at the top by the swollen feet inside. I found it very hard to get up off the toilet and onto my feet. I was unsteady on coming out and was brought back to the interrogation room where Swanepoel was waiting for me. Virtually unable to speak, I pointed to my feet. Richter did not have to explain how unsteady I was – he was propping me up. Swanepoel went off and came back with a bottle of small yellow tablets and told me I had to take two with a glass of water every few hours. They must have been diuretics for I then needed to urinate every twenty minutes or so. After a few hours of continuing talk in which they came back to Bethue's name again and again, not yet convinced they already had it, one of them put me to bed on a stretcher in Swanepoel's office and I remember being covered with a blanket.

Day 6: Wednesday 18 June

I was woken by Swanepoel in the early morning darkness, still on the stretcher in his office, and I was convinced we were in the Kruger Park amongst Afrikaans people. We used to go there regularly for holidays and would sleep on stretchers and converse with Afrikaners. This delusion gave such relief – I was back in the familiar bushveld, much like our home in Swaziland – until Swanepoel spoke. His voice was the sound of a nightmare. I was escorted back to the desk in the interrogation room and questioned until lunchtime. I kept asking them when I would be going to prison. Continued exposure was unbearable. I just wanted it to end. It seemed they wanted to keep me talking but my guess is that I could not keep my head up for any length of time and I do remember dozing with my head on the desk until one of them banged the desk loudly and got me to stand up, and he put my head in the basin to wake me up.

One of the others was curious as to why I wanted to be taken to prison. I would get very lonely there, he said, and would be only too pleased when one of them came to pay me a visit. In the blur of associations and memories, it is hard to retrieve any clear lines of enquiry except that in response to my repeated enquiries – as to whether or not I would be charged for anything – they only referred to the books they had found in my possession. It seemed as if there was nothing else of which I was culpable. I was persistent with this request for clarity until Swanepoel explained the procedure to come. Now he took on a new disposition – unctuous, ingratiating, solicitous and kind – as if he had nothing to do with these days of torture and would now comfort me for their consequences. It is hard to say which of his very different sides was the more loathsome – the rough voice of spleen and fury or the obsequious uncle. He told me that another Security Police major would take charge of my case from now on – a very nice man, he said, Major Coetzee, who had one blue eye and one brown eye. At some point in the future I would have some meetings with him to discuss my case, and a statement would be drawn up containing the information I had given them during the interrogation. Only when I signed the statement would they be in a position to inform me about what would be happening in my case. He went off then and I did not see him again for another two weeks. The interrogation was now concluded but they had no staff ready to cart me back to prison, so I sat dozing with my head on the desk where I saw several loose pens. I tucked one of them in my sleeve and, on one of the many visits to the toilet, I hid it between my legs inside my underpants.

When it was time to go, I could not walk properly because of the back pain and the oedema – the swelling in my legs and feet for which I had still been taking diuretics. I was given no medication to take with me as I struggled to get along the corridor to the back exit where a car was waiting to take me to prison. I was unbalanced and could not walk in a straight line. When I kept on walking into walls, one of them would guide me along, and then I believed that I was in the science laboratory at school where this kind master – the school teacher – was helping me with an experiment. The hallucinations were vivid and credible. When we got outside, the light was shocking. The car park was busy, traffic was coming in and out, and I was especially struck by the number of black Security Police in uniform. At one moment I wanted to challenge them about working for their own oppressors, and at another moment I thought they were the black staff in the canteen at my boarding school and wanted to talk to the one I knew well. He would make sure the other boys did not steal my food. Years on, here he was again! I was unable to tell the difference between a mad present and a threatening past – there was no regulator for consciousness. It kept tipping between different states of mind. Sensory detail was magnified, distorted and alarming. I can remember a police Land Rover coming into the parking area as I was being loaded into the car that was to take me back to prison, and saw a team of black policemen getting out of it – how ridiculous I thought they were, strutting about in the uniform of their oppressors. I can still see the dust on their vehicle, and I had in my nostrils the burnt rubber smell of tyres after a long journey. I wondered how far they had gone to arrest others. It did not occur to me that the offensive smell was my own.

Notes

1. See 'Apartheid Legislation 1850s–1970s'. It is a moving outcome to the abolition of this legislation to be able to report that one of those who helped me to reach Zureena Desai, through whom I was able to contact Susanne Klausen and verify the names and identities of Major Coetzee and Lieutenant Jordaan, is Professor Shahid Vawda, who holds the Archie Mafeje Chair as the Director, School of African and Gender Studies, Anthropology and Linguistics, University of Cape Town. See 'Prologue' note 9 and 'Interrogation II' note 4.
2. See 'Prohibition of Political Interference Act No 51 of 1968'. It banned political parties from having a multiracial membership. Later renamed the 'Prohibition of Foreign Financing of Political Parties Act', it was designed to prevent racial groups from collaborating for political purposes, and was enacted to undermine the Liberal Party's multiracial policy.
3. See Robert F. Kennedy's 'Day of Affirmation Address' 1966. This address (the 'Ripple of Hope' speech) was given to an audience of eighteen thousand at the University of Cape Town on 6 June 1966 on behalf of the National Union of Students on the University's 'Day of Reaffirmation of Academic and Human Freedom'. It received praise in the media, shook up the political situation in South Africa, and is considered his greatest and most famous speech.
4. See 'Tribute to Bill Ainslie', 2006.
5. See 'Dumile Feni in "The Constitutional Court Art Collection"'.
6. A comprehensive account of Mozambique, its long history under Portuguese administration and the battle for the country's liberation against the Portuguese alliance with South Africa, is available in *A History of Mozambique* (Newitt 1995).

SOLITARY CONFINEMENT
The Hanging Jail

Day 6: Wednesday 18 June

I have no recollection of the journey back to prison but do have a returning memory of being strip-searched outside my cell while, secretly, I did what I could to guard the treasure I had with me – the stolen pen hidden in my underpants. Protecting it brought me out of the sleep I must have been having on my feet. Once inside the cell I found the other treasure, the Bible that had been taken off my bookshelf – it was still here waiting for me.

As the door slammed, I collapsed on the 'bed' – a felt mat on the floor in one corner that had two woollen blankets folded on it. I struggled to get my shoes off and found that my feet were bruised and discoloured. Like my ankles, they were more than twice their normal size, so removing my shoes was difficult. I had not washed or bathed for almost a week and discovered that the smell – what I had thought was burning rubber in the Compol car park – was coming from my shoes, feet and socks. The bruising was extensive in the arch of each foot, rising on the instep and up around the ankles. The swelling extended to my knees. Propped against the wall in the corner of the cell and alone for the first time in days, I began to weep, stricken with a kind of crying I have never known before or since. The pen was my solace and I began the first of many letters to Janet, each written on two sheets of toilet paper. I had no idea if this would work, but I tried it out and found it would do. I tore one sheet off the toilet roll that stood beside the slops bucket and, tucking myself up in the blankets on the mat in the corner, I found that I could lay a sheet on the Bible and write onto the toilet paper's fragile surface with careful concentration. I can recall little of the content, but used words on the page to reach out in love and desperation. Then I rolled my message round the pen and stowed it away underneath my trousers which I used to make a pillow in the corner, and I then fell asleep for more than twenty-four hours.

Day 7: Thursday 19 June

I slept through Wednesday afternoon, the whole of Wednesday night and most of the next day. Late on Thursday afternoon as the light outside was fading, casting shadows of the barred window onto the opposite wall, I was woken by the evening meal being brought in by a black prisoner under the supervision of a white warder. The tray was placed on the floor beside the slops bucket, which stood in the corner by the door. I watched from my 'bed' as he collected the three uneaten meals that had been brought in over the previous twenty-four hours, one by one. They must have tried to rouse me and found it impossible. I had wet myself while asleep, and my underpants were now stuck to me. I could not put my shoes on as my feet were still painful and swollen. I had no change of clothing and still had only the garments I had been wearing on the morning of my arrest. It was getting cold and I had to keep on urinating in the slops bucket. I was also uncomfortably constipated but was unsure if that had to do with my reluctance to use the slops bucket. I took off my soiled underpants and rinsed them, and my smelly socks, into the slops bucket using drinking water from the jug. Then, putting the slops bucket under the window, I found I could get up on it and hang the pants and socks on the window ledge. I could just pull myself up on the bars in the window to get a view of the sky outside and see the roofs of the prison block and a distant row of jacaranda trees. I could not manage to stay up there long, and came down to eat.

Afterwards I began a pacing routine that occupied much of my time in the days that followed. There was nothing in my cell except a slops bucket for a toilet, a roll of toilet paper, a bottle of disinfectant, a water jug and a mug, two blankets on a felt mat against the wall and my Bible. The cell was six paces long and three paces wide. There was a barred window high on the outside wall in the top right corner though which I could see the sky. The cell had been painted a familiar hospital green in recent years. There was writing on the left-hand wall just above my bed. There were also other marks and initials elsewhere on the walls that had been covered over by paintwork, but this one inscription was fully readable: 'KNOX MASI FOR MUDER I WAS SENTENCE . . .'. He never finished his sentence on the wall. Did he finish his prison sentence? What was his fate? At least his message had survived. Who was he? What had happened to him? Where was I when he wrote it and where was I now, what was this terrible place?

Then I began to read the Bible. As the light fell, I heard singing from somewhere below. It was close enough for me to hear sorrow in the repeated melodic lines, but it was too far for me to hear the words. At that point I still had no idea who was singing or why, but I found it deeply consoling and it continued through the night. As the evening wore on, a warder outside doing his last patrol opened the eye hole in the door to look at me and called out in Afrikaans that the light would soon be turned off. I had no idea who was in the cells on either side of me, I never saw anyone and, from within my cell, I heard little local activity. There were regular cries and calls from further away, mostly in the night. It was very uncomfortable lying on the felt mat and sleeping on one rough blanket under the cover of another, and it never got easier. This mat was the only 'furniture' in the cell, but it gave me a corner refuge during the day, which I called the sofa, where I would often doze off while reading the Bible. And then it was a place to sleep at night, which I then called the bed. The pillow was made up of my shirt and trousers. During this first phase of recovery from sleep deprivation, I could not keep my eyes open after darkness fell. It would later take me a long time to fall asleep at night.

Day 8: Friday 20 June

This was to be the first day in my cell when I was able to stay awake through the normal prison routines. It began with a clamour of noise in the darkness outside and the steady sound of shovels grating on concrete as prison labourers stoked the furnace. There was singing in the background – slow, steady, sad, repetitive and beautiful – the same singing I had heard the night before. At dawn the singing stopped and so did all the other sounds around me, and for about half an hour there was complete silence. Then all the activity started up and all the other noises began again. The door was opened by a white warder who shouted, '*Kos!*' (food), and I collected the tray off the floor just outside the door where a black prisoner had left it. There was coffee with mielie meal porridge and a small square loaf of bread plus some butter and jam – as basic as anything could be, but despite that, quite edible, though I had little appetite. I was alert to sounds and noises all around, and I continued to struggle to find my bearings.

After breakfast the door was opened again, and I was told to clean my cell floor with the cloth that a black prisoner gave me. I then had to stand outside for the prison commander's inspection. He was a big, fierce man who strode past, cell by cell so none of us saw any of the others. My door was opened but I was not allowed out until the preceding door had been slammed shut, and then I was brought out and told to stand to attention as he passed by. Then I was sent back inside and locked up while the next prisoner was inspected – and so it went. This was to be a daily routine. The next time the cell opened the warder called out, '*Badkamer!*' (bathroom), and as I came out of the door he put a small white cotton towel in my hands and gave me a square of soap. But then he stopped me and pointed towards the slops bucket and the bottle of disinfectant that stood beside it. I did not know what he wanted me to do, and in a gruff state of impatience he directed me to bring them along. We left the cell door open and I followed him down the corridor with other cells on the same side as mine – there were some forty cells in all – and we arrived at the bathroom. My swollen feet were already getting better and, for the first time, it was possible to get my shoes on. I was directed first to empty the slops pail into the toilet and clean it with disinfectant, and then to get in the shower. The warder stood nearby. The little square of soap allowed me to wash myself and my underpants and socks, and it also served as toothpaste on my finger. At the basin I stood looking at myself in the mirror above it. I was still here! I did not know what to say to the person in the mirror except, 'I'm still here!' I looked like I normally looked and could see few signs of the ordeal in the face of the person staring out at me – except that I had lost weight, looked pale and my unbrushed hair stood wild on my head. To reassure myself and to master the fear I saw, I told the reflection, 'John, don't worry, you're still here. We'll get through this.' We were soon on our way back to the cell where the sound of the door slamming behind me was dreadful once more. Now I knew why solitary was called 'confinement'. The rush of air as the door slammed, its noise and the sound of its locks being turned from the outside, ended the short reprieve.

I sat on the blankets, now folded in a different way to turn them into my sofa, and began to read the Bible. I had already made a beginning the evening before, but I was still reading at random and finding it difficult to concentrate. I had been at a Church of England school and so knew passages from the New Testament. I had had a religious upbringing as a Jew and, from my bar mitzvah education, I knew the books of Genesis, Exodus and Kings, and was familiar with passages from elsewhere in the Five Books of Moses. But the Prophets and Psalms were new to me as whole bodies of text, and were to become absorbing and consoling. Because concentration was difficult, and because I later found the amount of violence in the Old Testament difficult to tolerate, I chose to read only from the New Testament in the morning, when I was at my worst. In some of the Gospels I found a benevolent spirit uplifting, but was unsettled by the accounts of Christ in front of Caiaphas, the high priest, and then by Pontius Pilate washing his hands before Christ's execution. I was brought face to face here with my own experience. I kept the Old Testament for the afternoon, and was again unsettled by its more punitive passages.

It was hard to find all of the Torah, the Five Books of Moses, readable. I was fully absorbed by Genesis and Exodus, and read my way through the beauty and concision of the language, with my attention held by the compelling storylines and their imaginative detail. But Numbers, Leviticus and Deuteronomy were almost unreadable. I came early to the account of Joseph thrown into a pit by his brothers and sold into slavery. His later ordeal in Pharaoh's prison led me to reflect on my own dreams, often fear-filled and alarming, and I wondered what a soothsayer could foretell that might reveal my fate. I forced myself to read progressively and not to choose random sections of text. I made my way through the Gospels systematically, and found the Sermon on the Mount in Matthew uplifting and consoling. The vivid narratives and storyline in the lives of the patriarchs picked me up, and so did the story of Moses, his brother and sister in Exodus, and the Israelites' redemption. The eventful passages in Kings that describe the prophets like Samuel and Elijah also held my attention, as did the historical sequence from Samuel through Saul to David and Solomon. I found the different challenges in David's life refracted through passages in the Psalms that build fortitude out of despair. The Nevi'im, the Prophets including Isaiah and Jonah, and the Kethuvim, the Writings, including Psalms, Proverbs, Job, The Song of Songs, Ruth Lamentations, Ecclesiastes, Esther and Daniel, were all new to me as whole texts and some of them seemed to open the bars of the windows.

Then a warder, a cheerful older man named Oom [uncle] Charlie, reappeared and called out, '*Oefening!*' [exercise], and when I did not understand, he said in English that I was going outside. We took a route along the corridor in the opposite direction from the one by which I had arrived, and we went through several locked grill doors, which the turnkeys opened and closed behind us. Then we went down two flights of stairs, through further sets of grills, and finally came out into a rectangular exercise yard with a blue sky. It was the first sky I had been aware of seeing for a long time. Walking into the sunlight was welcome but shocking. The warder pointed out where I was to walk and for half an hour I went backwards and forwards in a courtyard about twenty-five yards in length, framed by high brick walls. Black warders sometimes passed through it, but it was otherwise empty. Then he called out for us to return and I was soon back in the cell and, as the door slammed once more, the chill of the setting was overwhelming. I had to put my blankets around me to stop myself shivering. This was to be the daily routine for the rest of my time in prison.

Day 9: Saturday 21 June

This third day in solitary was unbearable. The confinement was suffocating. There had been no overnight singing and I missed the men's voices. I still had no idea who they were or why they sang through the night, night after night. On Saturday morning there were no voices. Each day, the periods after the shower and before and after the outside exercise were the most difficult because, each time I came back and the door slammed shut, the cell felt smaller and smaller. I did twenty-five press-ups and some other exercises, and then immersed myself in the Gospels. And then I paced. And paced. And paced. And then I would sit down and sing. I sang Simon and Garfunkel's 'Sounds of Silence' that had seen me through the interrogation. Their song 'A Most Peculiar Man' would bring me close to tears, though I could not remember all the verses. We had

had a gathering at our home on the Saturday night before my arrest, when we lit a fire in the grate and sang as one of our friends played this on his guitar. It gives haunting beauty to anonymity, confinement and death by suicide. Its desolation answered my state of mind, and I sang the lines I could remember repeatedly. They have stayed with me and I live to challenge their surrender.

If the desolation threatened to overtake me, I would break into 'The Volga Boatmen's Song', or Dylan's 'Mr Tambourine Man' – the verses I could remember – or 'Shenandoah', and I would sing them again and again. They have determination, resolve, purpose and drive. The first needed no words, the second took imagination to the sky and the third filled the cell with longing. 'The Volga Boatmen's Song' gave a rhythm to the pacing of the cell – six steps in one direction and three in the other. Everything became impossible after any period of application and I would have to stop after some time and then hoist myself up to the cell window to look over the prison roofs and see what birdlife there might be on the gutters that day. There were jacaranda trees in the distance, and the birds came and went between the trees and the prison gutters. I would usually see sparrows, doves and pigeons, but occasionally I saw less frequent lowveld birds – barbets and starlings – that did not come up to the Johannesburg highveld in those years. I could move the slops pail from the location in which it was supposed to be and, by putting it under the window and standing carefully on its rim, I could gain some height and then pull myself up to look out more easily.

Today was the winter solstice. In the afternoon I took myself in hand and drew up a calendar in the flyleaf of my Bible. The entry has Saturday 21 June as its heading. I drew it up for six months – June to November – and hatched across the dates from Friday 13 to Saturday 21 June to mark out the period over which I had already been detained. My markings are consistent, confirming that they were all done at the same time.

One of the surviving entries to my toilet paper diary reads as follows:

Dear Jan,
This place is so horrifying that the sensitive parts of one's self close up to shut it out, like certain flowers do at night. If one remained here for long enough, these parts would never be able to open again. But there are birds singing in the trees outside. Their songs penetrate even the heavy locks and unmitigated gloom of captivity.

Day 10: Sunday 22 June

Everything started up in a later routine because it was Sunday. As I lay in bed waiting for breakfast to be brought to the door, I could hear church bells ringing in Pretoria. I tried to keep the morning at bay to avoid the desolation, but

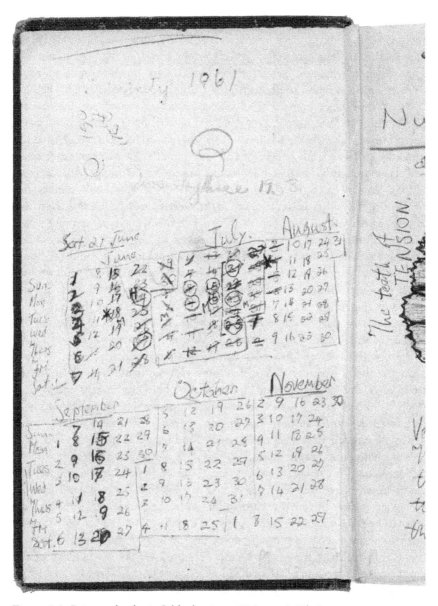

Figure 1.2 Prison calendar in Bible drawn up 21 June – Midwinter.
© Jewish Museum London. Photograph by Ian Lillicrapp.

it came on as it always did and there at the door was the usual morning warder, Oom Charlie, with the black prisoner bringing breakfast. He had invited me to address him as Oom Charlie some days before. He was a big man with a constant smile, and the most enormous feet I had seen on any human being. As we went down the corridor to the bathroom or, in the other direction, to the exercise yard, his boots on the polished floor clapped out a double-hit rhythm, step by step: heel and toe, heel and toe, heel and toe. He had the same build as my father but was six inches taller, and his cap gave him even further height. He was normally genial and, unlike everyone else I came across there, he was easy-going and accommodating. I needed him because I needed an exchange with someone, but his geniality did not give way to conversation. He would talk to himself as we went to the bathroom or, later on, to the exercise yard. Sometimes he would say, 'Ag ya' [Ah, yes] and at other times 'Ag nee' [Ah, no] and sometimes he would even say 'Ya nee' [Well, yes and no] in the course of a big sigh. I would ask him how he was, and he would tell me he was very tired today. I would ask him if anything had happened today that made him tired and he would smile and say 'Ag ja' [Ah, yes], and then look away and the conversation was over. That night there was singing again, and I welcomed it. I had been missing the consolation of those voices. I went to sleep comforted by the sad melodies and the carefully repeated vocal rhythms, but still had no idea who the singers were.

As the shock of the arrest and interrogation receded, physical recovery brought relief. I began to take real account of what it meant to be separated from Janet. We had been living as a couple for only five months and were in the first flush of love. We were in the first intimate relationship that either of us had known, and had been enjoying an active sex life full of the novelty of discovery and delight. I missed her terribly, and imagined her in our bed alone at home with our dog at her bedside. I was devoid of any sexual feeling while in prison. What I missed was the intimacy of our bodies' shared experience. The severance stripped away from me the tenderness that I cherished. The bed I now slept on, the felt mat, was hard and it was hurting my back. I wanted to ask Janet to help me with it and do some yoga exercises with me. By now she was likely to know if she was pregnant, but I had no way of finding out. Who was there for her to share the news with if it were positive? What would happen to her if I were to remain in prison, or if I never came out? And the baby? I wrote to communicate these things to Janet on the toilet paper, and then struggled to go to sleep when they turned the lights out.

Day 11: Monday 23 June

The clatter in the corridors outside and the sound of shovels scraping in the yard below opened the day once more. And then the singing – but then it came to an end . . . silence. After half an hour the prison noises began again without the singing. The warder who later collected me for the shower was a different person, someone I had not seen before. He spoke no English and looked like he had been crying. He was a young boy aged no more than eighteen or nineteen, and it looked like he had not started shaving yet. As we went down the corridor to the bathroom, I asked him in Afrikaans if anything was wrong: '*Meneer, is iets verkeerd?*' [Sir, is anything wrong?] He explained that he had helped to officiate at the hanging this morning. Normally it did not worry him but today it did, he said, and he went on: '*Die kaffer wat vandag opgehang is, was jonger as ek*' [The kaffir who was hanged today was younger than me].

He went on to explain that the people who sang through the night were the condemned, '*die veroordeeldes*'. We did not hear them on Friday or Saturday nights, he said, because the hangman did not work on the weekends. And now I knew whose voices had been consoling me and why they sang as they did.

The day had further differences. When taken into the courtyard for exercise later in the morning, I was directed to a chair and told to sit down while another warden put a towel round my shoulders and went on to cut my hair. There were no formalities and there was no discussion. I watched my hair fall on the concrete around me and then, when I got up off the chair, I watched them wash it down the gutter with a hosepipe. Seeing my hair going down the drain was now the lowest point of all the low points. So, the gallows were nearby and I was amongst the last to hear people's voices before execution. Violation overwhelmed me and stayed with me throughout the day, shaped by the picture of my shorn hair going down the drain. Violation was still with me in the evening. I did not sing at all that day, and spent it in a subdued state immersed in the Bible.

At some point in the afternoon the light from the window threw barred shadows onto the opposing wall as I lay on the blanket reading. The dust motes showed up and danced in the shafts of light. I watched the creased lines in my wrist that had propped up my head and wondered if I would ever get old enough to have creases and wrinkles that would not go away when I straightened my wrist out. The afternoon light was benevolent. I could even pray if I were religious. Ecclesiastes took me away and I withdrew into a state of reverie until the lights went out. I found the passage in its third chapter. We knew it sung by Pete Seeger, word for word. We had a much-loved LP of his folk songs, which included 'To everything there is a season' and other radical songs such as 'We shall overcome' that gave a fighting spirit to the vision of a just future. I had no sense of any future now. I read Ecclesiastes 3:1–8 again and again, and put words to the music that I knew under my breath.

> To everything there is a season, and a time to every purpose under the heaven:
> A time to be born, and a time to die; a time to plant, a time to reap that which
> is planted;

A time to kill, and a time to heal; a time to break down, and a time to build up;
A time to weep, and a time to laugh; a time to mourn, and a time to dance;
A time to cast away stones, and a time to gather stones together;
A time to embrace, and a time to refrain from embracing;
A time to get, and a time to lose; a time to keep, and a time to cast away;
A time to rend, and a time to sew; a time to keep silence, and a time to speak;
A time to love, and a time to hate; a time of war, and a time of peace.
(Ecclesiastes 3:1–8)

As the light fell and the evening came on, the singing started up again. Now that I knew what was happening it was no longer consoling, and only distressed me further. I tried to recall Fanon's defiant conclusion to his *The Wretched of the Earth* in which he says, 'Let us leave this Europe which never stops talking of man yet massacres him at every one of its street corners' (Fanon 1961: 235). Would there be any leaving of this place? Here I was at the state's own site of execution. We had been studying Fanon in one of the secret reading circles I belonged to. Although all of his writing was banned in South Africa, I had brought a copy of *The Wretched of the Earth* back from the USA and it circulated widely amongst my friends, coming back to me only just in time for the police to seize it when they arrested me. Now, I expected, it would feature in whatever case they were preparing against me. It had never occurred to me that I myself might be brought to the place of killing. People had their necks broken here on the direction of a judge. This was what Fanon called 'the dark heart of the Colonial machine' (Fanon op. cit.). Orwell described it as 'the Empire's despotic necessity' (Orwell 2003).[1] Fanon was now amongst the banned books they had taken from my home, and I wondered if my seized books could communicate with one another and give each other support while in the keeping of their enemies. And then, I wondered, what kind of night would those due for execution be living through? Still, I wanted them to stop so I could sleep, but I must have fallen asleep to their voices for I woke to discover I was still listening to them in the early morning before dawn – only to hear them stop.

Days 12–14: Tuesday 24 – Thursday 26 June

Now when the voices woke me in the darkness of the early hours, I understood why silence descended at dawn. As someone else was executed, I held my breath for the morning pause, along with everyone else. Was it one person or several? And the other voices? I learnt much later that those sentenced to death were kept apart from other prisoners and held in quarantine – literally death row – until their appointed time of execution. This might be weeks, months or even years after their arrival here. They would sing as the community of the condemned to support those of their number facing execution at dawn. Apparently, I later learnt, as many as seven people could be hanged at once.

Day 15: Friday 27 June

The day began with its normal routines until the inspection parade when the prison commander stopped in front of me and said, 'Schlapobersky?' 'Yes sir', I replied. 'You have visitors today and will be collected to be taken to Compol after your exercise.' He marched off without another word, and I spent the time worrying that I was going to be taken back to stand on the brick. After the exercise I had my nose in the Bible when Oom Charlie opened the door. '*Besoekers*' (visitors), he said. He told me to get dressed as there were people waiting to take me to Compol Building. I explained that I was already dressed and had no other clothes, so he took me downstairs where two familiar detectives were waiting in the Control Room. They explained that my parents were waiting to see me at Compol Building.

It is very difficult to report on this meeting. My mother and father were waiting in Swanepoel's office when I came in. I was overwhelmed by my mother's embrace and then by my father's stiff greeting as he strode across the room, stood ramrod straight like a soldier, and stretched his arm out for a formal handshake.

We used to tease my father about his 'parade ground march' that was put on for special occasions. This was one of them. He had been a soldier in the Second World War and could assume a very military bearing. I ask myself now, what was he saying to me, to us, by his manner and deportment? I like to think he was saying: 'I am Archie Schlapobersky, and this is my son; and no puffed-up policeman who won medals in peacetime is going to come between us or stop me from shaking my son's hand!' We were to later discover just how impressed Swanepoel had been.

Swanepoel was sitting behind his desk dressed in his full uniform. His clothes were all finely pressed and his leatherwear – shoes and belt – always shone with someone else's effort. On family visits like this he put on a jacket with medal ribbons. The two detectives who had brought me went off and we were left with Swanepoel's interrogation colleagues Richter and Baker. None of the others were in uniform. We were all very nervous. My father offered me a cigarette and I asked Swanepoel if I could smoke. Of course, he said. My own formality of deference to Swanepoel over cigarettes gave my parents the necessary information – here was Torquemada! This was coded communication that linked our situation to the discussions we used to have at home at the dinner table, about the Holocaust and the Inquisition.

During our teenage years we would discuss the Spanish Inquisition at home and knew Torquemada's name as the Grand Inquisitor of Spain. 'The hammer of the heretics', as he was known, saw to the burning of many thousands of Jews. Swanepoel carries his mantle in South Africa's history to this day, as Mengele does in the history of the Holocaust (Lifton 1986; Twiss 2002; Whitechapel 2003; Green 2007).

Swanepoel explained that we had forty minutes to talk to each other and were to keep our conversation limited to what he called 'personal matters'. If we strayed into any of the matters affecting my case, or anything about my detention, he would terminate the interview immediately and there would not be another. And then we had no idea what to say. I was determined my parents should see me strong and in command of myself. I could feel the desperation of their concern for me, and there was nothing I could do or say to reassure them. We had three strange onlookers who monitored our every word.

My mother got the measure of the situation by introducing outstanding administrative details – confirmation was needed for a minor traffic offence, there was a bill outstanding at a bookshop, and other details. Swanepoel assured us I could give my parents power of attorney to deal with these things in my absence. It was the last form of help we wanted to hear but the exchange got us talking. I wanted to know how Janet was, if the dog was alright, how my brother and sister were doing at school and how my brother was in Israel – my mother had been due to visit him just two days after my detention. Only now did I have confirmed what I expected to hear – those plans had been cancelled and my brother was waiting in Israel to hear what was happening. They passed on his greetings.

My parents tried to slow the time down by asking me repeatedly how my health was and if I was getting food that would not interfere with recovery from jaundice. My mother's references were pointed and deliberate. She talked to me so she could broadcast to the police, but when I tried to describe the food and prison routine I was stopped from replying.

When my parents told me the university authorities had held my reserved place, awaiting my return, this buoyed me up – but then, before we knew it, time was up. On both sides our helplessness was appalling. All I wanted to do was go home with my parents. My father wanted to know if he could leave me a packet of cigarettes, and was authorized to do so. We used that exchange to slow down the closure, and then Swanepoel helped us by encouraging my parents to take a change of clothes for me to the prison, which he identified for the first time.

I discovered later that this was the first point at which my parents knew where I was detained. They had done tours of Pretoria's prisons with food parcels and books, and tried to ascertain from the quality of the rejection they received at each jail, which of them might hold me. They had even delivered a parcel of clothing to Major Coetzee at Compol Building, but it never reached me. Records kept by my parents and those retained in the Correctional Services archive give detail, in my father's handwriting, of the number of clothing items submitted on my behalf that were never passed on.

As the interview was concluding, Swanepoel said I would need a suit for further visits. I was in the same clothes in which I had been detained. I had now been wearing them for two weeks and he did not like the way I was dressed, but he took no responsibility for the situation. He let my parents know what they could include with the suit: warm clothing, cigarettes and matches in any parcels brought to the prison, fruit, and some books. We all stood up and I was escorted out whilst my mother, father and I all struggled to keep our composure. And then I was back in prison and it was Friday afternoon. At least they now knew I was alive and coping. I knew that they loved me and would do what they could to see me through my ordeal. This was the first turning point, and it gave me strength for what lay ahead. The evening came on quickly and, as it darkened, I was less troubled because there were no condemned men singing on a Friday night and I found a passage in Chronicles that I wrote into the flyleaf of the Bible to honour my parents' visit and to mark the first sign of hope they had brought. Writing it down helped me to memorize it, and it is still there – a touchstone through my life:

> David: 'For we are strangers before thee, and sojourners, as were all our fathers. Our days on earth are as a shadow, and there is none abiding.' (Chronicles 29:15)

Decades later I found related words of David's from The Psalms, set to music in key passages of Brahms's Requiem:

> Lord, make me to know my end, and the measure of my days, what it is; that I may know how frail I am ... Behold, you have made my days as an handbreadth ... For I am a stranger with you, and a sojourner, as all my fathers were. (Psalm 39: 4,5,12)

This was a welcome discovery – I have continued to call on these passages when teaching others about therapeutic work with refugees

Day 16: Saturday 28 June

Today I woke to a different order – I had seen my parents! They were alright and would stand by me. They were doing what they could, that was clear. All might even be well. I lay in the blankets waiting for breakfast to be brought. As the hangman was off for his weekend, the men in the condemned cells were not singing and it felt less dangerous.

Once up and after my press-ups and exercise, I smoked while pacing, laying a pattern for a cigarette smoked to so many hours of pacing, and no more. The packet from my father was like a talisman and connected me to my parents. I had no assurance of when I might see them next, or if anything more would reach me, so was careful with what I had.

Day 17: Sunday 29 June

There were church bells in the distance in the morning's silence. Everything had a later start. In my reading during the morning, I came across a passage in Isaiah about releasing people from prison. His beautiful language was uplifting and, knowing little of what awaited me in its reading, I found great comfort in the passage: 'To open the blind eyes, to bring out the prisoners from the prison, and them that sit in darkness out of the prison house' (Isaiah 42:7).

During my upbringing I had seen people being carted off to prison and had given little thought to where they went or what happened there. Our gardener, Paul Moesethle, had been assaulted by police while in jail on a pass offence. We knew people who had been arrested during the State of Emergency in 1960 and then under the '90-Day Act' and '180-Day Act'. Mandela and many others were in prison on Robben Island, some for the rest of their lives. Why had I given no thought to their plight? And how would Isaiah help us now? The singing that began again in the evening was deeply demoralizing. Who was going to die in the morning?

Near the beginning of Isaiah, in Chapter 2, I found the passage, 'They shall beat their swords into ploughshares and their spears into pruning hooks; nation shall not lift up sword against nation, neither shall they learn war any more' (Isaiah 2:3–4). It served only to heighten my growing dejection. We knew these verses from prayer services in the synagogue, where they are recited weekly. I had then come across this passage while in New York three years before imprisonment. The words are inscribed in stone at the United Nations Plaza opposite the UN building on the East River in Manhattan. I had visited the Plaza regularly and, imbued with idealism by its vision and buoyant in the mood of the student movement, I would stand there with friends and colleagues from different countries, dreaming of the work we would do to create a better world in the different societies to which we would be returning.

Listening to the daily execution of others, the ideals now seemed so far beyond me and looked lost forever. I took greater comfort in Isaiah's later passages, especially Chapter 40, such as 'Comfort ye my people' (Isaiah 40:1) that I knew from Handel's *Messiah*, and I would sing its opening passages from memory again and again, reading them against Isaiah's text from my Bible. In later pages I found: 'How beautiful are the feet of them that preach the gospel of peace and bring glad tidings of good things!' (Isaiah 52:7), which I recited in hope of my own deliverance. Later still I found lines that have never left me, in which the author puts words into what he imagines to be the voice of God:

For a small moment have I forsaken thee; but with great compassion will I gather thee . . . for as I have sworn that I would not be wroth with thee, nor rebuke thee . . . the mountains may depart and the hills be removed, but My kindness shall not depart from thee, neither shall My covenant of peace be removed, saith the Lord that hath compassion on thee. (Isaiah 54:7)

Day 18: Monday 30 June

The usual clatter was again interrupted when the singing stopped and the execution took place. And then it all started up again. The day took a turn for the better when I received those things my parents were allowed to deliver to the prison – toiletries, clothes, cigarettes, fruit and books. They arrived too late to be of use for the shower today, but after the shower and exercise parade, my already-opened travel bag was brought to the cell with treasure. The toiletries included soap, a hairbrush, toothbrush, toothpaste, a razor without a blade, a change of clothing and a pullover, warm trousers and a suit for use on future visits. And there were some books. With these possessions stacked in the corner, the cell now felt like a different place. And now that I had a suit there would be more visits to come! The bag stood in a corner with everything folded into it carefully and the suit draped over it – after my bed this this was now my second piece of furniture. There was an upturn in mood despite the hanging this morning. With a good cigarette supply I now took to chain smoking, without concerns of shortage.

The encouraging turn allowed me to move on through the Bible to the Song of Songs, which I read avidly and reread when I could allow Janet's presence to walk with me in the pacing and imagine her at home in bed or going to work in the morning as she said goodbye to the dog. I wrote her a poem on my toilet paper diary outside the normal evening diary and sent it to her in my mind. Even the birds outside sounded brighter, and I hung from the window for a longer period than could normally be managed. It was cold in the cell, bright as it was outside, and I was relieved to have warm things. I had been wearing the same things for two weeks now. I was in a state of delight putting on fresh things and did my pacing in warm corduroy trousers that my parents had just bought. They had the seller's ticket attached, which reminded me about the outside world. I still have the trousers, unwearable and with multiple patches – they hang in the cupboard in a place of honour.

Day 19: Tuesday 1 July

The day's early morning clatter was as disturbing as ever and only stopped for the dawn pause. Later in the shower room I was delighted with the toiletries, and could brush my teeth properly. I was even given a razor blade that had to be returned once I had had a shave. The freshly shaved man who now looked at me in the mirror seemed to be in a much better state as he said to me in the reflection, 'So, you're still here!' The next few days settled into a manageable routine. I would come out of the cell first to use the bathroom and then later to go to the exercise parade. The morning was filled with the Gospels and the afternoon with the Old Testament. This ran in parallel with a beginning I was making in reading some of the new books. With an upturn in mood and more self-possession, the routine helped to make the days more bearable and I wrote this down in my nightly note to Janet before going to sleep, taking care to document the day in as much detail as my own handwriting could permit on just two sheets of toilet paper. Then I rolled it round the pen, put the pen into a fold in the blankets and went to sleep. The nightly discipline corresponded to the morning's routine of twenty-five press-ups.

The unexpected still took me by surprise and challenged my resources. I saw other prisoners occasionally, and only by chance. On my way to the shower this morning, passing rows of closed cells and with my own warder close behind me, I passed a black man just inside his open cell door being tormented by two white warders who held a toy snake to his face. His screams were mixed with the guards' derisory laughter, which echoed down the corridor. There were more frequent cries like this in the night.

Day 20: Wednesday 2 July

I was devastated by events that undid the coping routine in which I was settling. While out in the bathroom, I saw my escorting warden make signals to someone down the corridor from his station at the bathroom door where I was showering. It was unusual. When I came back to my cell, everything looked like it had when I left. However, when I looked in the familiar place inside the blanket roll for my treasure – the pen and paper – the pen was there but the roll of toilet paper sheets was missing. They had taken my diary and left me just the pen. The warden at the bathroom door had evidently been responding to signals from his colleague telling him the deed had been done. I checked my possessions in case I had left the diary in some unusual place, but it was nowhere to be found. And then I looked again. And again. I was still looking when one of them came to take me out for exercise. Now I took the pen with me when I went out. I thought that perhaps the diary might be there when I came back from exercise, but no, it had been stolen. They now knew what I was thinking, how I was faring, and they knew what propped me up – my relationship with Janet. Each sheet of paper had been addressed to her. It was a very anxious day, and I found it difficult to settle down to reading. That night when I could not get to sleep, I got into a worse state.

Days 21 and 22: Thursday and Friday, 3–4 July

There were changes in the routine. Oom Charlie was no longer doing the daily duties and there was no sign of the sweet-faced young man who had told me about the hanging. The current warden was severe and quite unpleasant, so I was worried when he stopped the exercise before I had had my full quota of thirty minutes, but I was in no position to argue. The day took on a sinister edge. I began to think that the man who looked into the eyehole in the door was able to communicate directly to the Security Police and give them a running commentary on what I was doing. He must have reported to them that I was probably keeping a diary when he looked in and – as he sometimes did – found me writing on toilet paper. I started to keep my back to the door when I was writing, but was then worried that this would only serve to confirm their need to take an interest in me; so I stopped doing that and wrote with defiance into the diary, expecting that they would later steal it from its location on the pen and read it for themselves. So, from now on it took a different form – it was still a cry from the heart to Janet, but it was also a piece of propaganda for the Security Police, who I expected would read it sooner or later.

Day 23: Saturday 5 July

There was another unsettling incident today when I went to the bathroom. As mentioned earlier, if I wanted to shave, I had to ask the warder for a razor blade which would then be taken back afterwards. Today, arriving at the basin, I found a blade pasted onto the side where I would normally put my toothbrush. Had it been left there carelessly when someone before me failed to turn theirs in? I pointed it out to the warder, who snapped it up and said in Afrikaans that they had forgotten to collect it after its use by the person before, but I went back to my cell with a feeling of disquiet. This hard-faced warder looked like a brute and I began to feel quite unsafe. Now the impact of the cell door closing behind me after the shower and exercise gave me a new, brooding worry that had no relief.

Day 24: Sunday 6 July

There was another razor blade plastered onto the wash basin this morning. Once more I pointed it out to the same warden who apologized and then snapped it up again. Going back to the cell from an unexplained razor blade in the bathroom (was it a sinister message?) to deal with close confinement in the face of another potential threat – my stolen toilet roll diary – I became more and more alarmed.

Now I was presented with evidence – repeated daily – that they would not leave me in peace, even in solitary confinement. I had to fight with every hour to get it to pass. My coded entries in the Bible diary highlight the daily threat. The toilet paper diary for the day reads:

> Dear Jan,
> The morning is false – the dawn is a false dawn and in the building the bustle of the day's awakening is preparing to prevent and destroy another day of life. The purpose of solitary confinement is to curtail the range and extent of one's experience. Its effects are in the disintegration of one's conceptual framework and the inability to think or comprehend.

They were tampering with my mind and imposing sinister suggestions. If they were inviting me to kill myself, then they wanted me dead. And if they wanted me dead and I did not oblige, then they would do it themselves. I paced the cell in a new state of agitation, and could find no peace. I could not sit and read and could do nothing except pace. And pace. And pace. At the end of the day when the lights went out, I half expected a team of murderers to come in to cut my wrists, so they could say I did it myself. I wrestled with the limited knowledge I had of the death in detention we had read about during a widely publicized inquest just three months earlier. James Lenkoe had died in this very prison. Perhaps he had been in the same cell? Perhaps he had used the same bathroom? They said he hanged himself in his cell. They allowed me nothing that I could have used to harm myself. They managed everything to the last detail – no belt, no shoelaces – and they made no mistakes. Had they not wanted him dead, they would surely have taken Lenkoe's things too! And then, they said, he hanged himself with the very belt that his wife brought to the Coroner's Court from his home. She said he left it at home when they arrested him, but the truth did not affect the conclusion. The coroner said that he killed himself with the very belt his wife held up in court. Facts and reality had nothing to do with the court's ruling. Would they do this to me too, set up a murder to look like suicide? We had followed the proceedings of the coroner's inquest held in March, just three months earlier. There had been vivid reports in the press that gave an account of how the barrister representing his family, Joel Carlson, had tried to confront the coroner with the reality that his only belt was left in his home at the time of his arrest. Yet this was put forward as the explanation for his death in a cell at Pretoria Local Prison just five days later.

In our reading of the press reports at the time, we took in the horror of a situation in which the police killed their suspects with impunity. This was the true meaning of the inquest's findings, which were broadcast through press reports around the country. I was later to discover that Swanepoel was implicated in this, as he was in some of the other six deaths in detention recorded that year. Joel Carlson, the lawyer representing those next of kin who could bring proceedings to bear, suffered death threats, attempted letter bombs and many other forms of police-based terror and intimidation during these very months and in the years that followed (Carlson 1973, Bizos 1989).[2]

It was hard to sleep and then frightening to be woken by terrible dreams. I dreamt that I was in a car accident that involved many vehicles and resulted in many deaths. There was a team of ambulances called to collect body parts that had been spread out on the road by this catastrophe. There was blood, flashing blue lights, cordons, sirens and police cars. But the body parts were all black and the ambulances only collected whites. What would happen now?

I had recently witnessed a street accident in Johannesburg in which an ambulance was called for a black cyclist. The ambulance driver and paramedic had not been informed that the injured man was a black, and the ambulance was 'slegs vir blankes' [only for whites], so the paramedics would not touch him, and he bled to death in the road. Perhaps he was already beyond help? Their disregard for the injury of a fellow human was appalling – they would have shown an injured dog or horse more compassionate attention.

The dismay from this incident filled the dream, which filled the day. Then my thoughts were shaped by later readings in the afternoon. So, they really wanted me dead. Would they come in to do it themselves? Until then I would live, damn them, and be alive to describe them for the murderers that they were! During the Holocaust in Lithuania, my grandfather's younger brother Tzodik, then leader of the Jewish community of Keidan, had been dragged to the graveside to face his executioners. They were told to disrobe, and the Nazi commanding officer came to get his coat off him, as he would not disrobe. As the Nazi was trying to pull his coat off, my uncle grabbed his revolver from his holster to turn it on him, but he could not work the safety catch, so he tried to strangle him and pulled him down into the grave. When some of the Lithuanian killers jumped into the pit to kill him with their knives – they did not want to shoot for fear of killing the wrong person – he tore out the throat of one of his assailants with his teeth before he was killed. By the time they finally killed Tzodik, he had killed the SS leader and one of the Lithuanians who had been doing the shooting (Chrust 1977; Oshry 1995; Lerer-Cohen and Issroff 2002; Levinsonas 2006).

Years later I visited the gravesite of our family in Lithuania to do them honour and, after saying the Kaddish, the prayer for the dead, I took a stone with me from the grave, which now sits in my home on the mantelpiece. Tzodik is honoured at Yad Vashem, and our name is honoured in the Jewish State Museum of Lithuania, where the handful of living survivors continue to give special regard to our family's name, on his account.

But that night in my cell I was at a loss, completely at a loss. How would I deal with a team of murderers when they came to kill me? Now, I thought, the singing from the condemned cells takes on new meaning for me. I thought that if the condemned can maintain their composure to face certain death, then I can do so too in the face of the unknown. I thought back to the early mornings as it was getting light, as I had done this morning, listening to them singing and then stopping. The anger set in, taking me beyond desperation, and I wrote a poem on the flyleaf of my Bible dedicated to the name of the unknown man who had written on the prison wall, presumably just before his execution – I construed him as Daniel, brought from prison to read the writing on the wall that prophesied Babylon's doom (Daniel 5:25). He did the writing, I thought, perhaps before he was killed, and I would be his Daniel. Their state, like Belshazzar's Babylon, was weighed in the balance, and found wanting.

For Knox Masi

He moved delicate patterns of
imagination among sunlight
and birdsong –
as mysteriously illuminating
as sunbeams
among tenuous wraiths
of smoke,
so when he died,
much, much of him was left behind
like a patch of sun
cast among many shadows
as if written on a wall,
but with no Daniel to
interpret it.

Through these continuing, desperate days, and for the week to come, the razor blades were there every morning, but I stopped pointing them out and resigned myself to facing them – the killers – when they came to kill me. I was carried by a new form of angry composure – cold, controlled and hostile – that dominated the week. On one of those days the exercise yard was busy with black warders standing talking to one another in clusters. I thought some sort of meeting had been taking place. Amongst them was a bigger man than the others who was dressed in a uniform that had marks of high office on it – including a peaked cap and a shining Sam Browne. As I walked my back – and

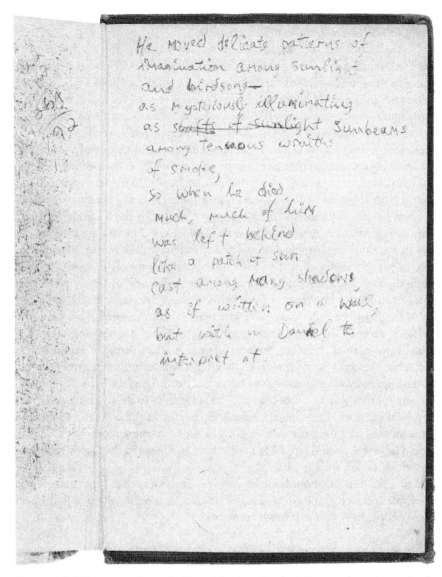

Figure 1.3 Writing on the wall: Knox Masi's unfinished fate prophesied apartheid's doom.

© Jewish Museum London. Photograph by Ian Lillicrapp.

forth routine there was a chance to walk straight at him, as he stood unwittingly in my path. In this 'test', it was he who gave way to my march. I muttered to myself how bizarre it was that even here, at the centre point of total police control, a black man of high authority still deferred to a white prisoner, only because he was white. Apartheid! A white *gevangene* [prisoner] stood above a *bantu* [black], even one who held high office.

The increasing sense of dread was aggravated by an eye infection that stopped me from reading. I reported this to the prison commander on his inspection. Later in the morning a medical orderly came by with eye drops and ointment, which left me partially blind, and he told me not to read for a day or two. The passing blindness was more alarming than the infection, and the inability to read put me completely at a loss. During the day it felt as if the tension was stretching me across my cell and that, like a taut drumskin, I would soon split.

There were more terrible dreams. In one, my mother was peering through the 'eye in the door' through which the warders inspected me on a regular basis. I must have begun to think they were waiting to find me dead at my own hands. Now in dreams my mother had joined them, and with the blazing eyes and a flare of rage that I remembered from childhood, she attacked me through the 'eye in the door' for bringing shame and disrepute to the family. Her uncontrollable rage was dreadful. There was no one left for me. The dream repeated itself through the week and I would try not to sleep in order to avoid it. It would sometimes be replaced by another dream, that Janet had a baby, our baby, the baby who was conceived just before I was arrested. I had gone to prison concerned she might be pregnant and worried about her every day. Now the dreams turned the worry into a different kind of reality. I would have a child, but the child would have no father. Janet was struggling, my mother was struggling, everyone was struggling, and I was dead. Then the baby was in trouble, my mother was in a rage and Janet was helpless to do anything constructive. Waking from these dreams was hardly a relief as the day yawned me into its confinement. Often my own cries woke me from these nightmares. Then I would lie on the floor wrapped in my blanket, and listen to the prison labourers shovelling coal in the early hours.

I found a passage about hope in the New Testament that I transcribed into the Bible and learnt to recite as I paced. It remains a personal guide that I pass on to people who see me for psychotherapy:

> For we are saved by hope; but hope that is seen is not hope: for what a man seeth, why doth he yet hope for? But if we hope for that we see not, then do we with patience wait for it. (Romans 8:24–25)

Days 25–32: Monday 7–Monday 14 July

The week that followed was made up of days of plunging anxiety and steady desperation, prompted by daily discoveries of razor blades on the bathroom basin and a growing sense of suspicion that saw the interrogators everywhere – I

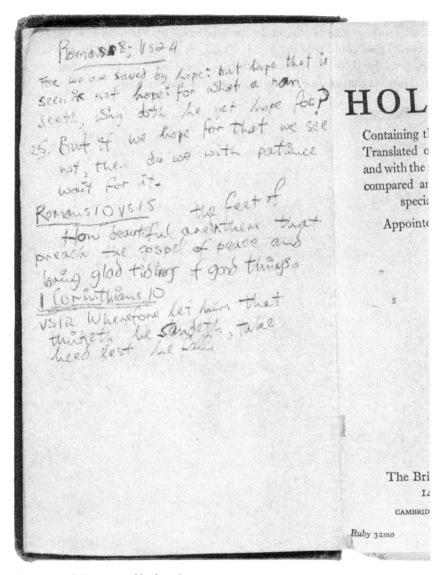

Figure 1.4 'We are saved by hope'.
© Jewish Museum London. Photograph by Ian Lillicrapp.

could find no place of refuge that was safe from them. One day, when I got back to the cell and began to read, I saw in the fly leaf of the Bible that, some weeks before, I had written a coded notation for those things I had revealed during interrogation that left me with special concern. What if they looked into the Bible after they killed me and found this notation? I thought they would know things about me and my associates that would be no good, and I fell into a real state. Finding razor blades on the basin filled me with bizarre anxieties – I was worried they could read my mind or read my intentions into the marks I had made in the Bible. So, I covered the notation with a densely shaded drawing and headed the drawing with a title, 'The Teeth of Tension'.

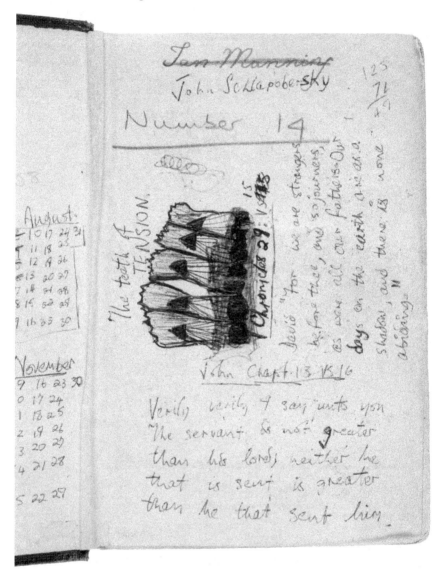

Figure 1.5 The Teeth of Tension hide anxious annotations.
© Jewish Museum London. Photograph by Ian Lillicrapp.

The Sunday night singing brought more foreboding to the daily desperation as the light faded in the cell, and on Monday morning, when the singing began again and paused, it was more difficult than ever to stay asleep with my breakfast on the floor beside me. Sleep was an easier state than being awake, and so I tried to sleep into the morning for as long as possible. As the anxiety mounted, that routine was progressively unsettled.

That Monday afternoon my reading of the Old Testament brought me to the book of Jonah, where I found myself more deeply absorbed in its narrative than I had been in anything else I had read so far. It gave me a focus and helped me to begin to get a grip on myself. At home we had a recording of it read by Leon Gluckman, a well-known South African actor and stage personality. On the LP, called 'Harvest of Israel', he read passages from the Prophets, Psalms and Chronicles. I had grown up listening to his voice tell the story of Jonah. Now I read it out to myself as if I were making the recording. I could never have foreseen just how deeply I would come to need the words of someone in a state of such despair. Jonah is 'cast into the depths' and 'engulfed by the floods' where his life 'was ebbing away'.

> The Lord provided a huge fish to swallow Jonah;
> and Jonah remained in the fish's belly three days and three nights.
> Jonah prayed to the Lord his God from the belly of the fish.
> He said:
> In my trouble I called to the Lord
> And He answered me;
> From the belly of Sheol I cried out,
> And You heard my voice.
> You cast me into the depths,
> Into the heart of the sea,
> The floods engulfed me;
> All Your breakers and billows
> Swept over me.
> I thought I was driven away
> Out of Your sight:
> Would I ever gaze again
> Upon Your holy Temple?
> The waters closed in over me,
> The deep engulfed me.
> Weeds twined around my head.
> I sank to the base of the mountains;
> The bars of the earth closed upon me forever.
> Yet You brought my life up from the pit,
> O Lord my God!
> When my life was ebbing away,

I called the Lord to mind;
And my prayer came before You.
(Jonah 2:2)

Judaism had been at the core of my upbringing in our early years but, in these later days, beliefs and prayers did not help to see me through. I never lost a sense of the sacred, or of natural events that could be awesome and transporting. I would happily climb a mountain to see the moon rise or watch a sunset, and found words for the sanctity of the natural world in poets like Wordsworth. But there were no Friday night rituals at my boarding school and, though we maintained a Jewish home on our farm, including kiddush and Friday night prayers, I had lost any personal sense of God's presence over those years. Jonah's plea for salvation and his gratitude at being spared were the most evocative of the passages we listened to on the Gluckman LP. Now they spoke for my own sense of life ebbing away. I had no purchase on any sense of faith and no confidence in prayer, but the desperation in Jonah's voice spoke to me. I got 'oxygen' from the graphic language in which he describes drowning. I discovered that his resilience gave me a foothold to strengthen my own. Hope could come from the impossible – a drowning man abandoned by his shipmates and lost in a storm at sea could even be saved by a whale. I read Jonah's words out loud again and again over the days that followed, and each time I did so they were like air for a drowning man.

I looked to other Biblical sources to find stories of survival through ordeals of different kinds. Another of Gluckman's recordings was a selection of passages from Job. Now I read them closely, and took up a position on his behalf to consider just how wronged he had been by God himself. According to the account, God tested Job's faith to demonstrate his own prowess in a wager with Satan, the Angel of Adversity in the Jewish faith. I decided that such suffering was unjust and therefore needless and unwarranted. Why should God need to 'show off' by causing a faithful man so much suffering? I found that David had been tested in a different kind of ordeal when Saul conspired to kill him and he hid in a cave. The spider that cast its web to conceal him gave me strength, and I found confidence and renewal in David's Psalm 27. The author is abandoned by his parents and surrounded by enemies. He cries in agony with a sentence he cannot finish, for it depicts the worst of all – the loss of his own community of faith, the loss of trust amongst his own. At a point of such desperation, he finds renewed strength reciting the Psalm's last lines, 'Look to the Lord, be strong and of good courage'. I was without faith then but found it later through my own survival and then on the birth of our daughter.

I had no way of knowing what was going on outside, and the letter that my mother wrote on my behalf to the prime minister, reproduced below, proved to be what I was hoping for but could not see.

Day 28: Thursday 10 July
(Outside the prison)

The letter written by my mother to South Africa's prime minister on this date is reproduced below. She was only free to disclose it to me after my release, once we were on the plane to Israel. It details some of the extraordinary lengths to which she went, and it must have played a key part in getting the police to grant the visit we were allowed on 15 July. A copy of this letter was retained in my mother's own file, and another copy was found amongst documents held in a declassified file in the Department of Justice which, thanks to Nobukhosi Zulu, has been secured from the Freedom of Information Programme of the South African History Archive. The actions of my family and our lawyer that lay behind this letter merit recording now. I knew nothing about any of this. My brother David, then aged 16, reports that the home of our loyal and devoted family friend Marcelle Feldman, documented below at 9 Cradock Heights, became a kind of 'family war room' where there were discussions about strategy and tactics, under the guidance of Raymond Tucker of Gus Friendly, Browse & Co, who was instructed to act for me. Others who joined them there included

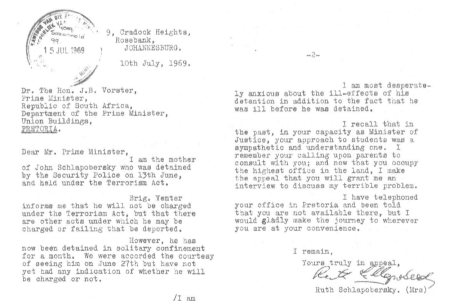

9, Cradock Heights,
Rosebank,
JOHANNESBURG.

10th July, 1969.

Dr. The Hon. J.B. Vorster,
Prime Minister,
Republic of South Africa,
Department of the Prime Minister,
Union Buildings,
PRETORIA.

Dear Mr. Prime Minister,
I am the mother of John Schlapobersky who was detained by the Security Police on 13th June, and held under the Terrorism Act.

Brig. Venter informs me that he will not be charged under the Terrorism Act, but that there are other acts under which he may be charged or failing that be deported.

However, he has now been detained in solitary confinement for a month. We were accorded the courtesy of seeing him on June 27th but have not yet had any indication of whether he will be charged or not.

/I am

-2-

I am most desperately anxious about the ill-effects of his detention in addition to the fact that he was ill before he was detained.

I recall that in the past, in your capacity as Minister of Justice, your approach to students was a sympathetic and understanding one. I remember your calling upon parents to consult with you; and now that you occupy the highest office in the land, I make the appeal that you will grant me an interview to discuss my terrible problem.

I have telephoned your office in Pretoria and been told that you are not available there, but I would gladly make the journey to wherever you are at your convenience.

I remain,
Yours truly in appeal,

Ruth Schlapobersky. (Mrs)

Figure 1.6 Letter from Ruth Schlapobersky to the prime minister, B.J. Vorster, 10 July 1969, with stamp of receipt by his office, 15 July 1969.
Courtesy South African History Archive, with thanks to the coordinator of its Freedom of Information Programme, Nobukhosi Zulu.

Raymond Louw and Benjamin Pogrund, editor and news editor of the *Rand Daily Mail*. Well aware of how limited his scope was for any direct legal intervention, our lawyer pointed my mother in the direction of the action she took in writing this letter. He then he guided her on the riskiest course of action – a direct approach to the head of BOSS, the Bureau of State Security, which she embarked on without an appointment, described on Day 33.

Day 33: Tuesday 15 July

The chief warder told me to get dressed because I would be going to Compol Building at lunchtime. There was no razor blade in the bathroom for the first time in more than a week. I put my suit on for the first time since its arrival three weeks ago. Going out on the now familiar journey from the prison to Compol Building took less than half an hour, but through the car window it was so good to be amongst people again. They were coming and going in the traffic – ordinary people doing ordinary things. I watched the business of the world going by in its ordinary way. What delight in the ordinary! We pulled up in the rear car park and went into Compol through its back entrance.

On coming along the corridor with my two-man police escort, I saw my mother at the other end – she had come in from the front entrance and was at a loss looking for Swanepoel's office. Evidently, she had been told where to go but could not find the office. I called out to her and left the detectives behind me as we ran to meet each other. The relief was overwhelming. I have never been so relieved to see anyone, before or since. We were standing outside Swanepoel's office and he must have watched us embrace. We went in followed by the two detectives who had brought me, but they then left. Richter and Baker were waiting with Swanepoel and we were invited to sit down, mother and son, overseen by the three watching policemen. Swanepoel took charge of proceedings to remind us that, as on the last visit, there was to be no discussion about my 'case' or any other political matters, and nothing about the prison. And then, in a quite formal way he said, 'Mrs Schlapobersky, was your husband a military man?' My mother replied that my father had been in the South African Army during the Second World War. Swanepoel went on to tell us that he thought my father had a most impressive military presence. It was clear then that my parents' strategy was working. I did not yet know their strategy, but she could see that it was working, and I sensed that something was 'up'.

I later learnt that my parents had agreed on a strategy for taking up discrete roles when they met the police. My mother was to simply be the concerned mother, anxious about her son's welfare. And my father was to be the stern and reproving parent, there to admonish his errant son in the presence of the policemen. He did not go quite this far, but his posture had clearly impressed Swanepoel.

Then they turned their attention to me. What I did not know at the time was that I was no longer able to talk properly. My mother said something to me, to which I thought I was replying, but her look of concern told me that something was seriously wrong. I believe Swanepoel tried to help by engaging with me, but he did not get any further. In a later report given to the press but never published, my mother described how I would answer a question by forming a sentence, but I seemed to have no idea there was no sound to my voice. I was bewildered, agitated and unaware of how distressed I appeared. When sound did come out it was in broken sentences with no sequence and no narrative content, and was interrupted by silence and the opening and closing of my mouth like a fish.

There was an exchange amongst them and then – with my mother and three policemen, Baker and two others – we were on our way out to a nearby restaurant. I was confused, and was carried along by an exchange and agreement that seemed to have passed me by. We walked some two hundred yards to a restaurant where the police and their 'customers' were evidently regular guests. We had a table to ourselves, set apart from everyone else. This was the very menu from which I had been fed while on the brick, weeks before. Watched by three sets of glowering police eyes and my concerned mother, I had a good meal and was the only one who ate anything.

In my mother's later account given to me after my release, she described how, after I had eaten and had several cups of coffee, she found that I could begin to construct sentences and vocalize, and could begin to talk again by describing trivia like the details of the food. This grew into a conversational exchange in small stages. We both made it last for as long as the police allowed, but eventually they told us we had to go.

We walked slowly back. My mother and I walked in front and the three police trailed us just behind. We talked loudly about the books I wanted her to bring for me on the next visit, and then had the chance in brief snatched moments for very quiet 'under-the-breath' exchanges, which were used to good tactical effect. She whispered that I was now legally represented by an excellent lawyer and that my uncle Willie Oshry– the barrister at the Johannesburg bar – was guiding them. I could be confident they were doing their best, and the Israeli ambassador had taken an interest in my case. I chose not to tell her that I thought they were trying to kill me. Grim as the situation was, I wanted her to see that I was coping. She looked so worried. I told her under my breath that there was compromising material in the bedroom wardrobe that had to be disposed of, and she only just had time to reassure me they would see to it. The authorities never did discover the cache of writing and political magazines that Wally and I had hidden there. When we got back to Swanepoel's office he wanted to know if I had had a good meal, and asked my mother if I had found my voice yet.

When we sat down with our entourage, she was controlled but fierce with him, and said to him in Afrikaans: '*Wat wil julle van ons seun hê?*' [What do you want from our son?] '*Wil jy hom vernietig?*' [Do you want to destroy him?] His jaw dropped – he did not know that she was fluent in Afrikaans. He asked her in Afrikaans how she came to speak '*Die Taal*' so fluently and she told him she was '*'n Afrikaanse Jood*' [an Afrikaans Jew], and that his language was her own. She had grown up amongst Afrikaans people on a farm in the Magaliesberg, not far away. He was curious, and she told him of the farm at Syferbult that her parents had renamed Ruthville in her honour when she was born. Her first school years at the Syferbult school were in Afrikaans. I followed everything closely without giving myself away to Swanepoel. An exchange followed about what was now going to be done about me. My mother wanted to know what would happen to my state of mind if I went back into a cell on my own. She wanted to know if I could be placed amongst other prisoners, but he insisted that was impossible. The exchange culminated with Swanepoel's assurance that he would phone my partner Janet from his phone now, and allow me to say hello to her. Tomorrow my mother could come back with her, so we could meet personally.

From the receiver at his desk and via a telephonist somewhere else, he quickly found his way to a line in the library at Witwatersrand University, and set the wind blowing when he told them who was speaking. He was one of the policemen who had arrested Bram Fischer, Ilse Fischer's father, and Ilse and Janet worked together in the university library. There must have been some panic, which we could see him enjoying. When Janet came to the phone, he introduced himself to her and told her he had me and my mother with him and that I wanted to speak to her. When she came to the phone, we did not know what to say to one another, but this was an immediate lift. When I asked if she had had any news, and she did not know what I meant, I had to remind her of our discussion on the way to the university on the last occasion we had seen each other. For the last month I had lived through isolated worry in the cell that she might be pregnant. I was able to pass on the enquiry without naming the concern and Janet reassured me that all was well – the news was negative. When we finished our discussion, my mother went off to the toilet at which point Swanepoel wanted to know what news I had been concerned about and I had to tell him.

Police use of this kind of worry to torment others came to light when I was in London one year later. I was being supported by the International Defence and Aid Fund (IDAF), who produced a pamphlet for publicity, 'Trial by Torture – The Case of the 22' (IDAF 1970), about the trial of Winnie Mandela, Joyce Sikakane and their twenty co-accused. My own article describing the use of torture, later republished in the London *Observer*, helped to discredit the evidence used against them. In 1970 I described to colleagues at IDAF how Swanepoel had gained access to my fears about Janet's pregnancy during detention. They described what they had learnt of how Swanepoel had later insinuated in the mind of a detainee the fear that a woman he had been friends with was pregnant with his child, while they were both under separate interrogation. These uncertainties were used to torment the man. Had she been pregnant this could have had embarrassing consequences, for she was married to someone else she had not been able to see for a long time. The police made calculated use of malice – misinformation drawn from one person's case to bring pressure to bear in another's – as a defining strategy.

I left our meeting in the company of my two detectives, and Swanepoel reassured us that we would meet again the next day, together with Janet, but not before I raised my own challenge – the theft of my toilet paper diary from the roll on my pen. I wanted it back. Swanepoel claimed ignorance of the matter but undertook to look into it.

What I did not know until some time afterwards was that, on my departure, Swanepoel interrogated my mother. He did not caution her or proceed with any formalities, but they talked in Afrikaans about Winnie Mandela. 'We understand', he said, 'that she came to your house for dinner in September last year.' My mother professed complete ignorance. He told her of the name of the person who had brought Mrs Mandela to our home, Mohale Mahanyele, the information officer from the United States Information Service, and he seemed puzzled that my mother had no memory of the occasion. My mother could be a very accomplished actress and, in an apparent state of shock, she said, 'Was that Winnie Mandela? Yes, he came to our home for dinner, but I didn't know that was Winnie Mandela with him. I thought she was his wife. No one told me that she was Winnie Mandela.' 'Yes,' said Swanepoel, 'that's what your son said too. And that's what Winnie Mandela told us also.' She turned the tables on him and said, 'So you've asked her about me? What did she say?' He replied – in Afrikaans – and quoted Mrs Mandela saying: '*Ons het my identiteit van sy ma weggesteek*' [We hid my identity from his mother]. '*Die seun is verlig, maar sy ma is verkramp*' [The son is liberal, but his mother is conservative]. And then they laughed together. The story was critical to the outcome of my own case, for it allowed him to go on and negotiate with my mother.

The truth was quite different. My mother was introduced to Mrs Mandela by name. I had never seen her so overwhelmed, as she was at the introduction, by the strength of another woman's presence. When my younger brother and sister went to bed that night, we talked politics late into the night. As described in Day 4 above, we also talked about Waterford Kamhlaba School, where my brother and sister would soon make a beginning – the same school that the Mandelas' two daughters were to attend later. It was located in Swaziland near where we lived, the only multiracial school in Southern Africa. That evening, in the spring of 1968, we were allies together in the living room of the Killarney flat. I would have expected nothing less from myself than the effort I showed while on the brick, to protect my mother. But with nothing to gain and nothing to lose in this case, Mrs Mandela chose to protect my mother and did so in a way that entertained her interrogator. 'Verlig' and 'verkramp' were the terms of division amongst the Afrikaners of the time and, with her characteristic wit and acuity, Mrs Mandela applied them to my mother's and my own, supposedly different, views. The upshot of this exchange was to play a crucial part in giving my mother credibility with Swanepoel in the events that were to unfold (Madikizela-Mandela 2014).

I was not to know until after my release that, despite their strenuous efforts under the guidance of our lawyer, my parents had been denied access to me since their first visit. My mother only got to see me for this second visit after a virtual 'sit-down strike' outside the Wachthuis, the office of Brigadier Hendrik van den Bergh, head of the Bureau for State Security. Under legal guidance, she took the calculated risk that the resolute presence of a mother pleading for access to her imprisoned son might have consequences, and it succeeded. She was eventually shown in to see him and disclosed her correspondence with the Prime Minister's Office, at which point he phoned Swanepoel in my mother's presence and the visit was set up for Day 33.

Day 34: Wednesday 16 July

I was taken out to see my mother again and, most wonderfully and surprisingly, Janet. We embraced and sat down close to one another in an intimate space we created that left out everyone else. What follows is Janet's record of our meeting. She wrote it up at home later that night and has kept a copy ever since. It is included here with her permission. We had the same preliminary warning from Swanepoel not to discuss anything about my case or any other political matters, or he would terminate the interview; and we had the same audience – Swanepoel, Richter and Baker. The two detectives who brought me in did not stay. Janet and I talked to each other while my mother and the policemen looked on and listened. Janet strayed directly into 'forbidden' territory by asking me details about the interrogation and about prison life. This was quickly interrupted, but not before I was able to tell her something about it. The detail emerges in her narrative below:

It's too personal to type – let me feel this pen and paper and feel you too, my love Yanka. I see you anew.

Pale, timid, almost baby-faced – I couldn't believe it was you – it was like some dream when the character isn't quite in keeping with the part – an actor that you know well who is wrongly made-up – gone was your swarthiness (that Brechtian stubble, that I was beginning to tolerate, even like), gone was your mop of hair and my haircut, gone your self-assurance and usual assertiveness. You were surprised by me, too, weren't you my sweet? One does forget the contours of face –

And we hugged and hugged, and it became a little more real – and hugged again – whispering so much, your face . . . I feel you . . .

'How do you do, Major Swanepoel. I'm pleased to meet you.'

When Ruth and Arch talked of an orang-outang like thug, I was allowing them a certain literary licence – conversational exaggeration – but it's horribly true; a kind of red-faced bloated ogre, so ugly that I felt sorry for him. That is one thing he is not responsible for . . . and Lieutenant Richter, suave, good looking, black suited; and another young steely eyed inquisitor on our left (Baker).

But, you know, I was so little aware of them that they soon ceased to exist – my whole being was centred on you – I am surprised to hear from Ruth that they listened to every word that passed between us. We sat so close together, holding hands, caressing, so close . . .

The house, Mehavya [the dog]; friends; Camus (I think of him a lot).

Past experiences? You are expanding moments?

I try.

You are going through such a unique time; the eighth dimension of hell, though it may be – but think of Laing, couldn't it be a type of breakthrough – not necessarily a breakdown? (We were reading existentialist writers, R.D. Laing's *The Politics of Experience and The Bird of Paradise* and Albert Camus's *The Myth of Sisyphus*. They forge routes through despair to find ways of affirming dignity and authenticity.)

Yes . . . but it is difficult. There are moments in the abyss . . .

After the chief warder has passed my cell in the morning – if he doesn't announce any visit, I know there is nothing, nothing and no hope for another 24 hours. And Friday afternoons, a weekend ahead of blankness. Last week it was bad for me at that time. Very bad.

No more interrogating?

No . . . Nothing after the first six days . . . I had one night's sleep in that time . . . [Interruption from Swanepoel that we are not to talk about this.]

. . . but we are not to talk of this . . .

Christ . . . Are you disciplining yourself? It's so important; exercise?

Yes. I do 25 press-ups a day. There is always that, and in the courtyard I walk up and down quickly, maybe do a mile each outing ... sometimes only once a day; sometimes twice. An old Afrikaner takes me; he's called Oom Charlie and is always smiling. Yes, I talk to him a little. Otherwise, to nobody. Nobody. The food is just left outside the cell. Someone shouts 'kos!' and I go to fetch it. Porridge and coffee ... I drink the coffee late in the morning. If I drank it hot with breakfast, I should not be able to go back to sleep; this is important – sleep helps to pass the time. I first awaken to a terrible clanging and battering along the corridor, doors crashing, until it culminates outside mine. It is still dark. I eat the porridge, with a little of last night's butter and sugar, and try to go back to sleep. Then I dress and at a certain time the cell is unlocked; I walk down to the washroom, down a long corridor, dark, passing perhaps forty barricaded cells ...

Do you ever shout out?

No ... I shower, shave if necessary, and look at myself in the mirror, still amazed that It is me! Clean my bucket and swill it out with antiseptic that makes it smell like a cattle dip.

Ruth: That must make you feel at home!

Yanka: That poem I wrote about two months ago ... you remember ...

Yes, that's it ... I sweep my room, my cell, and then drink the cold coffee. And then put on my ring – this is an important time, it means so much to me – I am thinking of you. Look at our rings ... look in the circle, how round and whole it is ...

Yes, yes. Beautiful and fulfilling. Do you think of our problem of how to reach the inside of the outside of a circle?

Ah, yes, Janitska.

The day passes. I know it is passing because the shaft of sunlight moves round my cell – each day it climbs in the window and only leaves in the evening – I am most hopeful in the evening because there will soon be a new day – until the chief warder comes round... Sometimes I climb up the cell window – I can see sky and birds, a few stars at night ... I have finished the Bible, read it from cover to cover. No, I haven't been learning anything off by heart – what is the point?

Discipline, Yanka. You must. Come on, let's both learn the Song of Solomon.

Swanepoel: Gids, man, no wonder women make the best secret agents.

No, I don't recite much aloud; can't remember any Shakespeare or my own poems. I sing aloud at night, loudly, when the prison is quiet. During the day there is continual noise. I had been writing that diary on the lavatory paper – but it was taken away, taken away – and I am confused now because, as I was writing it, I felt you were receiving it. Now I don't know what I've told you ...

You have given me a lot of details about your day. Tell me about the night.

Supper is at three – bread, butter and some jam and tea. That's all, but food is not important. The lights go out at 8 and then begins the problem of trying to sleep, and there is the fear of sleep because of the nightmares. Nightmares more horrifying than I can describe ... you must read 'The Idiot' ... the dreams of the man with TB ... dreams like your own – the gift.

Once I dreamt that you and Marian [my sister] kept changing places; it was frightening; I didn't know who I was engaged to ...

Ruth: That's incest! [A loud guffaw from Swanepoel].

But sometimes I feel safe in bed, wrapped in the blankets – like being in the womb?

Yes, but a hard womb. Felt matting on the floor and blankets. You must look up all those references – let me see the note again:

And now I can't remember any more details – let me just roam around in my mind – a mind heavy, heavy with concern to see you, Yanka, in the first stages of disorientation, slipping slowly. But I gave you hope, didn't I? And strength and will – it is a tunnel that has an end, you do know that?

I had brought Janet a poem, written on toilet paper, that I gave her when we met. I apologized for the paper, but the message said a lot. What is reproduced here is a fragment:

At Night

I see you in bed
gold hair splashed on the pillow
a shawl stretched across the wall behind your head
Alone.
But you know I'm with you
so sleep love, sleep –
it's where we'll meet
the only area of our lives they cannot enter.

Swanepoel asked to see what I had written before I could give it to Janet, and he took little account of the poetry. But he was embarrassed that I had had to write it on toilet paper: 'You shouldn't have to be writing on toilet paper. Here, we will give you some sheets of paper. Take them with you and do your writing on proper paper.' From then on, my diary, and the future correspondence I was to have, went down on A4 sheets, some of which I still have.

We concluded and were reassured that Swanepoel's colleague, Major Coetzee, would be taking charge of my case in the preparation of a statement and, after it was signed, they would be in a position to discuss the outcome of my case. They were planning to bring me out to see him from the beginning of the following week. Swanepoel again made clear that there would be no further discussion of future arrangements until I had completed and signed a statement.

Day 35: Thursday 17 July

The early morning shovels continued, as did the singing, but not the razor blades. There was a pause in the early morning song, a waiting period of silence, and then the prison clatter resumed. I was woken by the smell of Janet's perfume on my hands, and had her love and concern with me in the cell. I held her presence in my mind and she accompanied me through the following days. As the days became more bearable I regained composure, and time was taken up reading more of the Gospels in the mornings and the Old Testament in the afternoons. I was still in no fit state to read the fiction or the university books that my family had been allowed to bring in on their visits. During the afternoons I stuck to the discipline of an Old Testament reading and, depending on mood, I read Ecclesiastes if mournful or the Song of Songs if hopeful. I knew Janet was reading Solomon's Song at home. We had agreed to read certain passages and relay them to one another through the air. I memorized long passages, recited them to myself as I paced the cell, 'sent' them to her, believing she was doing the same for me, and transcribed some of them onto my new luxury – sheets of writing paper.

Now that I was reciting passages while pacing, other poems came to mind, and I recited passages I could remember, setting my pace to the rhythm of the poem. Roy Campbell's 'Horses on the Camargue' was the most strengthening. I found myself inside his poem:

> In the grey wastes of dread,
> The haunt of shattered gulls where nothing moves,
> But in a shroud of silence like the dead
> I heard a sudden harmony of hooves,
> And, turning, saw afar
> A hundred snowy horses unconfined,
> The silver runaways of Neptune's car
> Racing, spray-curled, like waves before the wind,
> Sons of the Mistral, fleet
> As him with whose strong gusts they love to flee,
> Who shod the flying thunders on their feet
> And plumed them with the snortings of the sea . . .

I had memorized this and many other poems while at school, and repeated them now, day after day. For my own renewal, I summoned up its closing verse. Four years earlier this poem's conclusion had been an inspiration in my last days at school and I continue to find strength in its 'spirits of power and beauty and delight':

> Still out of hardship bred,
> Spirits of power and beauty and delight
> Have ever on such frugal pastures fed
> And loved to course with tempests through the night.
> (Campbell 1930: 84)

Day 36: Friday 18 July

Now that there were no longer razor blades in the bathroom, even the weekend prospect was more bearable. I settled down to a routine of discipline and self-care in the loneliness, and I waited. On each occasion that I had a visitor, I was briefed by the prison commander doing his daily patrols. I would hear the door of the preceding cell opened as he marched up to the prisoner who was taken out to be inspected, and then I heard his cell door closed again as my door was opened and I was brought to attention outside it. He would come up to look at me in the way a farmer inspects livestock. Then he would either say, 'You will have a visitor today', and march on as I was directed to go back, while the next cell opened on the other side, or simply march on without a word. I had wondered if I should report the razor blades to him, but thought that he must be part of the conspiracy to see me dead, and so concluded that an appeal to him might do me more harm than good. Without the blades in the bathroom I had some sense I might survive. So, I reversed roles with this fierce man and stared back at him as if he was the ox and I was the inspecting farmer – I would not be slaughtered today. But there was to be no visit either, and it would be a long time before the weekend was over.

Day 37: Saturday 19 July

I spent the weekend floating through the hours. I had no idea if the police intentions were so devious as to offer me life and release but on certain conditions that they had yet to put forward and that I could not comply with, so I was still very apprehensive. I went to those Biblical passages I could find about hope, and assembled a catalogue for hope of different kinds. Hope in uncertainty. Hope without hope, like the men below, doomed but steadfast. Hopeless, like the men who cried out at night – utter despair. Looking for hope when there is no hope to be looked for, like the passage from Romans now written into my Bible – 'For we are saved by hope; but hope that is seen is not hope: for what a man seeth, why doth he yet hope for? But if we hope for that we see not, then do we with patience wait for it' (Romans 8:24–25).

I had no way of knowing about the efforts being made in the world outside, like the correspondence in progress between my mother and the prime minister.

Day 38: Sunday 20 July

The mornings were more bearable without the sound of the condemned men singing from below. On a Sunday morning without a hanging, the prison clatter started later. I was not woken at dawn and lay in my 'bed' waiting for breakfast to be brought. Then the sound of shovels started up as they scraped coal to feed the kitchen furnace, and then there were voices echoing around the corridors as locks and doors were opened and closed with slams and jangling keys.

Voices from the condemned cells had first been a solace, before I knew what they were, but they were now a reminder of what an appalling place this was. So, the hangman was having a weekend off. What did he do on his weekends? Where did he live and where did he go for his time out? Hartbeespoort Dam was near Pretoria. We used to go there to swim and to fish. Perhaps he went fishing there? Did he have a name? Would those who had their fishing lines in the water nearby realize they were fishing beside a hangman? If he met some-one new and they talked about their careers, would he introduce himself by his occupation? 'Oh, I hang people by their necks until they are dead.' I remem-bered childhood confusion about what a skull was, something like the spooky thing we saw on a pirate flag above the crossbones. When I was about five, our gardener Paul was arrested for a pass offence, and he came back from jail having been injured by the police. Our family doctor did a house call and concluded there was no fracture to his skull. This was the first I knew that 'skull' was not a scary thing like a ghost. I had come to believe that some people had skulls – very spooky things – inside their head. How terrible! Then I was told that I too had one, but I could not find where it was. And then I was told it was just made up of the bones in the head. I kept feeling my head to see where it was. And now, I thought, here I am in a place where they pull the skull off someone's spine, every day except for weekends. What a terrible job! Perhaps the hang-man deserves his weekend rest? Does the hanged person die straight away, or die over time hanging on the end of the rope? What does a condemned person think about the night before – like now – and where does the hope go when they come to collect him at dawn?

In the afternoon as the light began to fall, the voices were there again. There would be a hanging on Monday morning. Fading light through the barred win-dow cast its own image onto the opposite wall. It moved across the wall inch by inch until it disappeared in the evening. This was someone's last light.

I was to discover the next day that this very Sunday had also been the day that Neil Armstrong and Buzz Aldrin landed on the moon. Tomorrow was my brother David's birthday. He would be sixteen. Where was he? How was he doing at school? Was he being supported there? He and my sister Marian attended Waterford Kamhlaba School in Swaziland – an enlightened estab-lishment educating the children of a number of political activists. I was sure they would be supported there. I wanted to wish him happy birthday, and did so in my diary, which I no longer had to write on toilet paper – I had normal sheets of paper to write on.

Notes

1. Orwell, G. 'A Hanging' (2003). For further information see https://en.wikipedia.org/ wiki/A_Hanging (last accessed 23 May 2020).
2. Archive of deaths in detention during apartheid: 'Lists of Death in Detention', 2011/2019. South African History Online. Retrieved May 2020 from https://www .sahistory.org.za/article/list-deaths-detention. 'Truth Body Hears Testimony on Deaths in Detention', in Proceedings of the Truth and Reconciliation Commission, reported by SAPA (South African Press Association), 29/04/1996:

   Nicodimus Kgoathe died in police custody in February 1969 after allegedly slipping on a bar of soap while bathing. A month later, fellow detainee James Lenkoe also died, with police claiming he had hanged himself with his own belt [in the same prison]. On Monday, the Truth and Reconciliation Commission heard the two were among seven detainees who died within months of each other in 1969. Kgoathe's son Ben said an inquest magistrate had found nobody was to blame for his father's death, despite a district surgeon testifying he had found evidence Kgoathe was whipped and beaten.

   'To our surprise all the statements from the security police revolved around the fact that he had slipped on a bar of soap and that they had helped him up so that he could continue washing', he said. When he had visited his father at Silverton police station on January 18, several weeks before his death, he was lying on the floor of his cell. He was able only to raise his head to greet his son.

   'My father said he had slipped while he was bathing. Sgt. Geldenhuys who was there said he should tell the truth of what had really happened.' Kgoathe said his father had been transferred to security police headquarters in Pretoria several days earlier, where he was interrogated and tortured before being returned to Silverton police station. He said he had asked Geldenhuys to ensure his father was admitted to hospital to get treatment for his injuries. January 18 1969 was the last time he had seen his father alive. On February 5 police took his mother to HF Verwoerd hospital mortuary so that she could identify her husband. He said attempts to sue Prime Minister John Vorster and the Minister of Police failed after the family's attorney Joel Carlson disappeared.

   Witness Lorraine Lenkoe told the commission earlier on Monday that Carlson had been deported from South Africa because of his involvement in political cases. She said the family had retained Carlson after her father was arrested on March 5 1969 and detained without trial at a police station in Pretoria. Several days after his arrest, the family was told he had hanged himself with his belt.

   A doctor flown from the United States to conduct a post-mortem examination on behalf of the family found evidence Lenkoe had been tortured. 'He found that he had been burnt. I think they were electric burns.' She wept as she described how police stationed at the Ficksburg border post tried to frustrate the family's attempts to have Lenkoe buried in Lesotho.

   'They said no males were allowed to cross. My mother and my aunt had to carry the coffin to the other side where they were met by members of father's family.' She wanted to meet those responsible for her father's death so that 'I can forgive them and they can forgive me'.

INTERROGATION II
Johan Coetzee

Day 39: Monday 21 July

I was taken out this Monday morning at an earlier time than usual. In order to get me washed without clashing with the other prisoners' use of the main bathroom, I was taken to the warders' bathroom close to my own cell. It was an interesting exposure to their own working conditions. The facilities were austere and spartan, much like my boarding school and little different to those that we used as prisoners. Then I had my exercise early and we went down and out into the prison square. From there I was taken to the detectives waiting in the Control Room. On the way, Oom Charlie told me that men had been walking on the moon last night. It was hard to believe and difficult to take in. I had known nothing about it.

Then I was taken directly from the exercise yard to meet the detectives waiting to take me out, and by 9 a.m. I was at Compol Building where Swanepoel handed me over to Coetzee. I spent my first day in the new hands of these 'legalistic' detectives, which was threatening – because it was so exposing – but was nevertheless a welcome relief from solitary in the Hanging Jail. The experience is described in the entries that follow. At the end of this first day I was taken back to jail as it was getting dark and was back in prison before there was any sign of the rising moon. Passage back through the terrible prison doors did not trouble me as it had done on every previous occasion, as I could not wait to get back to my cell, from where I hoped to be able to see the moon.

When nightfall came, I looked for the moon by hoisting myself up to the window. I could hang there for only a short time and could see nothing except lights illuminating the prison roofs and silhouettes of the branches of the distant jacaranda trees. It was disappointing to have to accept that my cell faced north and so would give me no sight of the moon rising on the other side of the prison. I had begun to have some hope for a future beyond prison, but was cautious about what terms would be required and what price I might be called on to pay for a way out.

So, I had to content myself with a poem to the moon that I had memorized at school. Roy Campbell had become a committed fascist and fought for Franco in the Spanish Civil War, but I had grown up on his earlier South African poetry, and now recited fragments of *African Moonrise* to the empty window above my head. I could only remember the last two of these verses fully, but I had scattered words for the earlier lines that set out in verse the passage of the moon rising in the veld above a vlei, the kind of marshy area familiar to me from my upbringing in Swaziland, where we would go out in the evening to watch the moon rise. So, the lines went to an invisible, absent moon on which human beings were now walking. The dog's cry in these last lines echoed my own desolation in the cell:

> When the cold moon rose glinting from the fen
> And snailed her slime of fire along the hill,
> Insomnia the Muse of angry men,
> To other themes had chid my faithless quill.
>
> But wide I flung the shutters on their hinges
> And watched the moon as from the gilded mire,
> Where the black river trails its reedy fringes,
> She fished her shadow with a line of fire. . . .
>
> Till a starved mongrel tugging at his chain
> With fearful jerks, hairless and wide of eye,
> From where he crouched, a thrilling spear of pain,
> Hurled forth his Alleluia to the sky.
>
> Sing on lone voice! Make all the desert ring,
> My listening spirit kindles and adores . . .
> Such were my voice, had I the heart to sing,
> But mine should be a fiercer howl than yours! (Campbell 1930a: 60)

This last verse has always been with me. It gives words to anguish and ecstasy. It is an often-recited tribute to the rising moon and also, simply, a response to the howling of a dog in the night.

Days 39–42: Monday 21–Thursday 24 July

Coetzee was the man I had seen as a silent figure at the door of the interrogation room on many previous occasions. There was a regular procession of people who came to stare at me while I was on the brick. They seemed to be there out of either curiosity or amusement, as they made a sport of watching me walk into the walls of the little room when I became deluded and could not stay on the brick. Some of them sent for others to come and see, and the derision in their laughter stuck to me like spit.

In Coetzee's case it was all curiosity and no amusement. He had been studying me. He had eyes of two different colours, as Swanepoel described, set above a moustache with a flare in it. Years later I was to learn from one of the junior officers who served under him in the Special Branch that he was known as 'two-tone' because of these eyes.[1] He had a quiet, studious presence, a concentrated stare and a less pronounced Afrikaans accent than his colleagues. Above all, he was penetrating, intense and quite forbidding. He wore a tie and jacket whenever I saw him, and sometimes a suit. He was quick and focused, with an easy conversational manner and the bearing of a schoolteacher. During the week I spent with him going through my 'statement' I found him to be a more formidable presence than anyone else I have encountered, before or since. He followed through on every detail that might prove informative and he went for its unravelling, looking for consequences. He had an arrogance that took an affable form. He knew much more than I did – more than I would ever know – about politics and history, and he wanted to see me intimidated by his knowledge. He was also curious and enquiring, from the vantage point of very fixed views, and he had a number of questions to which he kept coming back, taunting me with my own inability to answer. Our time together was focused mostly on my association with my black friends. 'Why do you think they're your friends? They were using you and they're using you now. You were a promising student. Why did your family let you go to America when you were only seventeen?' And most probing of all, 'Why are you left-wing people all so maladjusted?' He named other opponents of apartheid of whom I had some vague idea, to let me see how their influence and their very personalities had been stripped out of public knowledge, as they would in time strip me out of the South African world. He was the stripper. He knew how 'maladjusted' all we left-wing people were, he said, because he knew of compromising information that he could secure about us, to serve as a way of silencing us. He was even more chilling than Swanepoel, whose force was all in the open. This man was like a crouching tiger.

I thought from memory that I had spent the whole week with him, from Monday 21 to Friday 25 July, but my Bible calendar indicates it may have been only Monday, Wednesday and Friday. We went upstairs escorted by an unfamiliar detective named Lieutenant Jordaan and took occupation of a large room on the side of the building. Coetzee and Jordaan got its phone lines sorted out, rearranged desks to turn the place into an office and set up the electric typewriter where Coetzee installed himself. He got me to sit down opposite him and introduced me to the younger man. They expressed some amusement that I had not already recognized him – I treated him as if we were strangers. 'Comparative African Government and Law', Jordaan said to me, still smiling. I was bewildered. Then he said, 'I was sitting near you in the lecture when you were called out for the arrest. I'm a student at Wits.' Only then did I recognize him. He spoke with no trace of an Afrikaans accent but broke into Afrikaans whenever he spoke with Coetzee. He took his jacket off to hang it over the back of the chair and made a point of letting me see the gun he carried in his shoulder holster. During the course of our time together he talked freely about his work as a detective – we were of the same generation – and he went out of his way to set my shameful misconduct against his brave career protecting the state and its people. He even undid his shirt at the front to show me the scar of a serious gunshot wound that he had suffered in the course of his duties, and he described the incident with some relish. Then Coetzee said, 'He's the man who arrested John Blacking.' He repeated this compliment as if he were giving him a medal – he probably did. I was speechless. 'I thought John Blacking was arrested under the Immorality Act!' I exclaimed. Indeed, he was – he was arrested, prosecuted and convicted, given a suspended sentence, and in the aftermath he left the country and returned to the UK.

The Immorality Act was one of the cornerstones of apartheid.[2] Based on a raft of earlier laws going back to 1927, it was consolidated into one statute in 1957 and made a crime of any sexual act between 'Europeans' and 'Non-Europeans', i.e. between whites and people from other designated races. In March 1969, Blacking was convicted of conspiracy to contravene this Act with Zureena Desai, an Indian doctor. He was already one of the world's leading musicologists and was our professor of anthropology at the time. We knew him and his first wife and children socially, which the police remained unaware of. People came from all over the country and beyond to attend his open lectures based on the original field studies he had conducted into the music of the Venda people who live on the northern and eastern borders of South Africa and in the south and east of Zimbabwe. After leaving the country, Blacking was divorced and he and Desai then went on to marry and had four children together. At appointments in Australia, the USA and Northern Ireland, where a lecture theatre is dedicated to John Blacking's name, they worked together to make a world-renowned contribution to musicology and social anthropology (Blacking 1973).[3]

Coetzee replied to my confusion with this explanation: 'We have many resources by which to keep the country safe. Your professor was running a nursery school for communists on the steps of the university. You don't think we are limited by security legislation to keep ourselves secure? The Immorality Act was very useful to us here. He won't trouble us any longer. And this is the man who led the team', he said, pointing to Jordaan. So, this was the man who posted photographers in the trees outside Blacking's home in Saxonwold to get compromising photographs through the windows, and then brought a case to court – widely reported in the press – that destroyed Blacking's university reputation in the country.[4] Coetzee's appreciation of his junior's success showed in his steady mentoring, in the interest he took in policing and security in general and, I was to discover, in the pastoral care of his own colleague's misdemeanours.

With that as our introduction, we got down to work, which consisted of reviewing the sheaf of interrogation notes that had been made by the team of six, five weeks earlier. He whipped through the material at a pace and recognized the individual handwriting of each member of the interrogating team, whom he knew by name. As he was browsing through the first set of notes he passed the rest on to Jordaan, who began to organize the material into topics. It was time-consuming, detailed and focused. From this vantage point I cannot recall content-specific narrative or topics.

With the help of lawyers at the South African History Archive I located a Security Legislation Directorate file number 69/2713 with my name on it. I waited for the chance to read its contents with a mixture of excitement, curiosity, disbelief and loathing, and was hopeful I could incorporate material relevant to this memoir in the text. But my investigation had an even more disconcerting outcome – the file was empty. The material that I watched these men build up about me had been destroyed.

Coetzee's disposition, outlook and approach were revealed also in the many asides that took place during the week. He had a topical knowledge of everything going on in the country, including, and especially, Zulu and Swazi history and people, and the Jewish community. He also had a wide grasp of the literature in political history. He let me know that he was busy with a PhD by correspondence with the University of South Africa and, though I do not recall its subject matter with confidence, I learnt that his special interests were in Boer and Zulu history, especially the Boer War – and Marxism, especially Trotsky. He appeared to be the mastermind of the operation that lay behind our arrests. He was governed by a highly organized, manic drive, and when I commented on the speed of his typing, he told me he had begun his police career as a court stenographer.

The material we reviewed together followed the interrogation notes, and he transposed what he thought relevant to (what he called) my 'case' into a first-person narrative that went down on the typewriter at a furious pace. He would pause to review a further set of notes, return to me for clarification where called for, and then type it down. I spent a lot of the time staring out of the window in an aimless state while the two of them worked their way through my material, one getting the topics organized and the other turning it into first-person statements. Coetzee would come towards the end of a sentence he was typing and then get me to finish it for him. He was clearly used to doing this kind of thing, and worked at extraordinary speed.

He opened out new areas of enquiry with me, or elaborated on subjects that his colleagues had not covered, in a focused and systematic way, and he had a penetrating curiosity to get to the bottom of everything that was covered. During breaks when tea or coffee was brought in, he would discuss the material with his assistant in Afrikaans and, like an instructor, he would point out to him evident flaws in the interrogation team's enquiries. 'We know this and it's clear, but why don't we know that, and why didn't they challenge him on it and get clarity on the link?' He had no idea quite how closely I followed his asides. Then, when we resumed our work in English, to include me, we would come to his own questions and I would be prepared. At times he saw how I watched them talk in Afrikaans and on one occasion he broke off from their dialogue about me and said to me in English, 'Wouldn't you like to know what we've been saying!' Well, I did know, but I had to profess that I understood nothing and would stumble and hesitate when he came to revise his enquiries with points that troubled me, as if I had been found out for the first time.

His mentoring disposition picked me up in its backwash. Later, on our first day together, after my visible discomposure and initial disbelief on hearing the John Blacking story, he said there were many other such cases I was probably not aware of. 'Your friend Fanny Klenerman, for example. Where you buy your books. She was a leading anti-anti-communist and attacked us for challenging the communists only because she was such a subversive herself. The shop where you get all your books is like honey for left-wing bees.' He picked out the opposition she organized against 'anti-communists', along with others he named whom I cannot now recall, and dubbed them all 'anti-anti-communists', enjoying his own designation with some relish.

Fanny Klenerman was the owner and manager of Vanguard, the only bookshop in Johannesburg that offered a range of political literature. She led the campaign of ridicule against the Publications Control Board, which had banned Thomas Hardy's *The Return of the Native* some years before. 'Native' had been the customary term for blacks before the state moved on to use the term 'Bantu'. Based on its title alone, the censors thought there might be something subversive about Hardy's novel, so they banned it.

Coetzee told me that Klenerman had been punished for bringing them to ridicule. He organized a police photographer to track her down to a remote mountain pool where she used to nude bathe. The compromising photographs they took of her could not stop her selling books, Coetzee said, but they did make her more cautious about challenging them in the press.[5]

Each of the topics covered in the first interrogation led him to comments and observations of one kind or another. What he was extracting from the notes is no longer within my memory. But he pursued me about a number of my associations with people in Johannesburg whom he regarded as politically minded – writing colleagues, fellow poets, jazz musicians and student activists. Along the way he would stop typing to look at me and ask: 'Why are you left-wing people all so maladjusted?' He presented this as fact, taunting me with it on different occasions through the time I spent in his hands. This second interrogation was less painful than the first but more exposing. It emerged that their primary focus – the one that led to my arrest – had arisen from their interrogation of the first group of detainees one month earlier; a developing friendship with a staff member at the United States Information Service had led Mrs Mandela to visit our family home the previous year. Further, I had taken young men from Soweto and Alexandra to work camps in Swaziland where we built a school in a rural area. Further still, I had a friend who was a jazz musician, who was trying to join his mentor in Lusaka, and when I spoke to a black journalist to ask for help, she must have assumed that I was part of an ANC recruitment pipeline. The police put all this together and, from their own calculations, I emerged as a dangerous underground operative.

At some point later in the process, when I felt cornered by something and could do or say little in self-defence, I spoke out against them both and said, 'You seem to have all the power here and your big system is set against me. There is nothing I can do. But you can't stop history and you don't control the future. It doesn't belong to you.' He replied: 'Mr Schlapobersky, this isn't Algeria with an inexhaustible supply of terrorists from the Casbah. The French had no chance of controlling the Arabs there. But they taught us enough about how to control our own population here. We don't have pass laws just to regulate influx control. They serve us as our primary source of intelligence. We know who lives where, what they get up to and where they go. And we always will. We have everything under control here. Your presence on that seat confirms it.'

What his over-clever taunt failed to address was just how misguided they had been in detaining me at all. The adverse publicity at the time cost them dearly; the expensive investment of police time brought no rewards; popular opinion in Johannesburg was mobilized against them, leading people to then take to the streets in demonstrations about each stage of the 'Trial of the 22' until their eventual release; and, finally, my article in *The Observer* embarrassed them profoundly at an international level.

The Natives (Abolition of Passes and Co-ordination of Documents) Act of 1952, known as the Pass Laws Act, made it compulsory for all black South Africans over the age of 16 to carry a 'pass' and later a 'reference book' at all times.[6] What Coetzee said to me then was not only confirmation of his role as an intelligence figure, but also pointed to what we have since learnt of the apprenticeship served by the South African Security Police in Algeria during the French colonial war. Kevin O'Brien, a distinguished historian of the South African security service, confirms that both Swanepoel and Coetzee received training in Algeria in interrogation techniques like the sleep deprivation programme that they had put me through (O'Brien 2011). This is also confirmed by proceedings of the Truth and Reconciliation Commission (TRC).[7]

There were other exchanges of relevance. Coetzee tried to get the measure of how I had come by my own left-wing outlook, and was curious about what there was in Jewish cultural life that led us towards Marxism. They had found Marxist books in my home that did not fit with the range of literature they were familiar with amongst South Africa's 'indigenous' Marxists – those like Rowley Arenstein, whom he described to me, who had a Communist Party background – and others from the different Congress movements. I had received no tutoring or mentorship in any such readings, but had come across the books they seized while I was taken up in the student movement of the United States. These police in South Africa were less familiar with all these new developments, but they treated me as a kind of 'find', someone whose case would prove informative in their further intelligence operations. He brought up Arenstein's name as an example of a Jew with a Lithuanian background who had not been satisfied with the legal profession for which he had trained (Arenstein and Johnson 1991). He was curious about the motivation that drew Jews towards the left. In the exchange that developed, several points of interest emerged.

Coetzee was familiar with Arenstein's current involvement in Zulu affairs, and he assumed that, coming from Swaziland myself, I would know something about this. I did not. But he took pleasure in displaying to me an extraordinary knowledge of Zulu history and a grasp of tribal and cultural issues. In the years that followed, as the Inkatha Freedom Party grew under Mangosuthu Buthelezi to become an opposing force against the ANC-oriented United Democratic Front, Coetzee's hand was, I believe, directly culpable in the shedding of the blood that soaked the country.[8]

He was interested in antisemitism in the country, and he went on to tell me of how, while responsible for protecting South Africa's Jews, he had made the startling discovery that Nazi graffiti on one of Johannesburg's synagogues had been placed there secretly by the synagogue's very own rabbi. He was intrigued by this discovery and made frequent reference to it. I later came to associate his preoccupation with this, and other such cases, with the case he himself was executing for the South African state. The widespread detentions that winter 'created' the threat they were intended to discover – there were communists everywhere!

'Discovered threats', he explained, 'work like nothing else to promote unity. The only things better are undiscovered threats, which are even more successful.'

The Afrikaners who broke ranks with their own people to side with the British, like General Smuts, earned a special hatred from the group who called themselves 'Die Bittereinders' (the Bitter Enders), who refused to accede to British rule after the Boer War. The population they were drawn from later went on to form 'Die Ossewa Brandwag' (the Ox Wagon's Sentinel), the Afrikaner underground movement that mobilized against Smuts's government during the Second World War. B.J. Vorster, the prime minister at the time the events in this book took place, was amongst the leaders Smuts interned. A further, more hidden and much more influential secret association of Afrikaners developed later called 'Die Afrikaner Broederbond' (the Afrikaner Brotherhood), which acted as 'the force within the force'. All the country's prime ministers and heads of state between 1948 and 1994 belonged to it, and they accounted for the leadership of many state bodies, especially the Security Police. Their hatred for Afrikaners' complicity with the British showed in the mini-lectures that Coetzee gave me as he illustrated Smuts's betrayal of what Coetzee called 'his own people's interests'. He told me to look at the bricks at chest height in the exercise courtyard of the prison I was in. The wall there was known amongst them as the Afrikaners' own 'Wailing Wall' – it was here, he said, that Smuts had the leaders of the Maritz rebellion executed when they opposed the country's entry into the First World War on Britain's side. In my own reading on the subject, I have found only one such Boer general to have been executed by firing squad, but in Coetzee's account there were many. I later inspected the exercise yard where I went daily, and saw just how many bricks at chest height had been removed and replaced – enough to cover the shooting range of a large firing squad (Plaatje 1916; Bunting 1986).

There are 'aside' stories about each of these policemen. When they took occupation of the office premises on this first floor in Compol Building – where I presume there was much more such work to come – I must have been the first in line for their interviews. The window faced out over Volkstem Avenue, and looked directly onto an office building on the other side of this narrow street. A team of young women could be seen doing administrative work and sitting at typewriters. Coetzee and Jordaan were uneasy about how visible they were to these women. Coetzee directed Jordaan to 'get busy', so he went through a series of phone calls to identify the company in the building opposite, and eventually got through to the pretty-faced young woman who would often look across at us. He invited her to look out over the street and find him. I was treated as if I did not exist. He did not know that I understood how he was chatting her up in Afrikaans, and once she had got over her embarrassment, he made a date to meet her one evening that week. He received praise and appreciation from Coetzee for doing this. I would never discover what became of this intelligence-courtship, but I knew it started as no more than a ruse, for he had told me of his own committed marriage, in order to contrast it with John Blacking's infidelity.

Coetzee had a phone on the desk beside him from which he often took brief calls and made others. I could not pay attention to everything that happened, as Jordaan was keeping me busy with other work on the document. But a point arose when Coetzee became agitated, and I realized he was speaking to a woman who was complaining to him about a man. I had not been monitoring the conversation but started to pay attention when I heard how concerned he was for this woman's distress. I could make out a woman's voice crying from the handset. I had no idea who she was – perhaps his sister, or the wife of his brother, or the wife of one of his junior staff. He got angry and irritated on her behalf, and replied to things she said with concerned outbursts against the person she was complaining about. Then he put the phone down and made loud exclamations against the behaviour of the man reported to him, using florid Afrikaans swearwords. And then he made a call himself, and I knew he was speaking to the offending husband of the distressed woman, but I was unclear if this policeman was one of Coetzee's relations or one of his staff. His reproach against him for marital infidelity was direct and powerful. He told him off in a number of different ways and warned him that he was putting his job in the police force at risk, and he could be transferred from Pretoria to a country office. '*Wees versigtig, anders word u na 'n vergete werk in 'n klein dorpie oorgeplaas*' [You've got to change your ways, or you'll end up in Oudtshoorn.] (A small country town in a remote part of the Western Cape once famous for ostriches but now fallen on hard times.)

Then he broke into English for special emphasis and shouted at him: 'She should be your pride and joy!' – and he put the phone down with a bang. He turned to Jordaan and shook his head with disbelief over what he was having to deal with regarding this man's misconduct – and then they both went out for a break.

Day 43: Friday 25 July

During my last hours with these two detectives on Friday afternoon, alarming things emerged that left me in disarray over the weekend. I understood we were due to conclude with the drafting of this 'statement' at the end of that working day. It was due for the typing pool to be properly typed on Monday when I would be expected to sign it. Only at that point would they be ready to enter into discussion with me and my family about the future of 'my case'.

However, as Coetzee worked his way towards the end of the set of interrogation notes, he came across a line of narrative about a student-based group of activists that I had been associated with that his colleagues – the earlier interrogators – had not taken seriously enough. We had been reading Fanon's *The Wretched of the Earth,* and our reading programme took in Che Guevara, Castro, Angela Davis and the Black Panthers. There had not been the same fierce line of questioning about white students as they had shown when investigating my association with blacks. Coetzee shared his concern with Jordaan in Afrikaans, saying there was an indication in the notes taken by '*Die Durban Manne*' (the Durban guys), of a grouping that he now realized they would have to take more seriously. It was well on into the evening, as it was already dark; we were all tired and hungry and they were in a rush to be finished. Swanepoel came in to see how they were getting on and Coetzee was clearly pleased to see him. Getting up from his desk where I had been sitting beside him, he went over to Swanepoel to discuss things some distance off, out of earshot, but as he got up, he said: '*Daar was nog ander dinge hier aan die gang waaroor ons moet praat*' [There were other things going on here that we need to talk about]. '*Daar was meer hier aan die gang as wat ons eers gedink het*' [There was more going on here than we first thought].

My heart sank. Perhaps they would put me back on the brick. Perhaps they would want to bring others in. What about their threats against Janet? Perhaps they would suspend their plans to review my case for an early release? They sent for a meal for me while they talked some way off, well out of earshot, and this heightened my anxiety. By then it must have been 7 or 8 p.m., and the car that took me back to prison drove through the darkness. At the prison the two detectives had to go through some enhanced security procedure to get the guards to open the gates and let me in. I was put in the hands of a night warder, who had a rifle over his shoulder and a revolver in his side holster. It was all much, much more alarming than the daytime experience, and the weekend wait ahead was due to be dreadful.

Day 44: Saturday 26 July

Now I anticipated the worst – I had some foreboding they would make some radical revision to the plan for my early release. I found myself strengthened by the two visits I had had from my family the week before, and even the week's exchange with Coetzee and Jordaan had done me more good than harm. I decided to stage a crisis over the weekend to aggravate their concerns about me, and to forestall any second thoughts they might come to about their plans to release me. I was due to sign my statement on the Monday. I was worried that they might decide to keep me in detention; or that they might attach conditions to my release; or that I might have to give evidence from this statement against the others they may put on trial. I was determined to be medically examined on the day of signature to try to disqualify my statement by saying that I had signed it under so much pressure that I had needed medical attention. I was in no position to evaluate how much trouble I was still in, or how serious the likely evidence might be that I might carry against anyone else.

The truth of the matter was the opposite of my own fears. As described below in 'Signing the Statement', an Israeli–South African journalist named Dovidi Fachler gained access to the archive records of the Israeli Foreign Office and published an account of the report made by Itzhak Unna, the Israeli consul general, to his superiors in Israel in the aftermath of my discharge. Fachler wrote an article about this in *Jewish Affairs* in December 2013 in which he gives us privileged access to records of the time (Fachler 2013). The records clarify that the Security Police were by now concerned to get me out of prison and off their hands without acknowledging any irregularity in their arrest of me in the first place. Had I but known this, I would have been spared the need for the drama I created over the next three days. But not knowing, and in fear of the contrary, I decided to stage a crisis. Below is the entry for my diary on the night of Sunday 27 July. As they had read my previous toilet paper diary, there was a chance they would read the next edition – so, based on this likelihood, I wrote into it material that I thought would confirm the drama I planned to create the next day.

Day 45: Sunday 27 July

Entry from my diary:

Hello Jan,
Oh, I tried Jan – and couldn't sleep. I was just too frightened of the things I might meet in my sleep. And when I did drop off, a horrifying, utterly horrifying dream fell before me, which I couldn't bear to describe here. This cell is unbearable, the silence terrifies me – the walls seem to come progressively closer – I feel as if a piece of steel is being driven into my skull. I woke feeling ill with a terrible headache this a.m. And when I went off to the showers, I fell asleep on the lavatory. Unbelievable. I fell asleep sitting on the lavatory. And as unbearable as the day has been, I am terrified by the approach of night, another horror in the dark. I don't know what's happened to me since yesterday – I'm trying to break through and not down, but being back inside this prison for the whole day yesterday, I just couldn't cope. Even the books don't help now. I try to read but can't get my mind off tomorrow – for, after signing my statement, I'll be returned to this cell to spend two weeks more of these terrifying nights and unbearable days – and then . . . if they decide to keep me here . . . the nights . . .

the dreams . . . how much worse can it get? This headache has been with me the whole day and I can't understand why, Jan. I'm worried, so so worried, about my mind – I just hope I don't go to pieces at this stage – I've been through so much – hold on tight, it might be just another week or two . . . I know being with you will help me put all these broken pieces of my mind back together – soon! Jan, soon we must be together again. I know I won't go mad if we do get together soon. Sleep well tonight, my love. Yanka

Notes

1. Paul Erasmus, a detective warrant officer in the security police, retired from the force on medical grounds in his mid-thirties, and in due course gave evidence to the Goldstone Commission investigating the violence due to the 'Third Force' in South Africa during the last days of apartheid and in the period of the 1994 election. He sought amnesty for his own conduct at the Truth and Reconciliation Commission, and later gave evidence to the commissions of inquiry held into the deaths in detention of Neil Aggett and Ahmed Timol. He was introduced to me by Frank Dutton, a private investigator, and has authenticated the names, ranks and identities of those security police officers named in this book. His own book, *Confessions of a Stratcom Hitman*, is due for publication in 2021.
2. See Immorality Act of 1957. See apartheid legislation.
3. See 'John Blacking', 2020.
4. Verification of Jordaan's name and the role he played in this case, together with his captain, Johan Coetzee, has been made possible through information provided by Paul Erasmus and by Susanne Klausen, Professor of History, Carleton University, Ottawa, who searched the trial transcripts and press cuttings that reported Blacking's and Desai's arrest and prosecution. Her book on South Africa's Immorality Act is due for publication in 2022 and she has a current publication in this field (Klausen 2021). I am grateful to Dr Zureena Desai, who introduced me to her, and to the following who have helped me with the investigation: Christopher Ballantine, Professor Emeritus of Music at the University of KwaZulu-Natal; Omar Badsha, South African History Online; Professor Shahid Vawda, Archie Mafeje Chair and Director, School of African and Gender Studies, Anthropology and Linguistics, University of Cape Town. See also note 8 of the 'Prologue' and note 1 of 'Interrogation I'.
5. See 'More than a Shop', 2019.
6. The Natives (Abolition of Passes and Co-ordination of Documents) Act 67, of 1952 required all men to carry 'passes' and later 'reference books' containing their photographs and information about their places of origin, employment records, tax payments and encounters with the police. Women were required to carry passes by the Amendment Act of 1956. Retrieved May 2020 from https://omalley.nelsonmandela.org/omalley/index.php/site/q/03lv01538/04lv01828/05lv01829/06lv01853.htm. See apartheid legislation.
7. The Truth and Reconciliation Commission reports that 'it was widely believed by many political activists of the time that, in the early 1960s, a special squad of security policemen received special training in torture techniques in France and Algeria, and

that this accounted for a sudden and dramatic increase in torture. The Commission established that the following officers received training in France at some point during the first half of the 1960s: Hendrik van den Bergh (then head of the Security Branch), TJ "Rooi Rus" Swanepoel, DK Genis, Lieutenant Daantjie "Kardoesbroek" Rossouw, G Klindt, a Major Brits (from the Railway Police), a Lieutenant van der Merwe and one Coetzee'. See 'The Use of Torture in Detention'.

8. The 'Third Force' was a term used by leaders of the ANC during the late 1980s and early 1990s to refer to a clandestine force believed to be responsible for a surge in violence in KwaZulu-Natal and the townships around and south of the Witwatersrand. The TRC found that while little evidence existed of a centrally directed, coherent or formally constituted 'Third Force', a network of security and ex-security force operatives, frequently acting in conjunction with right-wing elements and/or sectors of the Inkatha Freedom Party, had been involved in actions that could be construed as fomenting violence that resulted in gross human rights violations, including random and targeted killings. See 'Third Force (South Africa)'; and see Ellis (1998). More recently, Garson's *Undeniable: Memoir of a Covert War* (2020) documents the scale of violence and atrocity for which Military Intelligence and other covert apartheid hit squads and third forces were responsible.

SIGNING THE STATEMENT AND NEGOTIATING RELEASE

Day 46: Monday 28 July

When the warder came to collect me on Monday morning for my visit to the bathroom, I had my slops pail ready and walked off in the opposite direction – I went down the corridor towards the grill that led to the exit. He called out from behind and quickly caught up with me. I told him I had to take this to Major Swanepoel – the bucket of shit! I knew I was due for collection to Compol, and wanted to take my shit with me. The recall is none too clear. I had laid my plans, thinking of Richter's description of me in the concluding stages of the interrogation as someone who was not a communist but a madman. I talked in my mind to Richter and the others over the weekend, saying 'You think I'm mad? I'll give you mad!' I told the warder it was really important that he let me go so that I could give this bucket of shit to Swanepoel. I have limited recall of the exchange that followed, but he succeeded in redirecting me – we went to the bathroom instead. While there, I emptied the slops pail out and sat on the toilet to defecate, as I tried to do on a daily basis, in an effort to keep my cell as smell-free as possible. I had decided in advance that I would go into the toilet, close the door and sit down, and just not come out. I had further strategies in mind by which to target Swanepoel's own self-regard and unsettle him if I could. I have no way of knowing for how long I sat on the toilet. He eventually called out to me but I still did not respond. Then he banged on the door and I made an exclamation to say I had fallen asleep and would come out immediately. When I did so, I told him I had such terrible dreams during the night that I could not sleep, and in consequence I had now fallen asleep sitting on the toilet.

I got back to my cell, got dressed and was immediately taken out to the waiting detectives in the office below. They must have been given a report of my strange behaviour, though I do not recall if the detectives treated me in any different way. When we got to Compol, I was taken into Swanepoel's office where he and Coetzee were both waiting for me. I was here to sign the typed statement on the desk. Swanepoel was in charge of proceedings, and when he asked me how I was, I told him I had such bad dreams I could not sleep at night and then could not wake in the mornings. There must have been a discussion with them of some kind, for I was invited to sit down to have a cup of tea that had been produced. Swanepoel was seated at his desk and several others were standing around us – Coetzee, Richter and Baker. I told Swanepoel that I dreamt he had murdered my father, and I then became distraught. The cup fell on the floor and broke, the tea went everywhere, and I fell on the floor myself. They said I needed to see a doctor, and Swanepoel gave direction for one of them to find Dr Venter – the doctor I had seen on Day 2. They came back with news that Venter would not be available all day. Swanepoel became irritated and challenging, and he directed them to find another doctor who could see me immediately. Eventually one of them produced a phone number and I listened to Swanepoel ring the doctor and tell him that I needed Librium – a tranquillizer – and sleeping tablets.

Now the tables were turned. I had been pacing my cell fearful they had death in store for me. But now they were worried and thought they had to protect me from what they believed was the risk I posed to myself – the very risk they had been trying to cultivate. I chuckled to myself in a grim way from time to time. My plan was working.

Before they took me out to see the doctor, I was directed to sign the statement. I did so with as much of a tremor in my signature as I thought I could get away with. I did not read the statement and have not seen it since. I was now taken out by three detectives, each with his gun in his shoulder holster – Richter, Baker and another. There were two in the front of the car and one beside me on the back seat. We drove some way out towards Silverton, a residential suburb, and pulled up at a clinic. Time has cost my memory the name of the GP who saw me – a frightened Jewish doctor. How could he not have been frightened? I was brought into his consulting room by three Security Police wearing guns. He prescribed the benzodiazepine they wanted – the tranquillizer – and he told me that what they were doing to me was my own fault. He made sure the police heard him say this. I thought to myself, may his shame stand against him, and may Dr Venter's shame stand against him. But he was obliging to my purpose simply by seeing me, and at the time I thought it was all going according to plan. When I was offered deportation a week later, I knew I was outside police range and would no longer have regard for this doctor's record of my attendance, so I set any current memory of him to one side. It had been my intention to track him down in person from Israel, and write to challenge his medical misconduct.

On returning to the prison I found they had moved me to a different cell. I was now several doors down the corridor in a cell that had two doors. There was an outer sealed metal door just like my original cell's door, with double locks and an eyehole in the door, but this was opened back against the wall and left like that permanently; however, this cell also had an inner grill door made up of bars, which is what sealed me in. Once installed, I discovered that the daily guard who collected me for showers and exercise would now sit outside the grill as a permanent observer. It was very strange. He just sat there staring at me. Then he got bored and looked down the corridor. Then he seemed to doze off. And then he came round, only to stare at me again. Strange as I found it, this was a major advance in my case – they no longer wanted me dead. They were actually protecting me from what they believed to be the primary threat against me – myself! From then until my release there was an observer outside the cell night and day. He gave me the tranquillizer tablet in the morning and a sleeping tablet at night, and he made sure I swallowed them.

By this point I could immerse myself in reading beyond the now familiar passages of the Old and New Testaments. I had been going through those pages that offered me most, but the eye infection returned, brought on by so much reading of the Bible's small print in poor light, so I had to discontinue reading for a day or two. Once treatment had taken effect, I took relief in the larger print of the new literature.

Day 47: Tuesday 29 July

It was very strange waking in the morning with a warder stationed outside the grill door of my open cell, sitting on a wooden chair and looking very bored. He took no special interest in me and seemed to belong to a team who appeared used to work of this kind. When I needed to use the slops pail for the toilet, I would ask him to turn around to give me some privacy, and he did so without hesitation. They changed according to a shift of their own, but I was not on my own again at any point until I left the country. He took no special interest in what I did and now that I had sheets of paper, I spent a lot of time writing openly. I still had the roll of my toilet paper diary hidden in a pocket in my trousers, and I kept it with me at all times. I now had books relating to some of my university subjects and could diversify my reading timetable through the day. It was a relief coming away from the tiny text in my Bible, and reading a font size that did not cause such eye strain.

I was taken for a second time to the prison warders' bathroom, located at a different point along the corridor from my cell. With the warder walking behind me, we passed a cell that had no occupant and its door had been left ajar. I was startled to see a bed in the cell with an attractive cover over a mattress and a small desk on the other side of the cell. I was still sleeping on the floor on a felt mat softened only by the extra blankets brought in by my parents, and my books lined the floor. I later learnt – for the first time – that one other white had been detained during our arrests, Philip Golding, who was also being held in this prison. He was also a British subject and, I later discovered, was receiving visits from the British consul general. I assumed this must have been his cell. He was held until December that year, when he gave evidence for the state in the 'Trial of the 22', and he was then deported to his home in the UK. We have never met but when I published my *Observer* article in August 1970, I received a brief note from him through the *Observer* in which he congratulated me on giving such a full and accurate account of detention, interrogation and imprisonment, and he thanked me for holding my own position. It was charged with the remorse of much that was unspoken and I would like to meet him.

Dovidi Fachler's article, referenced on Day 44 above, was published in the Chanukah edition of the quarterly, *Jewish Affairs*, and called 'The John Schlapobersky Affair' (Fachler 2013). It draws on a report written about me by Major Itzhak Unna, the Israeli consul general to South Africa at the time of my detention, and sent to Mr A. Lourie, deputy director general of the Israeli Foreign Office on 8 August 1969, marked 'Highly Confidential'. Fachler gained access to these records, and published them in 2013. Further, he led readers to believe that I had authorized this release and given him an interview. I have no recollection of meeting him, and the report was unauthorized and therefore misleading. Nevertheless, its content now forms a closing and crucial part of this memoir.

Unna describes my mother's visit to his office on 29 July 1969 to seek help for her imprisoned son. My mother had explained that there was no support for me in the Jewish community. Friends had turned against her, as had those members of the Jewish community in South Africa who might have had influence in high places, and even her brother-in-law, the former mayor, had declined to help. She had described her visit to me in jail in Pretoria, attended by Swanepoel and Coetzee. They had explained there was no evidence to charge me under the Terrorism Act, but they would not release me in the country because of the risk that I might pass on information I would have learnt during questioning about the forthcoming trial. Although I had a British passport, they would tolerate no interference from the British Embassy, and the only option they would consider for my early release would be my departure to Israel through Major Unna, whom they knew and trusted.

Unna alerted his superiors to the identities of those named:

> Maj. Swanepoel is chief interrogating officer of the Security Police, and it is important to add that of late the South African English press had singled him out, especially since over the course of the last year four African prisoners 'under his care' managed to hang themselves in their cells. Newspaper articles have sug-

gested, however, that these inmates may have died from electrocution. Major Coetzee, on the other hand, belongs to the Johannesburg branch of the Security Police, and I know him from there.

Obviously Mrs Schlapobersky asked me that I contact Maj. Coetzee immediately in order to negotiate the release of her son. However I was forced to explain to her that since I was the Consul General of Israel and not of Britain I had no right to initiate contact with the security police on this matter, and if the police really wanted to talk to me they know where to find me. (Fachler 2013: 11)

Day 48: Wednesday 30 July

This morning I was told that I would have a visitor, and was later taken out to see my mother, who was waiting for me in Swanepoel's office. We had the same threatening warnings not to discuss my case or prison situation, but I was treated as a human being and he invited my mother to take me out for a meal before we had our meeting. We went out once more with the same three detectives. During the whispered conversation between my mother and me on the way out and on our return, I told her that I was pretending to be mad and she briefed me on what was to follow, cautioning me to be cooperative. Things were happening. The Israeli consul general had taken an interest in my case, and an early release was under discussion. I would have to be careful and discreet, as everything was still up in the air.

When we were back in Swanepoel's office he assumed the familiar threatening pose of the big man in charge. He explained, for the first time, that they would not be charging me, though in his view I had behaved wrongfully, many times over. I was a source of trouble to my good parents and a disgrace to my community and university – but they would not be charging me. A trial would take place in the coming months and the question to be faced now was whether I would prefer to remain in my cell for the duration of the trial, or if other arrangements could be made. They would not release me to go back to my home in Johannesburg in case I passed information on, by one means or another, to those who were still trying to protect the terrorists they were charging. They could take steps to make my cell more comfortable, and I could continue with my university studies by correspondence. That was one option. He then turned to my mother and said, 'Mrs Schlapobersky, you want to introduce another option.'

My mother explained that the Israeli consul general had taken an interest in my case. They had been to see him to ask him to look into my brother Colin's temporary release from military service there, in case he was needed to come back to Johannesburg to support the family while I was in detention. They had also raised with him the question of whether I would be allowed to emigrate to Israel if I were to be released from prison. (We call this making *ali-*

yah which my brother had done two years earlier.) I was at a loss. All I wanted to do was go home, resume my life in Johannesburg and return to my studies at university. I said so, and Swanepoel replied that I would only be released after the forthcoming trial, which could take a year or two. I raised the next question that came to me, which was whether I could be released to return to our family home in Swaziland. Swanepoel replied that they had already given this consideration, as they had the question of releasing me under a banning order and house arrest in Johannesburg. They would not consider either of these options. I was welcome to remain with them as a guest of the state in my cell over the period of the trial. If that was what I wanted, they could put a bed in my cell, and a desk on which I could study. Through the warder's oversight some days previously, I had already seen furniture set out in an adjoining cell, and assumed that this would be what awaited me if I did not leave on these terms now.

When I protested that they would be holding me without charge for an indefinite period, Swanepoel got inflamed and said I should be aware that under the Terrorism Act, which governed my detention, he and the minister of justice were the only ones who had any say in matters of this kind, and I had only just arrived. They were already bending regulations to allow me so many family visits and would make no more allowances. I asked whether, if I were to go to Israel now, I could return to South Africa afterwards, and Swanepoel assured me I would be free to return, providing I behaved myself, did not associate with communists and waited for the conclusion of the trial. I was not being charged with anything, he said; there would not be a record against me of any kind, and I could of course come home so long as I behaved myself. My mother came into the discussion more actively at this point to clarify that they had been in touch with both the British Embassy and the Israeli Consulate. Only the Israelis would be allowed to have access to me, and the British would not. She went on to explain how travel arrangements might be made for my departure to Israel. What I next wanted assurance on was that Janet could come with me. My mother assured me that this would be planned for, and so I agreed to these terms.

I was taken out by the standard team of two, and returned to my cell. I was not to know that Coetzee then joined my mother and Swanepoel in a further discussion about the terms of my planned release, and my mother was directed to take no further action until she heard from them.

Day 49: Thursday 31 July

The weekend to come of further waiting, held under observation in the cell, was to be the last in detention. It was so full of tension and anxiety that it cannot be remembered or reproduced. The only entries for the following days come from outside the cell.

Days 50–52: Friday 1–Sunday 3 August

The Israeli consul-general, Major Unna, reported that he was approached by Colonel Visser, head of the Johannesburg Security Police, on Friday 1 August. Visser explained to him:

> John Schlapobersky has been in solitary confinement for over two months and we are concerned that he may experience a nervous breakdown. You are a father who has children and so am I, and who knows better than ourselves how easy it is for children nowadays to fall into trouble. In truth we do not have any hard evidence against John Schlapobersky but since he was interrogated by us we cannot free him as he is now partly aware of what we know, and should we free him we will be unable to prevent him informing others that the police are after them. We also cannot free him until everyone involved is dragged in front of a court, and this will most definitely take another two years. There is a real danger that John will not be able to withstand solitary for such an extended period.

Visser asked Unna if he would be prepared to take me from them at the airport and place me on an El Al plane that was departing the following Wednesday. This was Unna's response:

> I answered Visser that I would definitely be prepared to help John make Aliyah if that is what he wanted to do but was not prepared to cooperate with them in an illegal deportation. I demanded that before I gave them my final answer, I needed to speak to John in jail so that I could personally assess his character and convictions. Likewise, I wanted it confirmed by him that after John made aliyah I was not to be held responsible for his actions or movements after landing in Israel. As far as we were concerned, he would be free to travel to whichever country he chose. (Fachler 2013: 12)

Visser had no confidence the consul general would be allowed to see me before making his decision, but Unna was adamant this would be a condition for his participation.

Day 53: Monday 4 August

The morning began with early morning singing and then the pause. After a weekend fluctuating between anxiety and hope for my own future, the voices the night before had troubled me, reminding me of the hopeless people below. Now there was another execution.

On the inspection parade the prison commander told me I was being taken to Compol later in the day, and I then looked forward to it in a delirious way. I made light-hearted jokes with the warders, and out in the exercise parade I ran up and down instead of walking. They came to collect me at lunchtime and we went back into Pretoria, where things unfolded in ways I could never have expected. I met my mother in Swanepoel's office and we talked for a short time, monitored by the watching team while we waited for the Israeli consul general's arrival. We all stood up when he was shown in and then I realized that he was already on good terms with my mother and also seemed to know Swanepoel. We agreed that our meeting was to consider terms for my immediate release and my subsequent departure for Israel on a flight this coming Wednesday. He explained that he would need to talk to me on my own, which led to some tension with Swanepoel, who insisted that he too would be present, but Swanepoel's crew left the room, as did my mother.

Unna and I had a brief discussion in which Swanepoel played a listening part only. Unna asked me if I wanted to be released to go to Israel and he made clear he was not party to any pressure to get me to go. What was open was an option, but he could not guarantee what would happen to me if I did not take it up. He was a gaunt, austere man with a proud bearing and a confident manner, and he had understanding, warmth and charm. I thought his English fluency had a British accent. He put me at my ease, and the process took no time at all. I told him I was ready to leave now and to make aliyah to Israel. He asked about Hebrew and I explained I had had years of instruction though I could hardly speak the language. Thanks to my bar mitzvah studies I was literate in the language and looked forward to learning more. He asked about the army and I said that if Israel was at war and I had made my home there, I would naturally take my place in the army, as my brother was doing with such distinction. He replied very sternly: 'Israel is not simply "at war". We are struggling for our survival. Our success so far gives us strength to help people in your position, but we continue to struggle.' I assured him that I would play my part, and he said that he was pleased to have met me. Now he wanted my mother to join us. She was sent for, and we set about discussing the practicalities. I was to be collected early Wednesday morning by the police and would be taken directly to the airport, where I would have time to say goodbye to my family. There I would be formally released from detention and he would see me on the plane to Israel. Unna wanted to know if my parents could afford the flight cost, and went on to assure us that, once I was there, living expenses would be minimal as I would be able to go to an *ulpan* (Hebrew language school) to learn Hebrew as part of the immigration process. My mother held out the prospect of my enrolment at university there, and he assured us I could resume my studies there at a university of my choosing. Janet had been consulted and would not be coming with me immediately. It would take her some days to pack up our home and effects, but she would follow some days later. My mother would come with me instead. She had been due to travel to see my brother nearly two months earlier and so would take up the ticket that the airline had kindly suspended. My mother explained that my father would bring my younger brother and sister, David and Marian, from Swaziland to say goodbye to me at the airport. Janet would be there too, and would bring those of my possessions I would be taking from our Johannesburg home, and my father would bring other things from Swaziland.

I was returned to my cell overwhelmed by the thought that I would be coming out alive, in one piece and without complicity in anyone else's prosecution. Thinking back now, it is not clear whether my greatest fear had been the pressure they might apply to get me to testify against those I knew to be in detention, or death itself. They involved death of different kinds and I was to be spared both. Nor was it clear what a trial might have involved or why I might have been called on to give evidence, but the shock and surprise of my arrest and interrogation had left me in no doubt that I could have been charged or called on to pay for my liberty by helping the police to charge others. I had no hesitation about going to Israel. What was around and just behind me was horror. I could see no other way out. My deepest concerns were for David and Marian. We were very close. During a visit to Swaziland over the Easter holidays I had seen them at home and then visited them at their school. The emotional climate at home was quite unstable, and they had come to rely on me in one way or another. I went back to the cell to spend the next day and a half writing letters for those to whom I would be saying goodbye.

Major Unna describes a visit to Pretoria to see Brigadier Venter, commander of the Security Police, on Monday 4 August, who wanted a word with him before deciding whether to permit him to meet with me:

> I found myself in a very odd situation. I was taking part in a meeting that was attended by twelve senior-ranking officers chaired by Brigadier Venter. The Security Police is comprised solely of Afrikaners. There is not one English-speaking person among the senior ranks, and the fact that I managed to acquire a superficial understanding of Afrikaans, so that they were able to conduct the meeting in their own language, contributed, in my humble opinion, to the friendly and informal atmosphere in which the meeting was conducted. At the end Brigadier Venter agreed to let me see John Schlapobersky, and after that we would all decide his final fate.
>
> The meeting between John and me took place in the presence of Maj. Swanepoel. Obviously at this stage I had already decided to make every effort to release John so that he could be transported to Israel. I will not go into detail about the contents of the meeting, for in truth it was no more than a charade. I spoke with John for about ten minutes, and obviously he immediately consented to make aliyah, and spoke of his future plans in Israel, showing that he had a good grasp of the country (*ulpan*, continuing his studies at university, the Israel Defence Force,

etc.). However, it was not difficult to discern that his two months in detention and the interrogation by Maj. Swanepoel had left their mark, and I harbour no illusions – had I offered John a trip to the moon, he would have jumped at the opportunity. . . .

Maj. Swanepoel and I then returned to National Headquarters where a meeting was once again convened with Brigadier Venter. I told Venter that John would be travelling voluntarily, and that from my perspective there would be no reason to prevent his trip. I nonetheless repeated what I had said to Col. Visser, that I could only be responsible for what happens to him up until his departure, and I would be unable to assume any responsibility in relation to his actions after he lands. Brigadier Venter accepted my position and thanked me for finding a humane solution to the John Schlapobersky affair. (Fachler 2013: 12–13)

Day 54: Tuesday 5 August

This was to be my last day in South Africa. It stands as a blank for which there is little record of my state of mind and from which I can retrieve little memory. I was more acutely aware of the singing in the morning now that I was in an exposed cell, as it gave me a chance to review the impact of the singing on the warders stationed outside and going past my open door. None of them seemed to take the least notice of what was happening. They must have played a part of some kind in the daily execution process, and were likely to have had a range of assigned duties that were rotated between them.

My own 'duties of the day' that it proved so hard to address had to do with the challenge of writing a farewell letter to each member of my family. My brother and sister were now at Waterford Kamhlaba School in classes two years apart. They had settled in well since their transfer from Johannesburg schools. My father would sometimes complain to me about how expensive the school fees were, but our parents were determined to see them flourish there. The matter that concerned both of my siblings was the state of our parents' marriage. There was a lot of conflict, they were frightened by the shouting, and I had a role to play in helping them to feel safe, even with the distance that separated us. They had each come to stay with Janet and me at different times, albeit never for very long, and we were always very close.

Although I left them behind without hesitation in the departure to which I was now committed, the sense of abandonment I appeared to be showing towards them caused me the greatest heartache of all. But I could do nothing to support them from prison, and if I perished there it would serve no one. I had to get out and face the challenge of finding security elsewhere that could prove to be a resource for all of us, and this was always in my mind.

In my *Observer* article in August 1970 I wrote: 'I betrayed my own principles in going along with this [release] – by accepting apartheid with its special treatments for whites, especially those with prominent names and British passports. But I rationalised this with the thought that if I could get out and publicise the details of my interrogation, it would help those remaining in prison. After being released I evaded publicity for nine months in the fear that it compromised people at home. I feel guilty at having kept silent for so long.'

In the letter I wrote to David, I gave him the gift of my motor scooter and told him I knew he would take good care of it until I could come back to join him once more in Swaziland. In the letter I wrote to Marian, I gave her the gift of our dog Mehavya as we were to be packing up our home in Johannesburg and Janet would soon come on to join me in Israel. I have little recall of what I said to my father beyond the inexpressible gratitude for the strength of presence he had shown me through these regular visits and the choice of things he had delivered to support me at strategic times during these recent weeks – cigarettes, university books and other reading. The correspondence kept me going through the day, and awake until late into the night. I could hardly get to sleep and was then late in waking up, woken only by the singing before I realized I had slept at all. These letters are included here:

Written to my father from prison (Tuesday 5 August)
Dear Arch,

Not long ago, timewise – only 3 years (almost to the day) but much longer in terms of what we've all been through in the last 3 years, you took me to the same airport – AFS [American Field Service Scholarship] – hopes, great expectations, many ideals that we all had then. Many of yours have crumbled, and far less painfully for me, many of mine have too in the last 2 months. But I will never forget what you said to me on the way to the airport last time – 'human beings, people, we, each other, are the only things to cherish or set any store by. The only valuable things are relationships'. I don't remember your exact words, but that was the substance of what you said. There's nothing particularly original in it and I'm sure it's been said many times before, but that was the first I heard it, and on leaving home for the first time – it made a tremendous impact. Despite all the chaos and bewilderment, I'll remember what you said as long as I live.

Second time round now – slightly different circumstances, spirited away with much shattered behind – but the important things – our relationships, all stronger than ever. It's a high price to pay for one's freedom and it's costing you a lot of hard earned, lost, and re-earned money, but far better than legal expenses and prison. Two of us gone now and both under painful and difficult circumstances for you – the Yiddish word 'nachis' (I don't know how it's spelt) is a meaningful one despite its misuse by most yiddishers – you haven't known much of it from us kids. I can't apologise for being the person I am, but I am sorry you haven't known more nachis. I don't know when we'll see each other again – perhaps next year in Jerusalem? (jokes).

Don't worry about me – as long as Jan is with me, and I can read and write, I'm free and well. We'll see what the future brings. I hope you've got to know her a bit better these last few weeks – I'm sorry that things were a little strained all round beforehand – especially when we were in Swaziland. We owe Jan's mother R150. I hope you can see to it. Also, a refund of R120 for Wits University for my second term's fees. Can David take my scooter over? Not to use at once but in one or two years' time?

Will you say hello to Pat Gcule for me? She has some slides of mine, which I would like back. Nicholas Glen also has some.

We're not going for ever – my return depends on our conduct (all of us) while I'm away, so no doubt we'll see you in Swaziland again – but I'm too excited to write much sense now – and will be even more so at the airport (that's why I'm writing now). So we'll write from Israel and let you know how things are, and tie up all the loose ends.

Shalom (and thanks),

John

P.S. There are many more unsaid things between us than there are spoken ones.

Written to my brother from prison
Hello Dave,

Happy birthday!! Sorry it's so late, but the police don't allow concessions, just to let brothers wish each other happy birthday. Sixteen! Just a year to go until you can get your license. If the folks will let you (though I doubt very much whether they will), you must take my scooter over as a birthday present. If they don't let you, write and tell me, and I'll send you a present from Israel. Okay?

How's school? Mom told me your marks are improving, which is a good sign. But I suppose your guitar is far more important to you at this stage. And it is! How well do you play? If there are any good books of folk-song music in Israel I'll send some across to you. I've spent a lot of the time in this little cell singing, but I wish I'd done what you're doing – learnt lots of songs. I've had to repeat the same songs over and over again because I know so few. What with that and my terrible voice, I'm sure the people in the next-door cells are sick and tired of my singing and will be glad when I'm out tomorrow.

I only heard yesterday, that I was going to be released tomorrow. You can imagine how long it took for today to pass. Maybe I'll write some poems about it all one day. How's your poetry? Written any lately? On condition that you send me some of yours, I promise to send some of mine to you, and we'll set up a whole poetry correspondence, as well as letters. Or is the folk singing more important at this stage? If you are more involved with it, how about sending a tape recording of some of your songs? I bet that'll embarrass you!

We'll be too excited at the airport to talk any sense, and that's why I'm writing to you now. Jan told me about how you didn't want to go back to school, but to find a school where you could study golf. I'll make investigations in Israel – perhaps they have such things there. By then it seems, half the family will have ended up in Israel.

Things haven't been very bad here in jail. At first, without books sitting alone with nothing to do, it was a bit grim. Once I got books things were okay. The tension is the worst part of the whole thing – not knowing what's going to happen. So the relief, when I heard the news yesterday, was incredible. I'll miss you all very much, and Swaziland too – but going to Israel is far better than remaining in prison. I don't quite know what we'll do when we get there – Janet and I – but when she arrives there next week we'll make plans.

It might not be for long, that we'll stay away – or if it is, maybe you'll come and visit us. I'll give your regards to Colin, and any messages. And as long as you do also, I'll send photographs. Okay? I've told Marian that she should take Mehavya over, but if she has already got a dog for her birthday and doesn't want another, why don't you?

Enjoy school, Dave – have a good holiday, good luck in the exams. I hope you're still keeping Marian protected from all her male admirers. And how are your female admirers – I hope all's going well and you don't need any protection from them or they from you. I'll write and let you know how things go.

HHHHAAAA,

John

Written to my sister (aged 13) from prison

Hello Soralina [little sister],

The last letter I wrote you was from 11 Queens Road, for your birthday. This one's from cell no. 1, on the second floor of the Pretoria local prison. And it's to say goodbye. Not a nice thing to have to do, when we don't know when we'll see each other again, but far better than spending months or years more in this prison. I'll be seeing Colin soon, will give him your love and tell him how you are. Jan told me that you'd enjoyed 'Thomasina'. She was so right in suggesting it as a birthday present. We'll send you more books from Israel, and will let you know how Colin is.

I'm glad your marks are so good at school. Good change from Saxonwold, hey? But don't get swollen headed about it! And boyfriends? Still seducing all the Waterford Kamhlaba boys, or did that last escapade put you off boys for the time being? If it has put you off boys, I'm sure it's only for the time being. I don't know what arrangements Jan's making about Mehavya, but I think the best thing is for you to take him over. What do you think? You were going to get a dog for your birthday, and if you haven't got one already, well – you can have a third dog on the farm to join the rabbits and Heidi and Strawberries.

Prison life has not been very bad – the food's not much worse than boarding school and they don't treat you badly. The worst part is being all alone in a cell, and waiting for the time to pass, not knowing what's going to happen. Yesterday I was told they would let me go as long as I got onto a plane and went straight to Israel. You can imagine how happy I was! Mom's coming with me and then Jan will come as soon as she can leave her job, and then Jan and I will settle down and make plans about what we'll do. Of course, we're not going for ever. I'll probably finish university there, and then maybe Jan and I will come back. In the meantime, you look after Mehavya for us, hey? Or maybe even, you'll visit us in Israel before we have a chance to come back? We'll see how things work out.

By the time you read this I'll probably be in the air on the way to Israel with Mom. Will you see that Jan doesn't worry too much? She's afraid of aeroplanes you know. Of course it's a very silly thing to be afraid of, but that's just how she is. And go ahead and tell her she's being silly if she gets upset. She'll probably catch next week's plane so she'll not only be worried about Mom and me, but herself next week too. So you will have to work hard to persuade her not to be afraid, otherwise she'll have a whole week's worrying to do. Please do remember all the things I wrote to you about last time about imagination? I'm so excited about tomorrow, that I can't write much sense now. But I'll write to you from Israel little sister, and we'll chat at the airport (though I'm sure we'll all be too excited to talk sense there either). Anyhow, there'll be much time ahead for us to exchange long letters about things, so that when we see each other again – in a few months or a few years – we'll have lots to talk about.

Write to me and tell me if there are any special messages to give to Colin, okay? Work hard at school, look after Dad while Mom's away (and when she gets back) and I promise to send photographs.

Much, much love,

John

P.S. Enjoy the holidays!

P.P.S. I'll miss you – but it won't be for very long that we'll be away.

RELEASE

Day 55: Wednesday 6 August

In those days there was only one midweek flight with El Al, the Israeli airline, and that was on Wednesdays in the late morning. I was due for collection at 6 a.m., and had been told that Coetzee himself would be driving me to the airport. I hardly slept that night. It had taken me much of the previous day and night to compose myself and say goodbye in writing to my father, to my brother and sister, and to Janet. I wrote out a list of what I felt would be needed from our home that she could try to bring when she joined me – things that would not fit in my own flight allowance. I did not have a suitcase in the cell and, despite my request the previous day, the warders had not been able to find bags of any kind for me to pack. I was finally assured that a warder would accompany me out of the prison to help to carry my things. We waited for nearly an hour beyond the collection time. I later discovered that when Coetzee and his assistant Jordaan had arrived without an authorized release warrant from the minister of justice, the prison authorities would not let me go. Apparently, they had to send another car to the minister's office to collect the release warrant and then, when the signal finally reached us upstairs, we had to scramble to get down because, we were warned, the plane would be leaving soon.

When I first came to prison, I arrived as what they called a 'bandiet', a term that captures all the detail of degradation. I was in a filthy and wretched state, delirious from lack of sleep, disfigured by days on the brick, and dressed in stinking clothes. I was then managed like a felon – insulted, stripped and humiliated. And yet now I was leaving wearing a suit, with a warder helping me to carry my things. What a strange turn of events! These warders normally spent their time escorting the condemned to the gallows, but now, on Wednesday 6 August, they were escorting someone out to take an aeroplane to freedom.

There was more to come. I had to sign a receipt for those things that had been taken from me on arrival – my wallet, belt, shoelaces and loose change, and the bag and the university notebooks it held, which had all been seized when I was arrested. It all took time and I was very conscious that the plane was leaving soon. There was more of the delirium that had been affecting me for some days now. I got quite 'high' saying goodbye to all the stony-faced staff in the main office, as if I were leaving a hotel. I did not quite say 'thank you for having me', but it felt quite manic.

Coetzee and Jordaan were keen to get away and I was placed in the front seat of the car, with a police major for my driver. How strange. Jordaan sat in the back. I have little recollection of any exchanges between us, but took in the passing scenes with feelings of grief about leaving the country. I looked with hungry eyes at the familiar brown winter landscape, the veld, the wattle trees in flower, and the khaki weed and blackjack growing along the roadside – I was overwhelmed. At the airport we went directly through a private entrance and I was suddenly in a room full of family. Marian at thirteen had been growing all the time and I could hardly take in how changed she was; David too was so much taller. Their eyes were full of worry. I discovered they had been waiting there for a full hour in a room dominated by Unna and Swanepoel, who was there with his Lieutenant Richter. David can still remember Richter's name, his black hair with a parting in the middle, his pencil moustache, swarthy complexion and smart double-breasted suit. Janet was there with my suitcase from Parktown, and my parents were there with another suitcase from Swaziland. The hour planned to allow our goodbyes was reduced by half. My father looked stunned. He had the same stoical face that I was familiar with from previous goodbyes. He had seen me on my way to university in Cape Town in 1966, and then to the USA later that same year. I had last seen him five weeks earlier. He was to tell me later that, after their first visit on Day 15 (27 June), they had left Compol Building not knowing if they would ever see me again. I never let my parents know how close I had been to death every day, but they knew. Now I was going to be safe. I could feel my father's relief when we embraced, and we all shared a lot of silent tears. I passed my series of written goodbyes to their recipients, and tried to turn my attention to sorting out personal effects from three different locations – prison, Parktown and Swaziland – to get it all into one manageable suitcase. Janet had brought my passport from Parktown, and my parents saw to it that my tallis bag and tallis – the prayer shawl we wear in synagogue – had come up in the suitcase from Swaziland. I was touched and grateful, and still have it to this day. It was a gift from my Uncle Ivan to honour my bar mitzvah. He had brought it from Israel, and I would now have it with me to go there myself. My mother, Janet and I were busy with these personal things when, from the other side of the room, there was an outburst of grief. Marian broke down weeping. She was crying for all of us. And then the dreadful Swanepoel – who happened to be the one standing closest to her – put his hand on her shoulder to console her, saying 'Don't cry, little girl.' She can still remember the moment at which he touched her. I would have killed him on the spot, but we were all paralysed and then it was time to go. As if he had not done enough to intimidate and alarm us, Swanepoel made a speech to everyone in which he told us, in his imperious and threatening manner, that if it were not for our consul general, Major Unna, I would have been spending a lot more time with him.

As best I could, I comforted my brother and sister, embraced Janet and my father, and was then rushed out with my mother by Unna, Swanepoel and Coetzee. In another adjoining lobby room, Swanepoel 'handed me over' to Unna as if I were a parcel, and I shook his hand and thanked them for making it less bad than it could have been. And then we went out onto the tarmac. There Unna took some minutes to talk to me alone. He cautioned me about the press, and wished me well from the bottom of his heart. Then he checked with my mother that she had the booking for our first nights in Israel and we both shook his hand and boarded the plane. I spent the first half of the flight talking non-stop, recounting what I had been through, and must have fallen asleep while talking.

What I did not tell my mother about was the sound of the condemned men singing before execution. I kept this tormenting memory to myself until I was talking to staff at the International Defence and Aid Fund in London in January 1970, when I gave them a full account. It is a puzzle to me from this vantage point that, when I wrote about my experience for the *Observer*, I made no reference to what was haunting me most in the memories that would not go away. I believe I was still so shocked by what I had lived through that I could not even write it all down. It is the memory that distresses me most to this day, and the one about which I say least. Knox Masi's inscription on my cell wall, described above on Day 7, was the emblem of the condemned. I later found others' experience of such exposure in Albie Sachs's book, *Stephanie on Trial* (1968), in the autobiographies of Hugh Lewin (1976) and Breyten Breytenbach (1984), and in Ingrid Gavshon's documentary for Angel Films, 'Facing Death . . . Facing Life', about Duma Kumalo and the Sharpeville Six facing the death penalty in Pretoria Local.[1] I had profound relief from the haunting consequences of this exposure when capital punishment in South Africa was abolished on 6 June 1995 by a ruling of the Constitutional Court in the case of *S v Makwanyane*, following a moratorium of over five years since February 1990. Readers will have seen Albie Sachs's own account of the judicial process by which the court abolished capital punishment in his Foreword to this volume. This memoir, which memorializes the lives of those who perished on Pretoria's gallows, is dedicated to their memory.

I was woken after we landed, and we came out into the August heat of Tel Aviv – it was summer, and for the first time in weeks I was not cold. There my brother was in his uniform on release from military service. He was strong and confident, at ease with himself and very welcoming. He soon had our baggage loaded into a taxi and we set out for a small hotel on the coast at Ashkelon. He told us, only half in humour, that the police should consider themselves lucky to have released me. He and his army friends had been planning to come over and break me out. After weeks of isolation it was deeply comforting to be able to share a room with my brother, and I was soon asleep.

Major Unna reports on these events at the airport in corresponding terms:

That Wednesday, I waited at the time and place that I had arranged to meet with Maj. Coetzee and John Schlapobersky. John's parents, brother, sister and fiancée were all waiting there; the mother in order to travel with John, and the rest to say their goodbyes. However, Maj. Coetzee and John arrived half an hour late, since the Security Police had forgotten to issue the release documents, and without them they could not release John from jail.

I suppose there is no need to describe the tension that we all felt when we were waiting for the 'man of the moment'. The Security Police provided us with a room in the airport where the family could take leave of John without arousing any suspicion. Even Maj. Swanepoel arrived at the airport to bid farewell to John, and he made the announcement in front of him and in front of all the family: 'Were it not for the consul general of Israel you would have spent a lot more time with me.'

I managed to speak with John privately for a few minutes. This time he left me with an outstanding impression, and I believe that he has sincere intentions of following in his brother's footsteps and settling permanently in Israel. I explained to John that although I have no control over his future actions, and even though I did not give any guarantee to the South African police that he would not be involved in hostile activity towards South Africa, the chances that I would be able to help someone else in a similar predicament was dependent on his conduct. I stressed the need for complete silence, especially when it came to the Israeli press. (Fachler 2013: 13–14)

Day 56: Thursday 7 August

I woke before anyone else and walked out to the beach at first light. In the prison the condemned would be singing someone to the end of his life. Dawn broke as I walked and watched the sea – and I thought about them, as I have done over the years that followed. The prison I left probably held some of my friends. Waves were breaking in the offshore wind that blew sand against my legs. I had not worn shorts for weeks, and for the first time in ages I found warmth in the air. Looking out to sea the rose colour of the sky behind me was picked up by the waves. Big waves in shallow water make a tearing sound as they roll in. It sounded like a tear in the fabric of the world that welled up and drew out into the next breaker – and broke again and again. I had never seen the Mediterranean before. So, this is where Jonah had set out in flight from God's directions and journeyed into a wild storm – and as his shipmates believed he had caused it, they threw him overboard. He would have drowned in this sea had he not been swallowed by a whale somewhere in this deep water. And here was the coast on which he was cast up. Mine had been a different story. Three hard-faced men came from nowhere to drag me out of my life. They put me before a face of terror, and I stood against this terror and his crew for a week. But I nearly drowned in isolation during the weeks that followed in the dark corridors of an unspeakable place, listening to people being killed every day. Was it behind me? Would it ever be behind me? There were to be twenty years and more of daily killing before the gallows were put out of action. And what courage it would take to wrest power from those whom Swanepoel and Coetzee protected. What now lay ahead of me? How many others found themselves washed ashore here? Had I come home? Could I be at home here? I was safe at least, and now we could move on from the ordeal that had torn our lives apart. My family needed a home and so did I. Where would we come to rest?

I could not have foreseen that I would be in the UK within the year and, within a few years of qualifying, would be engaged in work to relieve others of the misery I had known. It is now thirty-five years since I began with this kind of work, but I still remember vividly the words of one of our first clients at the Medical Foundation, whom I worked with for months to bring him out of a similar state to the one which I had been reduced to, so many years earlier. One year into his recovery he said, 'Yours is the hand of humanity that reaches out to save me from drowning in my sorrow.' I have described this in the story, 'The Hand of Humanity', in the Epilogue. Many such helping hands have been extended towards me over the years, and it has now become my honour to provide such hands for others. That morning on the beach at Ashkelon, I walked back to our hotel and found my mother and my brother up and ready for breakfast.

Note

1. See 'Facing Death … Facing Life', retrieved 20 October from https://vimeo.com/channels/887168/83743905.

EPILOGUE

London 2020

The events described in this memoir took place fifty years ago. There is another story to be told about my own professional journey from survivor to practitioner, which is not the subject of this book. If I have the good fortune to be able to write another book, it will be about that journey. This book is about fifty-five winter days and, for its epilogue, I have chosen six brief stories from my therapeutic work with other survivors over recent decades, to recount their journeys of healing and recovery. They have been selected to represent the range of people and problems I have worked with down the years. Some survivors go on to write their own accounts, and some of the agencies working in the field now employ storytellers and narrative therapists to help this process along. Some of my clients' stories have been published in my earlier book, and others will be published in due course. Their words speak for me and my own history, as I have learnt to work with them. Each of the following six stories is drawn from a long and complex therapeutic programme that was undertaken many years ago.

In 1981 I qualified in psychotherapy at the Institute of Group Analysis in London and, in 1985, I joined a pioneer health professional, Helen Bamber, to establish a centre for the rehabilitation of traumatized political refugees (Belton 2012). I was still in full-time employment at the London Hospital where I worked as a psychiatric social worker, and I did this development work with Helen in my own time. We set the organization up at the end of 1985. Some of our first clients were seen in the consulting room at my home as we had yet to secure suitable premises. The centre was then called the 'Medical Foundation for the Care of Victims of Torture' and, once we had a building, it was situated in a disused wing of the National Temperance Hospital in Camden. It is now known as 'Freedom from Torture' and operates from purpose-built premises in Islington, London. It is a self-funding, registered charity concerned with two key global social issues: one is the plight of refugees, their status as exiles and their need for asylum; the other is the effect of organized violence, including torture, on individuals, families and communities. The agency has developed therapeutic models for the physical, social and emotional rehabilitation of survivors of organized violence. Therapies including the use of groups have been developed for massive psychic and/or physical trauma, problems of displacement and exile, and transcultural problems. Clients include survivors of torture and politically organized violence of all ages from more than ninety countries. Services are provided by a multi-professional staff team who offer crisis intervention and long-term rehabilitation. They are assisted by a team of interpreters who provide a vital link between client and clinician in both language and culture. The clinicians comprise a core team of paid staff and a larger one of volunteer health professionals, many of whom hold senior clinical positions in other agencies, and they come in on a sessional basis. The agency provides a direct service to individuals, families and communities in need, as well as a specialist teaching and liaison service for professionals such as solicitors who require forensic and other reports, and for health professionals engaged in similar work in the UK and internationally.

Over the years I have also worked at the Traumatic Stress Clinic, the TSC, a resource in the Camden and Islington NHS Trust, where I have provided consultancy to staff. They also provided a clinical context for the group I had been running at the Medical Foundation with my co-therapist, Paul Burns, which we transferred to the TSC. I helped to extend principles of clinical practice from what we were learning at the Medical Foundation to corresponding practice here in the National Health Service. Through conference work and consultancy, this has been extended to agencies in the field elsewhere in Europe. These principles are described in Appendix 3.

I worked closely with Helen Bamber until her death, at the age of 89, by which time she had established a successor to the original organization, which she named the Helen Bamber Foundation. My first book, *From the Couch to the Circle: Group-Analytic Psychotherapy in Practice*, is dedicated to her memory. It describes many different applications of a model of group psychotherapy that we call 'group analysis'. We engage with people in therapy by helping them to engage with one another. The application of group analysis in providing services for survivors of torture and organized violence is described in Chapter 6 of that book (Schlapobersky 2016a).

The majority of those tortured do not survive. The testimonies of those who do, seen in agencies like these, cast a shadow upon us all. In his conclusion to *Spanish Testament*, Arthur Koestler, writing of his own detention while awaiting execution during the Spanish Civil War, described himself and his fellow inmates as 'men without shadows' (Koestler 1937, 1957). Waiting for death they felt themselves deprived of the substance to even cast shadows in the space they occupied in prison. Their lives had no substance in time either, for they had no sense of the future and struggled to protect their past from the eyes of their interrogators. We bear witness to the testimony of those who have had Koestler's experience, and mine, but who are without a voice. We see our responsibility in reclaiming time and space for those who have suffered the loss of both. We attempt to help those who have lived 'without shadows' to discover a voice through which to speak of themselves.

Names, ages and identifying detail have been altered to anonymize the people described here, in accordance with the Code of Ethics of the International Psychoanalytical Association and the Institute of Group Analysis.[1]

Six Stories of Healing and Recovery

1. My Brother, What Have They Done to You?

A group of eight men sit in a circle with two therapists for the first meeting of what will be a two-year group programme of some seventy sessions. They come from countries in which torture is endemic, and have all been profoundly injured. None of them know each other or have any prior association, but they all know one or other of the two therapists. Some are from the Horn of Africa, and include a Christian Ethiopian and a Muslim Somali. From Black Africa there is a Congolese and a man named Jonas, a Rwandan Tutsi who survived the genocide, both of whom were raised as Christians. The other four comprise two Iraqis who are Sunni Muslims and two Iranians who are Shi'ite, one of whom is Farid. Their religions, nationalities and ethnicities are given to stress their differences. What they have in common, however, is prior experience of traumatic loss and violence in their countries of origin. They are all refugees. We are meeting in a clinic established to provide such services for this population. All the group's members have already had extended periods of rehabilitative care followed by preparatory psychotherapy with either one of the two co-therapists.

To begin with we struggle through introductions that falter and halt. People refer all their questions to one or other of the therapists, from whom they expect answers. The two therapists are occasional and cordial participants, but we consistently refer back to the group. Then there is silence, followed by limited narrative sequences in people's fragmented stories of origin and arrival as refugees. We are as enabling as possible, but the edge to people's anxieties is inhibiting. All new groups begin this way, with a form of serial monologue. Thirty minutes into this fractious exchange, governed by seemingly unproductive pauses in which people look frequently to the therapists, one of the men, Farid from Iran, asks where the toilet is. He is directed by one of the therapists, and everyone sees him gather his crutches from beneath his chair and limp across the group room to the door. He was already seated when the other members arrived so – until now – only the therapists knew how handicapped he was.

We watch his every move in a kind of charged silence that remains unbroken while he is out. A few minutes later the door opens and, watched by everyone, he struggles across the room back to his seat and stumbles into his chair, perspiring from the effort. Finally, he replaces his crutches beneath his chair.

Jonas from Rwanda speaks with a commanding French accent. He has extensive, visible scarring to his face and neck caused by machete blows. He looks at Farid across the room and, leaning towards him, says, 'My brother, what did they do to you?' There is a long pause and then, with the reply, the room fills with relief and a real exchange emerges. Farid speaks in broken, faltering English to tell us about how soldiers at home broke his back with their rifle butts and boots, and how lucky he is to be alive. He goes on to tell us of how his family saved him, how he escaped from Iran with his wife and of the baby they are expecting. This is a truly relational moment that moves us from monologue to dialogue. The dialogue between these two men leads, in turn, to a non-directed discourse and random conversational exchange across the group, which informs us that the group is coming to life. It will falter, fall back and confound itself many times in the coming months of therapy – but in this first relational moment we all became witnesses, and in the act of bearing witness, group therapy begins (Schlapobersky 2016a: 68, Vignette 2.1).

In the question there is also an answer to yet another unstated question. I will be your brother, he says; will you be mine? In the moment of his question he begins to create brotherhood amongst us. General points can be extracted from this opening that are relevant to all group psychotherapy. These people had lost just about everything – their relatives, health, home and country, and their sense of integrity. Although they were preoccupied with their own losses, they could – through their compassion for one another – rediscover their dignity. Generosity emerged as a quality they had not lost, and from this discovery each of them would rebuild their world. This 'band of brothers' settled down to two years of productive work, in the course of which they stabilized their lives in a strange country. They began the mourning process of coming to terms with their past, and did so as displaced people in the absence of their customary rituals of mourning and grief, relying instead on the group itself. And finally, they began to generate together a real sense of future.

2. The Darkest Events in the Course of Human Conduct

A young man named Behrouz had arrived in London from his home in Iran after a complicated series of moves between various countries, and he was now living with family friends. He had been held in prison for some three years after his initial detention and torture, and he owed his escape and freedom to an accident.

Until his imprisonment at the age of 20, he was physically robust and problem-free in psychological terms. He was a sports enthusiast, played football and was interested in women. We found him anorexic, significantly below his optimal weight, incapacitated by a poorly healed fracture to one wrist and by soft-tissue damage to the soles of his feet, which had split while in prison after they had been beaten. Walking any distance presented a problem. He suffered from recurrent headaches, a disordered sleeping pattern and morbid ruminations. Exploration of traumatic associations aggravated a tremor that produced a dramatic convulsion, for which he had been admitted as an emergency to several casualty departments who then found him neurologically well. This was his story.

On being arrested he was blindfolded, taken to a building where the fold was removed, and locked in a cell where he found a friend who had had four toes cut off. He was later taken down some stairs to a small room covered with blood. There was broken glass on the floor, and he was put in the hands of three people without uniform, whom he would recognize if he saw them again. He was stripped naked; his hands and feet were bound, and he was hung upside down from a bar on the ceiling with a rope around his feet. Then followed vicious acts of burning, gagging and mutilation. Twenty-four hours later he was subjected to a mock execution. Together with five other prisoners, he was tied to a pole and blindfolded, and when the shots rang out, he alone was alive. He was then locked up in the back of a van with the corpses.

There are the darkest events in the course of human conduct to which, as witnesses, the only appropriate response can be the silence of respect or the indignation of tears. Testimony of this kind is quite representative, but we – as practitioners – are still very often left speechless or distressed.

Work with this man began with a detailed history taken by a caseworker and by one of our examining doctors. A great deal of time was spent establishing a relationship with some level of familiarity, and it was only when we were confident that a medical investigation would not be experienced as further bodily intrusion that more neurological tests were performed. These were done in the presence of the caseworker he had come to trust, and they confirmed the earlier findings that the convulsions were not due to epilepsy or brain damage. He was seen by a physiotherapist and an osteopath for treatment to his feet and to his wrist. Staff secured a special pair of shoes with built-up soles that reduced the discomfort of walking; and we found him a bicycle, which reduced the amount of walking necessary.

I began a course of individual psychotherapy with the assistance of a translator who was one of his family friends. The translator became part of the treatment process, and he continued the dialogue with him when they left us. Priority in our sessions was given to establishing a trusting relationship through dialogue in which the future was more important than the past. Close attention was given to his family history, early life and the period prior to detention. Only six months into his therapy were the details of his torture explored, at which point there was a reoccurrence – as we had anticipated – of the earlier convulsive seizures. Working together with the translator, we established a routine by which, when the seizures took place, our client was firmly held and massaged on those muscle sites that had gone into spasm. While doing so, the subject matter that had provoked the seizure was kept under discussion. The assistance of friends and family was sought to sustain this sort of response at home. During our sessions we turned increasingly towards an exploration of the symbolic content of his vivid and tormented dreams. Much later in our sessions, when he had learnt enough English to attend without the translator, we would pass a large dictionary backwards and forwards between us. It became a transitional object – a bridge by which to cross from his experience in the past to our experience now in the present. He made slow, consistent progress, as evidenced by changes in his mood and in his sleeping and eating patterns. His aversion to hot food – the consequence of, amongst other things, years of a cold diet in prison – steadily diminished, and he was able to begin eating solids after some dental reconstruction. We knew he was getting better when his weight went up, when narrative about imprisonment no longer produced seizures and when he was able to join a long-term therapy group, joke about an interest in women and use our staff to begin planning a career and study programme.

3. The Woman Who Could Not Relate to Men

Bhavana came from Ethiopia. She was a young, slight, frail person who spoke English well, but had a manner that was timid, shy and withdrawn, and she looked younger than her twenty years. She was obviously underweight and had trouble eating solid food. She was living in a hostel run by a church group, who had referred her. She was the youngest in a large family who enjoyed a privileged lifestyle, and she had had a good education. She was part of a small and innocent demonstration by some schoolgirls in their last year at high school who marched against aspects of their government's policy. They were detained by police who took several of the girls to their barracks where, over some three months, they were first turned into maids and then used for the sexual pleasure of the police, who passed them around. She lived through serial rape throughout this time. This was her first exposure to male sexuality, and she was left pregnant, venereally infected, anorexic and overwhelmed. One of the other girls died while being held there and, despite her release, Bhavana remained at risk herself because of the indictment she could still lay against the police. After a termination and medical treatment, her family got her out of the country but, entrusted to the care of strangers in Yemen, she was again sexually abused, this time by an older man who should have been looking after her. Eventually she got to the UK and into the care of a religious order. She was anorexic and, because of what had been put into her mouth over months by police, she could not tolerate solid food. She went into a serious decline with the news that her mother had died back home, and the ensuing depression was the basis of the referral.

During her first year with our agency, she had individual therapy with an experienced female colleague whose work I supervised. The therapist provided basic surrogate mothering and a quality of personal investment in her care and rehabilitation that was profound and touching. The most moving part of this experience was the day they went together for the results of the test for HIV/ AIDS. Bhavana collapsed into her therapist's arms when it was confirmed she was not infected, and the two women cried together.

Soon after this she joined a women's psychotherapy group with the same therapist. Working in the group with other women from Eritrea, Ethiopia, Iran, Kenya, Peru, Sierra Leone and Somalia, Bhavana was befriended, supported and assisted practically in many different ways. All the women had known profound sexual injury and abuse, but Bhavana was the youngest of them and, as such, they wanted to show her special attention; however, her basic responses scorned and spoilt it all. Her deep sense of hatred and rage about the violation of her youth set her apart from everyone and everything.

The first phase of her therapy, dominated by the repeated account of her experience, took the form of monologue in the group in which her suffering alone predominated in her own frame of reference. Outside the group she continued to see her psychologist. By her second year in the group, dialogue began to emerge in which she could relate to other women's injuries and histories, on a one-by-one basis. From the third year onwards, she could participate fully in the group's process. From then on, she could begin to see herself from the outside – as others saw her – and could generalize from the group's process to her own developing personal life outside the group. It was during this phase that she could take up and utilize the therapist's interpretations, and especially the construction of how her envy of those whose lives were not so damaged had led her to spoil any benefits she might have gained from them.

During her third year with us she had to cope with news of her father's death at home and, without contact with her siblings, she became more attached than ever to the women in the group. In addition, and for the first time in the group, she was open to discussion about men as fellow human beings. At the college where she was learning English, a young man who was a fellow Ethiopian kept on approaching her to offer friendship and kindness. She spurned every offer he made her, as she did to all the men that she had dealings with, and this story came back to the group repeatedly. At a certain point in the safety of the college classroom, where she had no reason to fear his contact, he offered her a traditional food they would have shared at home that was associated with their religious calendar. Her spoiling attack injured his feelings, and after the class, alone in the corridor, he approached her with tears in his eyes to plead with her to let him know what he had done to cause her to attack him whenever he offered her kindness. She apologized and cried with him and, for the first time amongst her peers at college, she disclosed that she would like him to be her friend, but was worried he would withdraw if he knew what the soldiers at home had done to her. At this stage in her therapy his kindness could not overcome her hatred, nor her fear of rejection, and the man's interest did not survive her damaging behaviour. But she was able to bring this range of emotion into the group where it gave a thematic focus to the discussions. Others shared related experiences and, as older women who had made further progress in their own therapeutic development, they modelled for her what recovery could offer. After a period, and for the first time since her arrest, she could begin to consider a man's vulnerability, and this marked a turning point in her development.

The real changes she lived through began internally, rather than with the man who first befriended her. Their bond was not maintained but she learnt a lot from it, as did he. Quite some time later she left the group and began training as a social worker, and she eventually went on to qualify and take up employment.

Her therapist kept in touch, and later learnt that she had begun a relationship with a different Ethiopian man whom she had met in the training.

4. The Man Who Could Not Relate to Women

Yunus came from a community of Alevi Muslims who lived in an area of Turkey populated largely by Sunnis, some of whom were extremists. He was the oldest child in a large family. When he was fifteen their father was murdered by a group of fanatics in the street for smoking during Ramadan. No action was taken against the murderers, and the family had to surrender their business interests to move to a less dangerous part of the country. There he looked for ways of avenging his father's murder and became increasingly associated with secular and left-wing causes. His group was betrayed, and he soon found himself in police custody where he was to remain for almost four years. He was twenty when we first met him, and he still looked like a young and beautiful boy. In custody he became the 'plaything' of the police – he had to wait on them, and they passed him round amongst themselves in their barracks for anal rape. Eventually his family were able to get him out of prison and out of the country. In London he was subdued, withdrawn, despondent and depressed.

After a sustained period of individual therapy with me, he joined a mixed psychotherapy group working at a deep level. During his second year of therapy his progress showed similar phases to those described above – there was a prolonged period of self-absorbed misery taken up as much with the father's murder as with his own lost years. During this phase his story just had to be heard – one detail after another – as all the details were repeated, again and again. There was then a second phase when he began to make real contact with the others and reciprocate their kindness, and he learnt to appreciate their common ground of injustice.

As the third phase of his therapy evolved, when he was able to participate in free-floating discussion and join the discourse, it became clear that he had known no age-appropriate maturation and had a limited sense of his gender identity and sexuality. The loss of his father and then the prolonged experience of abuse in prison had stripped him of his adolescence. As people's reflections on their common experience of violation put his own in context, he slowly learnt to play in the group, and began to 'play' with his own problems and history. Others were working on dreams in their analytic work and, after a period, he brought us one of his own. In the dream he was back in prison and had some of his fellow group members with him. Like the others, he had had good news – his family had received permission from the authorities to visit him. He could not believe it when he found it was his father who had come to see him in the prison's family room. Not only did he now have a living father, just like some of the others in the group, but the father was there with a large bunch of black grapes. He offered them to him and said to him kindly, 'Have some black grapes, my son.' He was in tears when he reported this. The group spent many weeks helping him to mourn the father's loss, to unpack the symbolic meaning of the gift of black grapes and to register with Yunus how this demonstrated his own sense of restitution, of bad things being made good once more.

This experience of being fathered, of finding an older man benevolent and generous, was understood as a marker of his newfound sense of acceptance in the group, and it led to new qualities of self-acceptance in his identity as a man. Central to this process were two relationships he had in the group – one was his relationship with another group member who was a few years older; and the other was his relationship with me, one of the two therapists. We did not explore the symbolic meaning of his dream through transference to ourselves as his new 'parents'. Rather, we took up the meaning of the dream through what he and the others in the group imagined his family at home would wish him to have – here were gifts of kindness that even his lost father could provide.

Things then emerged in the group that fostered his developing masculinity outside it. There was a woman at his language school who had been taking an active interest in him over a long period. He liked her but could not approach her, and would not allow her to approach him. The story came back to the group repeatedly. People joked about other such encounters outside, and they enjoyed their contact with one another across the gender divide in the group. Slowly Yunus began to see that his sense of shame at what had happened in the prison was cutting him off from any sense of legitimate participation in exchanges with women that could touch on anything sexual. As our analysis of his inhibitions progressed, he gained confidence with the woman at college, but at each point he came back to us with another account of withdrawal and hesitation. He was closely attached to the older man in the group who had known shame and injury of the same profound kind, and who constantly encouraged Yunus, relating to him as an older brother or mentor. When Yunus brought us a particularly vivid account of a warm and interesting exchange with this girl at college, in which he frustrated desire and withdrew yet again, the older man turned to him and said, 'Come on, you've still got it between your legs, they didn't actually cut it off!' There was an outburst of affectionate laughter in which Yunus was able to participate, and it revealed how he could begin to see himself through the eyes of the others.

The group's capacity to play with such extreme experience was only possible because it was shared. The confronting challenge was beneficial, and in the months that followed we saw him developing real relationships with women for the first time, beginning in the group with my female co-therapist. This was then slowly extended to the young woman at college who was waiting so patiently, and with whom he went on to develop an intimate relationship.

5. The Wounds of Injured Experience in the 'Sipology' Group

The Wounds of Injured Experience
During a discussion about language difficulties in one of our early mixed groups – composed of both men and women – one of the members, a Ugandan man who had a scarred face and neck after being burnt while in detention, said that that there was no problem about language. 'People who have been injured have our own language', he said. 'We communicate with each other like deaf people do, without hearing. Our experiences speak to each other in our own signs. The wounds have no words. If you've been wounded, then you don't need ears to hear. We speak with our own signs. This is our language – it is like this.' And he reached out and took the hands of the two people sitting on either side of him. They in turn reached out and took the hands of those who sat beside them. In a spontaneous moment all the members of the group were holding hands in a silent gesture of affirmation. One of the group's members was Anu, a woman whose husband had suffered permanent brain damage as a result of assault during torture in Sri Lanka. He had been a GP in the Tamil community and was suspected by the Sinhalese government of giving treatment to wounded guerrillas fighting for the Tamil Tigers. He never recovered fully from the torture, and they were assisted by their extended family to leave the country illegally and make application for asylum in the UK. One of their hopes was that something could be done for the husband's recovery so he might resume

medical practice, but they recently had news that only limited gains were likely. He had traumatically induced epilepsy, was subject to unpredictable and continuing seizures and would be reliant on anti-convulsant medication for the rest of his life. She was wretched and disconsolate, and the hands that reached out to her were of real assistance. She thanked us for making a circle round her, and said through her tears that she needed to feel our strength together. The Ugandan man referred back to the hand he had been offered earlier as a link. He described his own as another. 'This is a chain,' he said, 'one link and then another. It will be a great chain. When we eventually shake this chain, it will be like thunder. You will hear thunder. The world will stop to listen, humanity will come to its senses and there will be no more torture' (Schlapobersky 2016a: 265, Vignette 10.8).

'Sipology' with Soap and Bubbles
Amir was an Iranian Shi'ite and, though fluent enough in English to be eloquent, he had endearing quirks of miscommunication due to his Farsi diction. He first joined us with florid post-traumatic symptoms and fractured relations with his family, some of whom were with him in London and others in hiding at home. After two years of group therapy we were reviewing our time together in the closing sessions when he came forward with the following: 'This sipology group', he said, 'is like a band of brothers (the film *Band of Brothers* was being screened at the time on television), but it's not for war. We come together each week like a band of brothers who go to the laundrette, and you therapists climb in the machine with us after you put in the soap powder and turn on the switch so we go round and round in soap and bubbles for ninety minutes. We come out each week cleaned by the sipology of talking and listening so we can go home safely, love our families and give thanks to God' (Schlapobersky 2016a: 6, Vignette 0.3).

6. The Hand of Humanity

One of our first clients at the Medical Foundation was a teacher from Iran named Mustafa who spoke only broken English when he came to see us in 1986. His father was a respected cleric in Teheran opposed to the established rule of the ayatollahs, but he was too widely regarded in their society to be attacked personally, so the Revolutionary Guard persecuted his sons instead. There were four sons and two daughters in the family and our client was the youngest. The oldest son had come to the UK on a university scholarship some years before and had been here for some time. He brought his youngest brother to our centre and acted as the interpreter. After arrest and interrogation, one of the middle brothers had been able to get away but was stranded in Syria. The other was held with our client in Evin prison in Teheran, where he was killed.

The interrogators exposed our client to the mutilated body of his dead brother to apply further pressure to get him to talk, but he had nothing to disclose. Some years after release he was able to get a temporary permit to travel to Turkey, and from there he came to the UK hidden in a container.

Soon after he joined his brother in London, they got news of the father's death at home, and they attributed his heart attack to the suffering they had been put through. Mustafa fell back into the state in which he had been found on discharge from prison one year earlier, and this led his GP to refer him to us. He had a form of complex post-traumatic stress disorder that interfered with his eating, sleeping and concentration. He was acutely anxious, had florid nightmares, could not sleep at night and so dozed off during the day while conversing. He lost his appetite, was hypervigilant, looked for threats everywhere and found it difficult to converse in coherent sentences. I met with him and his brother on a twice-weekly basis for supportive psychotherapy, and one of my psychiatric colleagues provided him with anxiolytic medication. As we developed a bond of trust, we created a space in which he could talk about the years he spent in prison and about their lost family members. He gained in strength over the months, to the point at which he could begin to grieve. He and his London brother wrote Farsi poems of dedication to their now dead father, and sent them back to the family, who read them over the grave. The reports he received of his family's recovery aided their own stabilization in London. A key part of our therapeutic work involved a testimonial approach to his time in prison. What follows is one from amongst his many prison stories.

While Mustafa was in Evin prison he shared a cell with an elderly peasant who had been brutally beaten by the guards. The old man was an illiterate farmer who posed no risk to anyone. He was suspected of giving shelter to opponents of the regime, but he did not know who they were or where they went. He had nothing to confess, so they left him in a punishment cell with our client at the top of the prison, which was open to the weather. There they had no shelter through the winter, and from time to time the beatings continued. After one of these beatings our client went to comfort him and said: 'Old man, we can't strike them back, but while we're both here I will teach you to read and to write, and that will be our victory against them.' This kind of wisdom earned him regard amongst other prisoners. He taught us a basic principle that now informs our work with survivors of organized violence. He found his own way of fighting back by reaching out as a teacher towards others. In order to survive he had called on the coping strategies and natural resilience of his past life as a teacher, and reached out and shared this resilience with others. He had survived by working as the teacher; he taught others to survive, and by helping others he was able to survive himself. He was guided by value positions that were not the symmetrical reactions of hatred or vengeance. Their victory against barbarity was the struggle for literacy in the most hostile conditions.

As the intensity of his grief for his lost father receded, we were able to build up a picture of his resilience while in prison. He was then able to call on those experiences to deal with the different demands of loss and exile in the present. Finally, in the relative safety of his life in London, we could call on the narrative – the story of past times – to help to free him from its consequences. The work progressed through testimonial detail that was remembered on behalf of his lost brother and the many others.

After a year of regular sessions, when he could converse well enough in English to attend on his own, we looked together at the epitaph he had written to his father in the Farsi poetry that he had sent back for his family to read over the grave. It was spring, and his mood lifted. We began to discuss the next phase of his therapy and the prospect of joining a group. As we brought our individual sessions to a close, he wanted to thank me – and he did so, again in poetic language, by saying, 'Yours is the hand of humanity that has reached out to save me from drowning in my sorrow.'

The six stories above reflect the work by which I answer my own former torturers and inquisitors. I have learnt to harvest the gifts of adversity from my own experience, guided by the inspiring figures of Nelson Mandela and Albie Sachs and others, who have turned their own experience of adversity into humanitarian principles that reach out even to their former adversaries. 'The hand of humanity' that reaches out to save us from drowning in our sorrow, shifts the groundwork of our fight back – from retaliation to rehabilitation and the pursuit of justice. This is the long road towards what Albie Sachs calls 'soft vengeance' (Sachs [1990] 2014).

Note

1. Two of these stories have been published in my earlier book, *From The Couch To The Circle: Group-Analytic Psychotherapy In Practice* (Routledge, 2016). Story 1: 'My Brother What Have They Done to You' is reproduced from Chapter 2, Vignette 2.1, pp. 68–70; Story 5. 'The Wounds of Injured Experience in the "Sipology" Group' is reproduced both from Chapter 10, Vignette 10.8, p. 265; and from Introduction, Vignette 0.3, p 6. I thank my publisher, Taylor and Francis, for their permission for the re-use of this material. Two of my stories are based on accounts of work I undertook jointly with my colleague Helen Bamber and saw published by Diana Miserez in her publications, *Refugees, the Trauma of Exile* (Martinus Nijhoff Publishers, 1988) and *Trauma and Uprooting* (Matador, 2020). Story 3: 'The Darkest Events In the Course of Human Conduct' is reproduced from p. 102; and Story 6: 'The Hand of Humanity', is reproduced from pp. 97–98. I am grateful to her for publishing these stories and for releasing copyright for their re-issue here. For Story 3: 'The Woman Who Could Not Relate to Men', I am grateful to my colleagues and former supervisees, Rachel Tribe and Susan Levy, for the work they did in cases like these. This story is a tribute to their work, and I am grateful for their permission to publish it here.

AFTERWORD
Memory and Testimony

In writing this account I have been guided by the same principles that I was trained to work with as a forensic psychotherapist when giving testimony in court hearings to ascertain the truth – or otherwise – of a survivor's evidence. I have written reports for many hearings of the Immigration Appeal Tribunal in the UK, and for other courts, and I have often been required to attend in person as an expert witness in the subject of trauma, its history and its context. My account has followed the same principles. It has been based on my own first-person narrative set out as clearly as memory has allowed. My own memories have been investigated through such documents of verification as these fifty years allow – the prison Bible and those surviving fragments of the toilet-paper diary that were transposed into good copy. This has then been augmented by the memory of others, such as my parents, my former partner Janet, and my brother and sister. Then there is corroborative material from others who have endured similar experiences. Albie Sachs's account of Swanepoel subjecting him to sleep deprivation is consistent with my own account and so are the accounts of Mongane Wally Serote and Ezekiel Mokone, who have, over the years, corroborated the detail of my experience with their own. Our own experience is then set in the context of documentary and other historical source material from the Truth and Reconciliation Commission and elsewhere, and these sources are given in the endnotes. A living and contemporary witness from 'the other side', Detective Warrant Officer Paul Erasmus, who in the years following served under the Security Police officers I have identified, has verified their names, ranks and positions of office, and so his reading of this manuscript and his corroboration of how the Security Police worked gives my account further authentication. Finally, I reached out to Zureena Desai, widow of the late John Blacking, thanks to a series of introductions described in the Prologue, note 9, and in Interrogation II, note 4. She in turn put me in touch with Susanne Klausen, a professor of history at Carleton University, Ottawa, who has made available to me the fruits of her own research into the responsibility of (then) Major Coetzee and Lieutenant Jordaan for the arrest of Blacking and Desai six months before they interrogated me. During my interrogation they identified themselves as the police responsible for those earlier arrests. This line of enquiry now closes the circle of verification.

On reviewing literature about what a memoir should be, I have found that an author's memories at its source should themselves be of interest. But if memory was my only source, testimony and fiction would have no distinction. I have been guided in my drafting by the way in which others have gone about their task. I have found Thomas Merton's *The Seven Storey Mountain* the most profound contemporary memoir – its subject is his autobiography (Merton [1948] 1990). Koestler's *Spanish Testament*, already quoted in the 'Epilogue' above, describes his own experience living amongst 'men without shadows' waiting for execution by Franco's forces during the Spanish Civil War. His purpose as a survivor is to give substance to the lives of those who did not survive (Koestler 1937). Sharanksy's *Fear No Evil* describes his own endurance, survival and release as a Jew through Soviet imprisonment, and he gives testimony to the lives of countless others (Sharansky [1988] 1998). Farbstein's summary of the vast Holocaust literature focuses on diary consistency and personal memory as forms of testimony in and of themselves (Farbstein 1998),[1] and I now bring these perspectives round to the South African story.

The struggle against apartheid in South Africa was prolonged. The courage of those by whom it was led created a unique literature of engagement. When I was young, its leaders stood far beyond and above me. I never thought I would find myself standing under interrogation in circumstances of forced confinement. We knew little about the literature of the struggle because the banning orders and restrictions destroyed our context and current history.

The Literature of Imprisonment and Resistance

My voice comes late to the literature and is one amongst many others. I now wish to pay homage to them. Growing up where and when we did, we knew nothing of this literature – most of it was banned. The work of the Security Police stripped our literature of these authors. I began to learn of them only after reaching the UK in 1970, and I have been making discoveries ever since. It is hard to catch up with an erased history, and I have been guided by the determination to do justice to those others who have written about it. Albie Sachs's writing has prominence in my story, first because of its merit but also because of the parallels he has honoured me by making, between my work offering psychotherapy to survivors and his own life's work in human rights. I will continue with the towering figure of Nelson Mandela. His early writings and speeches, including his celebrated oration when facing the death sentence with the other

Rivonia accused at their trial, were published by the African National Congress in London – *Nelson Mandela Speaks* (Mandela 1965a) – just one year after he went to Robben Island with the others convicted. A further such compilation was published later the same year, with a foreword by Ruth First, *No Easy Walk to Freedom: Articles, Speeches and Trial Addresses of Nelson Mandela* (Mandela 1965b). The second edition has a foreword by Ahmed Ben Bella, President of Algeria, and is introduced by Oliver Tambo, President of the African National Congress (1973).

Mandela began drafting the text through which he would one day speak to the world about his own and South Africa's struggle – his autobiography, *Long Walk to Freedom* (Mandela 1994) – while he was still in the bitter captivity of 'The Island'. Despite its stringencies, the prisoners were able to support each other and they developed study programmes through which 'The Island' became known as 'The University'. Life there is described in Athol Fugard's celebrated play *The Island* (Fugard 1993: 193–227), and in the writing of Neville Alexander (Alexander 2014). Amongst so much else, Mandela's autobiography records the severe penalties that he and his comrades suffered there when the authorities discovered sections of the manuscript that he was trying to smuggle out. The later issue of his testimony makes clear that he and others were mostly successful in their efforts to document their histories and experiences in the struggle, and to get them out ready for publication when the time was right. Mandela's autobiography was released in the year the country went to the polls for the historic election of 1994. It is the single most inspiring account of any one person's struggle for their own and their people's freedom. It also included a commitment to redeem his captors, and it has had a sustained and worldwide readership, which led many of us to nominate him as 'Man of the Century' at the millennium – an award that *Time* magazine conferred instead on Albert Einstein. A compilation of his prison letters was published in 2010, covering the full span of his 27-year imprisonment (Mandela, Venter and Dlamini-Mandela 2010).

Narratives documenting the early years of imprisonment during the struggle begin with Ruth First's account of solitary confinement during the State of Emergency in 1960 (First 1965; reissued in a posthumous edition by her daughter Gillian Slovo in 2010). Albie Sachs's *Stephanie on Trial* (1968) and his *Jail Diary* (1969) followed. In Albie's Foreword to my memoir, he gives us his own account of the literature of resistance and imprisonment that influenced and inspired him during his own development.

There are further accounts of political imprisonment and resistance by Hilda Bernstein (1968), Denis Brutus (1969), Hugh Lewin (1976), Breyten Breytenbach (1984), Jeremy Cronin (1987), Albie Sachs (1990, 2009, 2018), Raymond Suttner (2017) and Winnie Madikizela-Mandela (2014). In the last of these, Winnie Mandela describes the experience of 491 days of solitary confinement in the wave of arrests that included my own. My 55 days described here should be understood in comparison to her own – a much greater span of confinement and torture, and one that was also endured by those prosecuted with her and by many of the others. Hilda Bernstein's account cited above describes her earlier imprisonment during the State of Emergency in 1960. She describes their lives in Johannesburg during the years afterwards, leading to the Rivonia Trial in which her husband was one of the accused, and her later escape to Botswana. The account she gives of her own early imprisonment, first in 'The Fort' and then in Pretoria Local, includes a poignant description of her diary: 'I managed to keep a daily prison diary written in tiny, almost illegible pencil, and smuggled [it] out of prison when I was released. I still have it,' she writes, 'seven years later' (Bernstein 1968: xvii). She later wrote a comprehensive account, *Rift: The Exile Experience of South Africans*' (1994), which is based on the testimony of more than 330 people, including me, with descriptions of the conditions – including imprisonment – leading to their exile. It concludes with a chronology of the security authorities' many atrocities in their fight back against the struggle (ibid.: 510–16).

Benjamin Pogrund's original account of Robert Sobukwe's life and times, including Sobukwe's years of solitary confinement on Robben Island, was published in 1991, followed by a second edition in 2006 described below (Pogrund 1991, 2006). Mapanje's compilation, *Gathering Seaweed: African Prison Writing*, was published by Heinemann in 2002. He includes many of those described above, and widens the frame further to bring in many writers from north of South Africa's borders.

Many of the South African stories take their inception from Herman Charles Bosman's account of his time in the same prison in which many of us were detained – Pretoria Local, 'The Hanging Jail'. The building and its gallows were a British construction after their conquest of Pretoria, formerly the capital of the Boer Republic of Transvaal. Bosman's own account of the regular hangings there, a fate that almost befell him, describes the same pall of despair that touched all of us who had this exposure (Bosman 1969). The death sentence imposed on him for killing his own brother in a fight was repealed, and he was eventually discharged after a long prison sentence. His writing gifts were forged in that terrible foundry. Many years later he was recruited by the parents of Lionel Abrahams to offer their child, compromised by cerebral palsy and unable to participate in normal education, private education. Bosman became his tutor and mentor and, in the years that followed when Abrahams found his own voice as a writer, he became Bosman's editor and champion. The poetry that flowered in Abraham's hands had its seeds in Bosman's imprisonment. Abrahams taught me to read and write for a second time and he became a pathfinder through whose voice many of us found our own. He founded Renoster Books and was the first publisher for the writing of Oswald Mtshali (1972) and Mongane Wally Serote (1972). He continued guiding us until his death. I have written more about Lionel in 'Acknowledgments' below, as I have about Hilda Bernstein. Here I wish to record how honoured I am that my book's account includes Albie Sachs's description of the legal process through which that terrible 'death drop' was brought to its own end.

The events described here took place fifty years ago. When I described them for the British *Observer* months afterwards, the South African authorities responsible did not just dismiss this as fiction. The head of the Security Police, Brigadier Venter, issued a press release in which he called my account 'emphatic lies', insisting that 'we did not harm him'. And then, I later discovered, they destroyed their own records about me. The events were real enough at the time. They altered my life and the lives of the others who were detained, and the lives of our loved ones, families and friends – which is what state terror is designed to do. But the changes they led to in my life were not what the enforcers had intended. On leaving school three years earlier, I had gone to university to train to become a doctor but was twice derailed by the life events described in the narrative above. Now I am a psychotherapist with a specialist competence in the rehabilitation of those who have endured atrocity. The writing of this memoir is a further act of defiance against the authorities of my day, and against others like them in other countries, past and present. I have dedicated many working years to the rehabilitation of other survivors, helped to train generations of other psychotherapists to do this kind of work, and, in writing this memoir, I want to ensure that the names of the chief perpetrators are never forgotten.

The police did not find evidence to include me in the two trials that followed. While they otherwise fabricated evidence to suit their own devious purposes, they set out to close my case down to minimize the damaging publicity it raised, and they chose instead to deport me. They seemed to believe that I was sufficiently damaged to cause them no further trouble. The testimony I gave for the *Observer* during the trial that followed put an international spotlight on their use of sleep deprivation as a systematic torture. Putting this testimony forward was an obligation and an honour. It was first drafted as a fully documented day-by-day account for a pamphlet called 'Trial by Torture – The Case of the 22' produced by the International Defence and Aid Fund, who were mounting publicity on behalf of those I had been arrested amongst, who were then facing charges (IDAF 1970). It was then reissued by the *Observer* on 23 August 1969. The ferocious reaction from the Security Police forms part of this memoir. The record I gave remains a deep source of pride and self-respect, despite the unauthorized headline that the *Observer* editor introduced. It read: 'How Vorster's Jailers "Broke" Me'. I was appalled when I first saw it, and for the rest of his life I had nothing further to do with this editor. I was injured but I was unbroken, and I had put my account forward to protect others. The pages of the newspaper might be yellow with age, but the details remain solid and the emotions of the time are brought out now in this book.

In writing this account half a century later, I have called on the *Observer* article to shape it and have reconstructed events on a day-by-day basis, guided by the surviving toilet-paper chronicle and the Bible calendar and its annotations. The drafting of this memoir has occupied much of my writing time over the last two years. I could only get to grips with it for limited periods of time, and would then find I had to return to the world of the present to recover. When immersed in this narrative, when holding the old Bible, or when looking at the toilet-paper diary, the material had a strange quality that corroded my well-being. Radioactivity must be like this. Its effects are invisible, but they can be harmful. I remain intensely curious about the events of the time but, on looking into their detail, I found I could get distracted and moody and become careless about people, arrangements and possessions. During the writing of this memoir, I lost my mobile phone several times, lost my bicycle once and was repeatedly brought up sharp by other self-inflicted misadventures. If I worked late on the manuscript, sleep could sometimes be disturbed or impossible. I fear my work as a psychotherapist must have been hampered, on and off, for a period of time. Now that this task is done, I look forward to being on better terms with my past in the years ahead, and without so much threat from its shadows. I can now open the file on the computer that contains this memoir, without having to brace myself. The 'trauma radiation' has abated and I am increasingly able to reckon with my own past, as I reckon with the past of my many patients who have endured trauma of one kind or another. My brothers Colin and David and my sister Marian have played a supportive part, as we have always done for one another. Recently my sister commented, 'When we hear what it has cost you, it is clear why you have not written this before.'

While in detention my survival was shaped by the belief that I could protect my life by describing what was happening. At the time I knew nothing about the earlier experience of those who had strengthened their own resilience in such conditions by writing about it. As described earlier, I stole a police pen from the interrogators' desk and took it with me into solitary confinement. There I kept a daily chronicle on toilet paper, kept a calendar on the flyleaf of the Bible that I was allowed, recorded lines of Biblical text and poetry of my own, and kept further coded notes and an aide-memoire on what had happened during the interrogation. When I became fearful of what this could still give away, I destroyed the aide-memoire by drawing an image over it called 'The Teeth of Tension'. Photographs of this material from the Bible – now on permanent loan to the Jewish Museum in Albert Street, London – illustrate this memoir.

On reviewing this *Observer* article with Albie Sachs beside me recently, I noted with his help just how traumatized I must have been at the time of its drafting in 1970. As well as the evident outrage and anger, there is also fear between the lines. As we read the article together, Albie's presence carried authority from legal sources that predate the police state and succeed it with the strength of a just and legal constitution. He has been one of the architects of the struggle for justice. I am comforted by his lucid commentary based on his own earlier, related experience, by his own knowledge of apartheid's dark creatures and his clear eye for the courageous role played at the time by the different people in my story. His personal strength is inspiring. This is the strength that has beaten swords into ploughshares in the Truth and Reconciliation Commission, in the drafting of the country's constitution and in the work of its Constitutional Court. And so, the work goes on!

In the records, Albie sees my parents struggling to do what they could for me, and finds notes to Raymond Tucker, the lawyer they instructed. I note Albie's special appreciation of the running press commentary. There were brave journalists like Margaret Smith and especially Benjamin Pogrund at the *Rand Daily Mail* who tracked my detention and release with closely focused articles. One year later these journalists brought the implications of the *Observer* article to light inside the country, where it was illegal to publish any of its content. What they did was repeatedly to reference the stir that had been created by my article in the press abroad, and they then interviewed the police and prison authorities to test the limits of what they could say. They put all this to press as they went. Police impunity was challenged by this kind of courage during the sharpest years of the struggle, but the journalists who did the work put themselves on the line. I did not know these journalists at the time, but in the years following I became friends with Benjamin Pogrund in London, where he consulted me on the new edition of the book that he was reissuing about Robert Sobukwe. The contribution I made to the understanding of how solitary confinement had unsettled Sobukwe's faculties was based first on my own detention and then on my years of experience rehabilitating others. I am honoured by Benjamin's acknowledgement of my contribution in *How Can Man Die Better* (Pogrund 2006). This association with others who have lived through such experience, and with other authors and clinicians, is another source of authority in the documentation of my history.

On rereading the *Observer* article for the first time in decades, I note how my own position towards those events has changed down the years. In 1970, the article conveyed a sense of devastation, whereas now I find that I can write about this past with a sense of agency that has been gained over the years by clinical service in the field. This is the gift that has come to me from my clients and patients, past and present. In most cases I can choose what to remember from my own history, how to remember it, or whether to remember it at all, and I have found how to put it to use. Helen Bamber was first a colleague and then she became a close and lifelong friend. Working with her at the Medical Foundation for the Care of Victims of Torture, she taught me what I could do with this history and, by putting it to use for others, I have been able to make it into one of the gifts of adversity.

There is a puzzling absence of reference in the *Observer* article to my own exposure during detention to the regular execution of others. Memories of this exposure must have been present when I wrote the article in the months after release. Those in the field who work with trauma might explain this as dissociation – a person's unconscious eradication of their own memory, when it is too painful to bear. That exposure remains on the horizon of memory to this day, and it can still be brought back by innocuous and unexpected events. Pretoria Local Prison was built by the British after the Anglo-Boer War and was closely modelled on the UK prisons of their day. During my working week in London I go past Pentonville Prison quite regularly, and sometimes have patients there who need to be visited. Execution by hanging was refined here before its export to the colonies. Its enormous gate can still bring back to mind the overnight singing of the condemned in Pretoria Prison all those years ago, as can a game of 'hangman' by a group of children. Memory can come back from hidden places to haunt the present. A flight attendant on a plane leaning over me unexpectedly to adjust my seat belt can put himself at risk if he does not stand back when I insist on doing it myself. Echoes – like Edvard Munch's painting *The Scream* – can still overtake ordinary events, and then I have to work hard to send the shadows back to where they have come from.

The most heartening antidote to the 'white noise' of bad memory came on learning from Albie of their determination to rule against the death penalty in the Constitutional Court as soon as they could. When he and I looked together at artefacts kept in my mother's file of the time, we found a note in her handwriting, dated early June 1969, with telephone numbers for Raymond Tucker – the lawyer instructed – and for his senior partner, Jack Browse; and for Swanepoel in Compol Building. Albie said, 'This is a mother's memorandum. And how many mothers there were!' We looked further into the file and found another of my mother's notes, this one with phone numbers for the minister of police, Lourens Muller, and another for the prime minister's office. There were other notes, one with an inventory of clothes delivered to prison for me, documented in my father's handwriting. So, this was a father's memorandum, written as only an old soldier could: '2 vests (two), 2 shirts (two), 2 prs socks (two), 2 prs underpants (two), 1 parcel food & fruit'. And there was my father's signature and the date when he handed the clothes over to the prison authorities. There is a copy of this very piece of writing in the prison records discovered in the National Archives, together with a receipt for these clothes, signed for by Lieutenant Dirker 836/6461 and Major Viktor 836/6465. They match exactly. I did not receive the clothes at the time they were signed for by the prison authorities. It took another two weeks for them to get to me, but these are the details that authenticate memory, and there is much more besides.

Amongst the most significant of the other memoranda is an earlier receipt from my mother signed by Major Coetzee, Pretoria 14/06/1969, in which he takes receipt from my mother of '(a) Two blankets, (b) Two jerseys (c) Foodstuffs'. My parents would have had no idea that on the day these items were signed for, just one day after my arrest, I was standing on a brick in Compol Building, the very place to which they had brought these items. I never saw these things then or afterwards and only knew about them when I came out.

There have been previous accounts of my story by others – journalists, commentators and others on radio, on film and in print. As already mentioned, Hilda Bernstein included an account of my arrest, the time in prison and my deportation in *Rift: The Exile Experience of South Africans* (1994: 81–87). Peter Marshall, a good friend, included an account of my time in detention. It was filmed as I stood talking to him outside Compol Building for a television documentary he made, *Voyage around Africa*, while Compol was still the headquarters of the South African Security Police in Pretoria (Marshall 1994; see 'Peter Marshall', retrieved 28 December 2020 from: https://wn.com/_peter_marshall_(author)/Peter_Marshall/_Peter_Marshall). My cousin and good friend Norman Rosenthal included some of the story in his book, *The Gift of Adversity* (Rosenthal 2014). In the title of his book and in his text, he developed descriptive terms for the benefits that we ourselves, the therapists, get from the work that we do. We can turn our own historical injuries into sources of strength for our clients and patients. Swords and spears can become ploughshares and pruning hooks when revenge is replaced by reparation and the quest for justice. Another good friend, Shelley Katz, gave me a chapter in her book *Turning Points* (Schlapobersky 2016b), which I devoted to the children of apartheid who feature above in Day 1. The work of drafting these books and my return to South Africa for Peter Marshall's film have helped me to come back to my origins, for which I am grateful. Dovidi Fachler published an account of what he called 'The John Schlapobersky Affair' in the Chanukah 2013 edition of *Jewish Affairs* based on access to Israel's Foreign Ministry's archives (Fachler 2013). It describes the role played at the time by Itzhak Unna, the Israeli consul general to South Africa, who negotiated my release. Fachler's article has been called on to inform this memoir, which includes passages from these archives.

The South African History Archive – Correspondence

9 May 2018
Dear John,

We are excited to be able to somehow assist you in finding the information you are searching for. Your memoir promises to be a good and meaningful addition to the much-needed accurate historical accounts of the lived experiences of many people during apartheid.

We have searched our documents and found there indeed does exist a Security Legislation Directorate file with your name on it, file number 2713. These files are kept at the National Archive. In order for us to gain access to the file, we need to make a Promotion of Access to Information Act (PAIA) request on your behalf. Having read what it is that you are searching for, we will also be sending a request for your file to the South African Police Services as well, in case they also have some records.

In order for us to make the PAIA application we require that you please provide us with a copy of your ID – it does not matter that it is not a South African ID – as well as a signed copy of the attached SAHA consent form.

Just to let you know, unfortunately, records can sometimes take a little long to release. There are times they come within a few weeks, but sometimes it can take a little longer, so we can only hope the response is quick.

If you have any further questions, please do not hesitate to ask.

Warmest regards,

Nobukhosi N. Zulu

FOIP Coordinator

SOUTH AFRICAN HISTORY ARCHIVE (SAHA)

19 May 2018

Dear John,

I hope you have had a good week. I wanted to update you on the PAIA process concerning your request.

At the beginning of week, I submitted three records regarding your inquiries: one to National Archive for the security file they have on you; one to the South African Police Service for the police record detailing the events around your arrest; and a third one to the Department of Home Affairs (previously Ministry of Interior).

We have an online tracker system that allows individuals to track their applications on our site, but unfortunately we are expecting technical difficulties. As soon as the tracker is up and running, I will send the links and you can follow.

The National Archive and SAPS have acknowledged receipt of our requests, which is a good sign.

Have a blessed weekend.

Regards,

Nobukhosi N. Zulu

26 June 2018
Dearest John,
  It is my pleasure to inform you that the National Archive has released your SLD file. The records are currently with our archival team and I should able to forward them to you before the end of the week. Parts of the released files are in Afrikaans; I am not sure if you are fluent and would be able to read it on your own. If you would like the records translated, SAHA would be glad to assist in finding a translator and let you know the related costs; it should not be much as it is just a few pages.
  We are still waiting on the other government departments – they are often less efficient than the National Archive.
Kindest regards,
Nobukhosi N. Zulu

27 June 2019
Dear Nobukhosi,
  I am deeply moved by your continuing kindness towards me in keeping me so closely advised. This is truly remarkable news. I await the material with great interest and some anxiety, of course, and will look closely for your next communication. I am writing a Memoir about my history, and as you've already had some access to this material, you will appreciate how much it all matters to me, 49 years later.
  I studied Afrikaans right through school for 12 years. We attached to the language our hatred for what we saw its people doing to the African population. But it was my mother's first language as she grew up in a small Jewish population in the countryside and went to an Afrikaans medium school. When the National Party came to power in 1948, the year I was born, all her associates in that Afrikaans community rejected her because she wasn't one of them, so eventually we moved to Swaziland.
  In the Memoir, when it is finally published with the material you've found for me, you will see what a big role the issue of Afrikaans played during my detention and interrogation. While in the hands of the police I insisted I understood nothing, so they had to question me in English, but discussed my case in Afrikaans in front of me, so I knew a little of what was going on and did what I could to protect myself and my friends.
  When Nelson Mandela was inaugurated as President in 1994, and De Klerk was inaugurated as one of the two Deputy Presidents, along with Mbeki, De Klerk himself took his oath of office in Afrikaans and he wept as he did so. Watching on TV here in London, we wept with him. Since then I have been able to tolerate and indeed appreciate the language for the first time, and its

speakers, and I now take pleasure using the little Afrikaans and siSwati that I know, whenever I am back.

All this lengthy explanation is to help you understand why I will take receipt of this archival material in Afrikaans, with pleasure. If I need translation I will of course come back to ask for your assistance, as you have offered it.

With gratitude, Ngibona Kakhulu,

John

28 June 2019

Dearest John,

I am glad to read a brief account of your history with Afrikaans. I have had my own journey with the language and through a great sense of humour (I suppose) God gave me some of my dearest friends to be Afrikaans, which began a healing process in me.

I am glad to say here attached are the files that were released from the National Archive. They are not that comprehensive, but I sincerely hope they will shed some light and will add to what promises to be a worthy account.

I will keep you updated with the other requests as any news arises.

Warmest regards,

Nobukhosi N. Zulu

28 June 2019

Dear Nobukhosi,

Thank you so much for this material. It is much, much appreciated. Unfortunately, it is also very meagre. From what I can make out, the file is composed only of 'declassified' material comprising the warrant for my arrest, and associated documents; correspondence from a visiting magistrate who saw me in prison; correspondence between my late mother and the Prime Minister's office following her request for an interview with him while I was still in detention; and a series of newspaper cuttings about me at that time.

The fact is, I signed a lengthy statement after days of interrogation under torture. There is nothing in the material you've sent from the Security Police themselves, and my own signed statement is not included. There must have been extensive documentation, and I know the kind of records they had because I watched them drawing them up.

Do you think there is any chance I could gain access to the classified material, in particular the working notes and records of the Security Police themselves, which are simply not here, and also their names and identities?

Kind regards and many thanks,

John

30 July 2019
Dearest John,

I hope this email finds you well. It is with sadness that I have to inform you that we seem unable to get any other records. I contacted the National Archive and they affirmed that the records they sent us are the records they have. And the South African Police Service got back to us and informed us that the requested records do not exist. The Department of Home Affairs (former Ministry of Interior) has not so much as acknowledged our request. We are in the process of appealing to higher authorities to force a response, but our chances are slim of getting any positive feedback. In some very rare instances, the Department of State Security would have some records of their own, we have sent a request to them and hopefully something will come from there.

The apartheid government destroyed a lot of their records; and for those that do exist, in some instances, the files cannot be found because of bad file management, and in other cases there is an unwillingness to release the information. Unless we know for certain that information does in fact exist, it is difficult to dispute the government when they say the records do not exist.

I wish I was bringing better news, but sadly this is the unfortunate state of access to information in South Africa. I will keep you updated with the DSS request and if anything materializes from there.

Warmest regards,
Nobukhosi N. Zulu

What the Press Said

In 2009, my brother David, still living in South Africa, set out to track down press cuttings relating to my detention on its fortieth anniversary. He was advised by Raymond Louw, former editor of the *Rand Daily Mail*, to contact Michelle Leon, a staff member at Avusa (now called Tiso Blackstar), where the *RDM* archives are kept. She helped to trace many references and David put them into a portfolio. We have found many of these articles replicated both in my mother's original press file and in the file extracted from the police record at the National Archives. The cuttings in the Security Police file all have handwritten codes and brief directions in Afrikaans, which I presume would have directed their readers to other sources in their intelligence archive. They did not have the legislation by which to close down the opposition press during the years of the struggle, but they used the press itself to mine information and track opposition. The press cuttings relating to my detention that were found under my name in the Security Police archives testify to their intelligence work. In 1985 they succeeded in closing down the *Rand Daily Mail* through commercial manipulation of its company holdings. Other sources of press opposition came into focus at this point through the brave work of succeeding journalists, for apartheid's end was still almost ten years away.

In London, my brother Colin and his wife Simone spent a lot of time with me organizing my mother's press file containing the cuttings compiled at the time, memos and notes, and her correspondence with the state authorities. This file also contains a draft account of an interview with my mother in Swaziland conducted by a journalist from the *Rand Daily Mail* – acting for their news editor, Benjamin Pogrund – that took place in the weeks after I published the *Observer* article. Here she gives detail of the state in which she found me when given access to me in prison for the second time on Tuesday 15 July. Her account is incorporated in the daily narrative. Its detail challenges the discrediting claims against me by Brigadier Venter after I went to press, that 'we did not harm him'. She also describes how, in the days leading up to my release, she was taken aside by Major Coetzee and subjected to threats that the South African state could deny my parents access to the country from Swaziland, or could freeze their financial assets in South Africa, should they choose to make disclosures to the press of any kind at all. It was in view of these threats that the *Rand Daily Mail* chose not to give public voice to my parents' statement of support for my own account.

What follows is a full inventory of press headlines relating to my detention, in chronological sequence. It is collated from the identified sources: the Security Police Press Archive under my name; my mother's press file; and my brother's portfolio compiled from the Avusa sources in 2009. The articles underline the safeguarding role played by the brave and independent journalists of the time. The inventory is both an archive of my history and a tribute to these journalists. I have set it out here as a statement of gratitude from a former political prisoner to the investigators who safeguard our freedoms and who – in today's climate worldwide – can sometimes pay for the truth with their own lives.

Saturday 14 June 1969. *The Star*, Johannesburg: STUDENT IS HELD BY SECURITY POLICE.
Sunday 15 June 1969. *Sunday Express*, Johannesburg: SECURITY POLICE HOLD FORMER MAYOR'S NEPHEW. Express correspondent.
Sunday 15 June 1969. *Sunday Times*, Johannesburg: EX-MAYOR'S NEPHEW IS DETAINED. Margaret Smith.
Sunday 15 June 1969. *The Sunday Times*, London: DETAINED ART STUDENT MAY BE BRITISH.
Monday 16 June 1969. *Rand Daily Mail*, Johannesburg: DETAINEE JOHN SCHLAPOBERSKY: STUDENTS' CALL FOR TRIAL. Staff Reporter.

Tuesday 17 June 1969. *Rand Daily Mail*, Johannesburg: 30 HELD UNDER 'TERROR' ACT. Staff reporter.

Tuesday 17 June 1969. *Rand Daily Mail*, Johannesburg: SCHLAPOBERSKY SPIRITED AWAY, SAY FRIENDS. Staff reporter.

Tuesday 17 June 1969. *The Star*, Johannesburg: STUDENTS HOLD MASS PROTEST.

Wednesday 18 June 1969. *Rand Daily Mail*, Johannesburg: DETAINED STUDENT BRITISH SUBJECT. Political reporter.

Wednesday 18 June 1969. *Rand Daily Mail*, Johannesburg: STUDENTS AT WITS RAISE MONEY FOR DETAINEES. Staff reporter.

Wednesday 18 June 1969. *Eastern Province Herald*: MASS WITS PROTEST FOR HELD STUDENTS.

Friday 20 June 1969. *The Star*, Johannesburg: MULLER ON RUSSIAN THREAT (justifies detention of two British subjects, including Schlapobersky). From Our Bureau.

Saturday 28 June 1969. *The Star*, Johannesburg: GOLDING AGAIN SEEN BY BRITISH CONSUL (Schlapobersky, though a British passport holder, is also a South African and cannot therefore be represented by Britain: Questions raised in House of Commons, London).

Sunday 13 July 1969. *The Sunday Times*, London: MAJOR THEUNIS, JACOBUS SWANEPOEL AND HIS TEAM OF INTERROGATORS (first-hand stories of systematic sleep deprivation used in SA as a form of torture, leading to deaths in detention).

Sunday 20 July 1969. *Sunday Express*, Johannesburg: SECURITY BRANCH CHIEF VENTER DEFENDS MAJOR SWANEPOEL. Patrick Weech.

Thursday 31 July 1969. *Rand Daily Mail*, Johannesburg: CHEER PARCELS FOR DETAINED STUDENTS.

Friday 8 August 1969. *Rand Daily Mail*, Johannesburg: DETAINED STUDENT FREED – FLIES OUT.

Friday 8 August 1969. *The Star*, Johannesburg: STUDENT DETAINEE LEAVES SECRETLY.

Sunday 10 August 1969. *Sunday Express*, Johannesburg: SCHLAPOBERSKY LEFT S.A. BY CHOICE, SAYS VENTER. Margaret Smith.

Friday 22 August 1969. *The Star*, Johannesburg: CHIEF INTERROGA-TOR SWANEPOEL SAYS 'I'M NOT A GESTAPO OGRE'.

Wednesday 29 October 1969. *Rand Daily Mail*, Johannesburg: 22 SENT FOR TRIAL UNDER 'RED' ACT: REMANDED FOR TRIAL IN SUPREME COURT: CHARGED UNDER SUPPRESSION OF COMMUNISM ACT. SCHLAPOBERSKY CITED AS CO-CONSPIRATOR.

Sunday 23 August 1970. *The Observer*, London: HOW VORSTER'S JAILERS 'BROKE' ME. John Schlapobersky.

Saturday 29 August 1970. *Rand Daily Mail*, Johannesburg: ILL-TREATMENT STORY IS AN EMPHATIC LIE – BRIGADIER VENTER DENIES SCHLAPOBERSKY'S ALLEGATIONS.

Wednesday 2 September 1970. *Rand Daily Mail*, Johannesburg: DETAINED STUDENT IN NEWS: JOHN SCHLAPOBERSKY'S ARTICLE ABOUT POLICE TREATMENT AROUSES WIDESPREAD INTEREST. Staff reporter.

Tuesday 15 September 1970. *Rand Daily Mail*, Johannesburg: PRISONERS OF PRISONS ACT: JOHN SCHLAPOBERSKY'S STARTLING ACCOUNT OF DETENTION IN *OBSERVER* BURST ON BRITISH PUBLIC – JOURNALS, RADIO & TV. BUT NOT ONE WORD ALLOWED INSIDE SA.

Note

1. Farbstein provides one of the most informative discussions about the relationship be-tween diary and memoir as historical source material in 'Diaries and Memoirs as a Historical Source'. She writes that 'only the multiplicity of facets and strata manifested in the diaries and the memoirs may bring us closer to the universal history of the time. This is because a witness's account, like any historical narrative, "sheds light on a certain part ... (and) discusses certain aspects. None of these reports is complete or perfect, but all contribute to the advancement of knowledge." [A. Firan, 1985, 'What Are the Historians Trying to Do?', in Avraham Weinryb (ed.), *Historical Thinking*. (Tel Aviv: Open University), pp. 235–60.] We should give the memoir literature the place it de-serves – a loftier place than that given it thus far – and rid ourselves of excessive sus-picion, especially when additional tools may confirm a reasonable degree of reliability' (Farbstein 1998).

ACKNOWLEDGEMENTS

The acknowledgements due are extensive. They take in those who played a part in supporting me and my family during detention and afterwards; those who saw us through the initial experiences of life in exile; and those who have supported me and helped me to tell this story.

I begin with my parents. Without the courage, ingenuity and continuing commitment of my mother Ruth and my father Archie, my chances of survival would have been very different. They gave me life twice over and, from a mother and father, who could hope for more? As I have stated in the dedication on the opening page, this memoir is dedicated to their memory.

I offer my special thanks to Marion Berghahn, my publisher, without whom the memoir would not exist as a book; and to Jeremy Boraine, my South African publisher, who took the project on later, just as soon as he saw the manuscript. Marion's team at Berghahn Books have been receptive and helpful in turning the manuscript into the book that lies between these covers. I was introduced to her by my close friends Phyllis Cohen and (the late) Walter Goldstein of New York, who recognized there would be synchrony between publisher and author. I have celebrated their friendship many times over. This book now also pays homage to their good judgement and stands in memory of Walter, who did not live to see it published but understood what could be made of the manuscript.

The Berghahn team in New York, Chris Chappell and Mykelin Higham, began the editorial process, which was taken over by Tom Bonnington in Oxford, who has seen the book through to copy editing and into production with Caroline Kuhtz. I extend my sincere appreciation to all, and to Nigel Smith, the copy editor. They have joined me in making this more than a commercial or editorial enterprise, and I thank them all for their shared commitment to unravelling the history of apartheid and its iniquities. Jeremy Boraine has taken responsibility for the publication of the South African edition on behalf of Jonathan Ball Publishers. His further editorial guidance has been of great value. I thank him on my own behalf and especially on behalf of the book's future South African readers for bringing it home – where it began and will always belong. His colleague at Jonathan Ball, Caren van Houwelingen, has given the Afrikaans used in the book authentic colloquial form, and I thank her too. Their role and the publishing house they represent continue to inspire us through our shared appreciation that there is much yet to be done through the printed word, for freedom in South Africa. The review of the Afrikaans used here was initiated by Francois Louw to whom further thanks are extended below. I extend my sincere appreciation also to Paul Wise, the South African proofreader and fact checker.

Closely advised by Marion Berghahn, the designer at Berghahn Books, Andrew Esson, produced the cover illustration. It will speak for all who have looked for light from inside a prison cell. I trust it will set the book well on its way to a wider public. The designer at Jonathan Ball Publishers, Marius Roux, created the South African cover design that opens a window of hope behind the cell door. I extend my sincere appreciation to both designers.

My partner at the time of my arrest, Janet Beattie, who later became my wife, joined me in exile in Israel, and then wrote to the South African prime minister to surrender her South African passport and renounce her citizenship as a protest against their treatment of me. Her correspondence on file gives lasting strength to our bond, cemented by our daughter Hannah, her son and my stepson Josh, and our grandchildren, Maia, Leo and Elodi.

In the days following my arrest, my fellow students at Witwatersrand University mounted a series of demonstrations, protests and fund-raising events for those of us in detention. The import of the Terrorism Act and the terms under which I was deported, prevented me from ever publicly acknowledging the stand they took and the courage they showed, at the time and in the months and years following. The mobilization of protest at the time of our detentions helped to bring public opposition onto the streets, to the benefit of those who were to spend much longer in detention. People in Johannesburg and elsewhere protested against the continuing detentions and the abuse of justice in the trials that followed. I am very pleased to be able to give public recognition to this now, and to extend my thanks and friendship across the years to Denis Hirson, Ian Margo, John Wacks, Pat Schwarz and others.

My parents instructed a lawyer on my behalf, Raymond Tucker of Browse, Tucker and Associates, who became my legal representative. I only met him personally more than a year after my release when he visited London on another case, by which time he was married to Pat Schwarz, my old friend of university years. He played a key part in supporting us legally and through good counsel over many years, until his untimely death. Major Iitzhak Unna, the consul general to South Africa for Israel, negotiated with the Security Police to secure my release and arranged for my departure to Israel. My indebtedness to him, and to the authorities he represented in Israel, remains profound and lifelong. On arrival in Israel the extended Schlapobersky family in Tel Aviv, and the Kadashai family – some of whom we had known in Swaziland – played a big part in making us feel safe and cared for. We went on to live and work on Kibbutz Beit Alfa, where we experienced deep hospitality and close political affinities with our own values and political outlook. When we arrived in the UK six months later, Janet's family were waiting to receive us, and we knew lasting kindness and hospitality from her Uncle Derek (Beattie) and her Aunt Jane and Uncle Charles (Gordon). On arriving I myself knew only two families in the country. One was the Szur/Stoller family, including old Mr Label Szur, who was a political stalwart, a founding figure in South Africa's trade union movement and night school programmes, and a committed member of the ANC. The other family was Rafi and Kath Kaplinsky, who were then at Sussex University. They were the first people to whom I could give a full account of what had been done to me. Raafi and Kath provided an introduction to staff at the university, which then admitted me to a degree programme. They also opened their homes to us and, through their different connections, I was introduced to Albie Sachs and his then wife Stephanie Kemp. They in turn showed me great personal kindness and understanding, and *The Jail Diary of Albie Sachs* (1969) helped profoundly with my own recovery. They went on to introduce me to the International Defence and Aid Fund where I met Rica Hodgson, and later her husband Jack. Thanks to Rica I was able to put my story into print in their pamphlet 'Trial by Torture – The Case of the 22', and was introduced to Colin Legum of *The Observer*, who saw to the story's publication in that newspaper. Thanks to Rica, I was introduced to the International University Exchange Fund, which raised a scholarship for me that supported us and allowed me to resume my studies at Sussex University. This university was my first and primary point of reference in the UK, and my gratitude to the staff in the School of African and Asian Studies, and in the departments of English, Philosophy and Psychology is abiding.

After qualifying as a psychotherapist, I joined Helen Bamber to help establish the Medical Foundation for the Care of Victims of Torture in 1985. The first location from which we worked was my own consulting room at my home in Highgate, and the next was a loaned suite of offices in the decaying buildings of the disused National Temperance Hospital in Camden. Some years later we moved to a building of our own in Grafton Road, Camden, and then finally to grand premises in Isledon Road, Islington. Helen was an inspiration throughout, and then, following her retirement there, she went on to establish her own Helen Bamber Foundation which is now also located in Camden. It carries forward the perspective on testimony, advocacy, rehabilitation and recovery that we pioneered together over a long period. My first book, *From the Couch to the Circle: Group-Analytic Psychotherapy in Practice* (Schlapobersky 2016a), is dedicated to Helen's memory. There were others I was closely associated with during our years together at the Medical Foundation, and here I wish to thank Rachel Tribe, Erol Yesilyurt and Sheila Melzack for our years of joint endeavour and their continuing commitment to the struggle for human rights. In the provision of services of this kind, I wish to honour the work of Mary Robertson, clinical director of the Traumatic Stress Clinic, a service in the Camden and Islington NHS Foundation Trust. The service provided a setting for my group work over a period of years, and Mary went on to provide group work placements for our trainees from the Institute of Group Analysis. She continues to lead an inspiring agency. She has kindly reviewed this manuscript before publication. Mary's husband Francois Louw, a London-based psychoanalyst with an Afrikaans background, has kindly reviewed and corrected my own use of Afrikaans in the manuscript. My grateful thanks go to both of them.

I wish to express my special thanks to other friends and colleagues in the world of psychotherapy and especially the group-analytic movement in which I have been trained and nurtured, and where I locate my professional home. Our association has helped me to develop three simple precepts for our work with people in groups, which guide us in all we do. The approach rests on the challenge involved in helping people to find a voice for themselves; to bear witness to the voices of others; and, through discourse, to come together out of the shadows. I have come to the simplicity of this understanding – and to appreciate its centrality in all therapeutic work – through the writing of this memoir. So, I thank my associates in group analysis for the journeys we share, and my colleagues in the wider field in many countries who have put my first book to work for the care of our patients and the training of our colleagues. They include friends and colleagues in the following: the International Association for Forensic Psychotherapy; the Institute of Group Analysis Athens and the Institute of Psychosocial Development, Greece; the American Group Psychotherapy Association and its affiliate, the Eastern Group Psychotherapy Society, New York; the Derner Institute of Advanced Psychological Studies at Adelphi University, New York; the Australian Association of Group Psychotherapists; the Bloomsbury Psychotherapy Practice, London; the CAP Programme for Group Psychotherapy, Beijing; the Institutet for Gruppeanalyse, Aarhus and Copenhagen, Denmark; the Deutsche Gesellschaft für Gruppenanalyse und Gruppenpsychotherapie; Freedom from Torture, London; the GRAS Seminar in Group Analysis, Bonn; the Ljubljana Institute of Group Analysis, Slovenia; the Institute of Therapeutic and Applied Group Analysis, Muenster, Germany; the European Federation for Psychoanalytic Psychotherapy; the European Group Analytic Training Institutes Network; the Group Analytic Society International; the Israeli Institute of Group Analysis; the Irish Group Analytic Society; the Nederlandse vereniging voor groepsdynamica en groepspsychotherapie; the Romanian Programme in Group Psychotherapy, Bucharest; the Gruppanalytiska Institutet, Stockholm, Sweden; the Traumatic Stress Clinic, Camden and Islington NHS Trust; the Ububele African Psychotherapy Centre, Johannesburg; the Centre for Group Analytic Studies, Cape Town. It all began at the Institute of Group Analysis in London, where I have been a staff member for decades. I honour fellow therapists, teachers and supervisors at this institute, and the generations of students who have come to train with us down the years and who continue to give new vitality to the developing field.

I have had a lot of therapy down the years, and there are four practitioners to whom I owe special and lifelong gratitude – three are my former therapists and one is my former teacher – and I express my heartfelt thanks to all of them. I first went into long-term therapy with Robin Skynner at the Group Analytic Practice. The experience first gave me a grounding from which to embark on training at the Institute of Group Analysis, and many years later I became his literary editor. Malcolm Pines was a mentor to me at the Maudsley Hospital in London, where I had a student placement, and I went on to learn much from him about the practice of group psychotherapy – first from his teaching at the Institute of Group Analysis, then as a co-author in the papers we wrote and then as a co-conductor in the large groups we ran together. I am now concluding the task of editing his collected papers, which has been another privilege in learning. Many years after qualifying, I went back into therapy and chose to do so with two successive members of the British Psychoanalytical Society – first with Christopher Bollas and then later with Caroline Polmear, with whom I had a long analysis. I could not have written either of my books without their close and continuing guidance, and they have my deep and lasting thanks.

My extended family has always been important to me and I honour this wider network. Many of the family are still at home in South Africa, while others are now widely settled round the world and some are no longer alive. There are five people I wish to thank publicly and sincerely. Marcelle Feldman was a distant cousin by marriage and my mother's closest friend. Over many years she made her home into a sanctuary for our family during troubled times. There were no times more troubled than the period of my detention, and during this period, when some members of our family and friendship circle shunned contact with us, out of either fear or shame, she was steadfast, fearless and committed, as was her daughter Barbara. Their address in those days, 9 Cradock Heights, Rosebank, is the one from which my mother wrote her letter to the prime minister on 10 July 1969, as described in 'Solitary Confinement', Day 28. I would put a monument there if I could; but for now, as Marcelle is no longer with us, I extend my deep thanks to her daughter Barbara Stein – who was like my older sister when we were little – and to her husband Peter and their children, Nicholas, David and Lucy. My cousin Norman Rosenthal, with whom I used to play in the gardens of our homes in Johannesburg's northern suburbs, is now a professor of psychiatry in the United States. His original studies into the relationship between light and depression have broken new ground in the field, and he has applied his originality to the study of trauma in his book *The Gift of Adversity* (Rosenthal 2014). Here he put my story into context for the first time, for which I thank him. I hope we still have much more to do together. My Uncle Ivan is the only surviving sibling of my father's generation, and his gifts have inspired me all my life. His gift for storytelling is amongst them. Through his intimate knowledge of our family history and his fond memories of his father Harry and his mother Janie, his own storytelling has come into mine and confirms its authenticity. My thanks go to him and to his children, Paul, Nicholas, Hannah and Alex. I will conclude these words of appreciation to our wider family by honouring the late Esta Rosenthal, my father's younger sister and our Auntie Esta. After my grandfather's death in 1964, my grandmother went to live with her, and their home in Oaklands became the centre of our family's life. Her home was always open to me, as was her heart. She would be pleased to know that this memoir has now been written and would also be pleased to read the Introduction, which describes our family life and upbringing, and to know that the four of us – the children of Ruth and Archie and our children and grandchildren – continue to fare well. My thanks go to her and her husband, our Uncle Charlie, and their children, Norman and Susan, and to Jennifer, who is sadly no longer with us.

The journalists whose brave reporting on political detentions played such a crucial part in protecting us, merit thanks and special recognition. They include Margaret Smith and especially Benjamin Pogrund, whom I first knew from a distance in his dedication to the work of the *Rand Daily Mail*. Many of the articles cited in 'What the Press Said', arose out of the work of these two journalists. Benjamin followed my detention with closely focused articles, and I acknowledge his courage in those years, his stamina in maintaining a South African perspective in the work of his later years, and his inclusion of the modest guidance I could offer to him in the drafting of the second edition of his book on Sobukwe (Pogrund 2006).

The figures who guided and inspired me in the writers' world of Johannesburg in the late 1960s included Lionel Abrahams, Bill Ainslie and Mongane Wally Serote. I honour the friendship of those years. I had hardly made a beginning there when I was detained and deported. The good things of those years – fraught with danger and fertility – lay in our close collaboration with one another as we faced challenges we knew we had to make, against a system that seemed unassailable at the time. Bill introduced me to Mongane Wally Serote, and I in turn introduced him to Lionel, whose writers' group I had been attending for some time, and we went on to attend the group together. Lionel published Wally's first anthologies, but Bill was lost in a motor accident years before his time. His passing has been honoured by what we have seen visual art represent in the new order of things in South Africa, and by the flowering of graphic art in the work of a number of his distinguished protégés like Dumile Feni and William Kentridge. Many years later I wrote for Lionel's public obituary, organized by his wife, and I said that he had taught me to read and write for a second time.[1] The seeds of opposition and creativity have grown with grace into the new cultivation of our time. Who could have foreseen what was to come as we struggled to find words in the desert of the unspeakable? In the wonderful output of poetry in the writing of Mongane, there are trees standing representing the new literature of South Africa. I thank him for the poem he has authorized for use in the Introduction, 'When Lights Go Out' (Serote 1978a). More deeply still, I honour the youth we shared and his own personal courage in the way he defied an unacceptable order. I continue to find inspiration in the hope by which we were mobilized and in our search for poetry in the most improbable of places – even in prison. I honour the friendship that survived our interrogations and endures even now as we move in these later years between writing and healing. On the last occasion I met our mentor, Lionel Abrahams, some years before his death, I expressed regret that I had never found my own voice as a poet. Lionel's kindness went beyond the obvious. A poem must have come about in the life of every person who benefits from your therapy, he said. I refer this now to Mongane, and acknowledge that while living out the dreadful terms of 'a dry white season', he knew that 'seasons come to pass', and his vision continues to guide us. This was amongst the first of his many fine poems. May we still walk together through the words of our time.

I make further special mention of the other friends with whom I was detained – Ezekiel Mokone, whom we called Moji, and Bethue Folie, whom we called Pepe – and to others I mixed with at the time like Milner Moroke, who came with us to Swaziland to help to build the school at Makwana in 1968. It is still standing, and this is written as our story.

Several close friends looked at this manuscript while it was taking shape and have helped to give me the confidence to make the story into a book. I give thanks to the following:

– Ken Margo, a childhood friend from Johannesburg, who joined the ANC during the later years of the struggle and now lives in Israel. The loyalty of his friendship and the integrity of his person have always been an inspiration. He has long encouraged me to write, and his guidance has been crucial to the writing of this book.

– Stephen Frosh, my London friend and academic, fellow clinician and a university teacher who taught me how to teach at university level, has been a generous guide in the writing process and has seen this manuscript through to production, as he did with my previous book.

– Erol Yesilyurt, whom I worked with at the Medical Foundation in London for more than two decades, encouraged me to persevere with this manuscript and has been a steady, reassuring presence.

– Brian Harris and Shelley Katz in London have shown me continual support, and my thanks go to Shelley especially, for giving me permission to redraft material from the chapter I wrote for her book *Turning Points* on the children of apartheid (Katz 2016).

– Rabbi Jonathan Wittenberg, the rabbi of my synagogue community at the New North London Synagogue, a companion of the spirit and soul, a mentor and a guide, has helped me with the drafting of this book at many crucial points and, by his own writing, has helped to show me the way with my own.

– Peter Marshall, a close friend and inspiring writer, and his wife of later years, Elizabeth, continue to give me faith in the writing process, and we share a continuing love for each other's children.

– Finally, Jenny Zobel, the wife of Peter's earlier years, was a wonderful mother to her children and mine, and a proud daughter to her father, Joseph Zobel, who was one of the founders of Afro-Caribbean literature in French (Zobel [1950] 2020). Sadly, she is no longer with us. Shortly before her untimely death she listened with me to 'Senzenina' and 'Asimbongana Mandela' – songs she knew through her own singing group – and confirmed for me that they had to go into this memoir (see Prologue). I wish to acknowledge Emily and Dylan Marshall, Peter and Jenny's children, who have grown up beside mine, and I thank them for their writing and teaching output, which, like the work of my own children Hannah and Josh, extends their parents' vision and strikes out with new and original developments.

I extend special appreciation to the South African History Archive and to their Freedom of Information Coordinator, Nobukhosi Zulu, for their diligent search for archive documents, and for Nobukhosi's permission to include our correspondence in this memoir.

I thank the people who have helped to authenticate my use in this book of the names of the Security Police who had responsibility for my arrest, interrogation and detention. Frank Dutton, the Chief Investigator of the Goldstone Commission, specializes in war crimes and crimes against humanity and has a specialist knowledge of Security Police archives and history. He was not available to read this manuscript in time for its publication but he introduced me to Paul Erasmus, formerly a detective warrant officer in the Security Police, who joined them nearly a decade after my detention and served under those I have named. He left the force on medical grounds but later testified against those he had served with, first to the Goldstone Commission of Inquiry into a hidden state-sponsored 'Third Force' responsible for the country's violence during the last years of apartheid and in the period of the 1994 election. He has also testified in the inquiries into the deaths of Ahmed Timol and Neil Aggett. He was unable to furnish the missing names in my account, but he has confirmed the names and ranks of those I have identified. My account has thereby gained in authenticity, and I extend my sincere thanks to both Frank and Paul. Erasmus's own book is due for publication shortly (Erasmus 2021). I thank a succession of others for their recent help with the enquiries I made to verify the

Security Police named and identified in this memoir. They include Marianne Tham, of the *Daily Maverick*, Jacob Dlamini, author of *The Terrorist Album* (2020) and other books, and Christopher Ballantine, Professor Emeritus of Music at the University of KwaZulu-Natal. Together with John Blacking, she was arrested and charged with conspiracy to contravene the Immorality Act six months before my own arrest. This action was led by the same Security Police who interrogated me – Major Coetzee and Lieutenant Jordaan. I have described above, in Interrogation II, the conspiracy of these police to use the Immorality Act to silence political opposition. Christopher introduced me to Omar Badsha, a photographer with South African History Online, who then introduced me to Shahid Vawda, Arthur Mafeje Chair, Professor and Director in the School of African and Gender Studies, Anthopology and Linguistics, at the University of Cape Town. He introduced me to Zureena Desai who – finally – introduced me to Susanne Klausen, Professor in the Department of History at Carleton University, Ottawa, Canada. Susanne's research into South Africa's Immorality Act gave her access to transcripts and press cuttings in the arrest and prosecution of Blacking and Desai through which she was able to confirm the names and identities of the police officers concerned. I thank all the above-named most sincerely.

I thank the South African Jewish Board of Deputies and the editor of their *Jewish Affairs* quarterly, David Saks, for their authorization of the reproduction in this book of extracts from the article about me that was published in *Jewish Affairs* (Fachler 2013).

I thank Louise Crane, my editorial assistant in London, most sincerely. She has contributed to this book as she did to my last, with a steadfast commitment to the manuscript's detail. This book represented a different kind of challenge and I thank you, Louise, for your generosity of spirit in bearing with the painful content of the writing that has made it an easier journey for me.

I thank Kate Pool and the Society of Authors for guidance in the publication process that, as with my previous book, has allowed safe passage through its technicalities.

I thank Faber and Faber Publishers for their permission to reissue extracts from two of Roy Campbell's poems, 'African Moonrise' and 'Horses on the Camargue', both published in *Adamastor* (Campbell 1930).

I thank Bloodaxe Books for their permission to reproduce an extract from Anna Akhmatova's poem 'Almost in an Album' in Appendix 3 (Akhmatova 1988).

I thank the Jewish Museum in London for giving a permanent home to my Prison Bible, which is on display amongst other artefacts brought to the UK by Jewish immigrants. My thanks go first to their director of that time, Rickie Burman, who received the Prison Bible and incorporated it in their permanent display of artefacts; to their subsequent curator, Kathrin Pieren, who saw to the photographs that illustrate this memoir; to their photographer Ian Lillicrapp, for his permission to publish the photographs he took of the Prison Bible and the calendar, illustrations and annotations written into it; and to their current director, Frances Jeens. I thank Lynn Joffee and her brothers, Frank, Cecil and Peter, for the care they and their late parents showed us – and especially our father – at difficult periods in our lives. I thank Lynn for re-introducing me to their former housekeeper, Maggie Moeletsi, who remembered our former gardener Paul Moesethle – described in my Introduction above – who worked for their family after leaving our own employment. Maggie confirmed Paul's family name so I can extend my sincere thanks to him. He was a man of great character who came to us as a gardener, stayed to help raise our family and passed away some ten years ago. And I extend further thanks to Maggie for her care and for this verification.

In August 2011, I invited Albie Sachs to open an international psycho-therapy congress as its inaugural speaker. He gave us a lecture illustrated with a film about South Africa's new Constitutional Court, where the search for justice is built into the fabric of the building. The account he gave us, 'A Man Called Henri', was based on his own reparative work with a former perpetra-tor documented in his *Strange Alchemy of Life and Law* (Sachs 2009), in which he describes the work of the Constitutional Court and the Truth and Recon-ciliation Commission. He brought our audience of some five hundred people to their feet, and many who heard it found his voice a call to engagement in the affairs of our time. Later, when he spoke at the Cape Town launch of my previous book in 2017, our contact helped to confirm my plan to write this one. I was invited as a guest to his home, where I met his family – his wife Va-nessa, their son Oliver and the son of his earlier marriage, Michael, together with Michael's wife, Gadi, and their children, Mahlasedi and Lewatle – and other friends. I came away feeling I had visited the rainbow at the end of the storm.

Albie has now written the Foreword to this book. A long-time activist in the South African struggle, he has come to occupy a worldwide position as a leader in the continuing struggle for human rights everywhere. He has lent his weight to this book through what he has written and through helping me to find words for my own account. I regard it as a privilege to also claim him as an older brother who has helped to show me the way and who continues to walk with me. Albie has also introduced me to Karen Press, a long-standing friend and colleague of his. Karen is a poet of rare and distinctive grace, who has privileged this book with her own gifts of clarity, incision and elegance. She and Albie were this book's first readers and became my most important guides in its drafting, for which I thank them both.

More recently, Shirli Gilbert, Professor of Modern Jewish History at Uni-versity College London, read the manuscript for a pre-publication review and offered me discerning guidance on its presentation and content, for which I am most grateful.

I give thanks to my children and grandchildren for their forbearance during my distraction as a writer; I honour their presence in our lives and the future they look to safeguard with their youth and their promise. My thanks go to my daughter Hannah Sherbersky and her former husband Simon, to their children Maia and Leo, to Hannah's husband Martin Gill, and to my stepson Josh Beattie, his partner Sarah and their daughter Elodi. Many of my family were with me when I was honoured by the request to deliver the commemorative Foulkes Lecture in London in 2015. Its title was 'On Making a Home amongst Strangers: The Paradox of Group Therapy' (Schlapobersky 2015a).[2] This was our story as much as it was about our patients. I am gratified and proud to see my daughter Hannah continuing this tradition through her work in child psychiatry and family therapy. By the time this book is published she will have a clinical doctorate in a related area, and she is making a major contribution in her field (Sherbersky 2020a, 2020b). And I am proud to see my stepson Josh continuing our investigative tradition through his work as a documentary filmmaker, alongside his partner Sarah Lambert.[3]

I offer my sincere thanks to my siblings for standing by me – to my brothers Colin and David and my sister Marian, who have long encouraged me to give this account. David and Marian were with me at the time of my release, when I said goodbye to my family at Jan Smuts Airport at the time of deportation on Day 55, and Colin received us in Israel later that day. Our bonds have seen us through so much. They have now provided me with emotional support and drafting guidance in this memoir that includes us all. Their children, Kate, Diana, Andrew, James, Simon, Alice and Jane, and grandchildren, Fred, Erin and Aaron, are a source of joy and pride for all of us. My concluding thanks go to my partner, Claudia Arlo, who was with me in Houston at the conference when I visited the NASA Space Center in 2018 – as described in the Prologue – and she knew that I had to tell this story now. This is not just another book. Claudia's presence in my life has helped me to find the strength to write it down.

Notes

1. Leveson 2004; and see 'Lionel Abrahams: Mischievous Guru of South African Letters', 2000.
2. Available at https://groupanalyticsociety.co.uk/39th-foulkes-lecture-may-2015 (last accessed 22 April 2020).
3. See www.JoshBeattie.com (last accessed 22 April 2020).

Appendix 1
Arrest Warrant,
English Translation

ARREST WARRANT
PLACE AND TERMS OF CONDITIONS UNDER SECTION 6 OF THE TERRORISM ACT, 1967 (ACT 83/1967)

Under the jurisdiction granted to me by Section 6 of the Terrorism Act, 1967 (Act No. 83 of 1967)
I, **JOHANNES PETRUS GOUS**, Commissioner of the South African Police, determine the place and conditions set out in the Schedule hereto as the place and conditions where
JOHN ROBIN SCHLAPOBERSKY, a person referred to in that section (hereinafter the called the detainee), shall be held for interrogation.

BYLAWS

1 The detainee must be held in a prison as defined by Section 1 of the Prison Act of 1959. PRETORIA PRISON is hereinafter referred to as the place of detention.

2 No person, except an official in the service of the State acting in the performance of his official duties, has access to the detainee except with the consent of the Commissioner of the South African Police or the Head of the Security Police.

3 Subject to the provisions of Section 6(6) and (7) of the Terrorism Act, 1967, the detainee may not contact any other person without the prior con-

sent of the Commissioner of the South African Police or the Head of the Security Police.

4 No daily newspapers, Sunday newspapers, or other reading material of whatever nature shall be provided to the detainee, without the prior permission of the Commissioner of the South African Police or the Chief of the Security Police.

5 Except with the consent of the Commissioner of the South African Police or the Chief of the Security Police, the detainee shall not receive any food or drink items sent to him by family or friends of the detainee, or by any person, body or organization.

6 A reasonable amount of personal clothing may be held at the place of detention for the sake of the detainee and kept at his disposal.

7 Personal clothing must be washed and cleaned at the place of detention.

8 Medical or dental prescriptions prescribed by a medical or dental officer or district surgeon prior to detention must be approved by letter by a medical officer appointed under the terms of Section 6 of Prison Regulations of 1959.

9 Subject to the aforementioned conditions and the provisions of Article 6 of the 4th Convention on Terrorism, 1967 (Act No. 83 of 1967), the provisions of the Prisons Act, 1959, and the regulations made in terms of Section 94 thereof, and the Prison Orders and Official Orders of the Commissioner for Prisons applicable to unconvicted prisoners awaiting trial for alleged offences, apply mutatis mutandis to the detainee.

10 Given under my hand in PRETORIA on the day: 13th June 1969.

**JP GOUS, GENERAL, COMMISSIONER,
SOUTH AFRICAN POLICE**

Appendix 2
The Sword and the
Ploughshare
The Terrorism Act and the Bill of Rights

The Sword: Terrorism Act of 1967

'THE SWORD' SECTION 6, TERRORISM ACT OF 1967	COMMENTS BY ALBIE SACHS
(1) Notwithstanding anything to the contrary in any law contained, any commissioned officer as defined in section 1 of the Police Act, 1958 (Act No. 7 of 1958), of or above the rank of Lieutenant-Colonel may, if he has reason to believe that any person who happens to be at any place in the Republic is a terrorist or is withholding from the South African Police any information relating to terrorists or to offences under this Act, arrest such person or cause him to be arrested, without warrant and detain or cause such person to be detained for interrogation at such place in the Republic and subject to such conditions as the Commissioner may, subject to the directions of the Minister, from time to time determine, until the Commissioner orders his release when satisfied that he has satisfactorily replied to all questions at the said interrogation or that no useful purpose will be served by his further detention, or until his release is ordered in terms of subsection (4).	Section 6(1) is the provision under which John was detained. It is written in technical legalese, in one unbroken sentence, intended to be unintelligible to lay people. The gist of the verbiage is that it allows senior police officers, without having to get a warrant, to detain and interrogate suspects indefinitely in secret places.

(continued)

'THE SWORD' SECTION 6, TERRORISM ACT OF 1967	COMMENTS BY ALBIE SACHS
(2) The commissioner shall, as soon as possible after the arrest of any detainee, advise the Minister of his name and the place where he is being detained, and shall furnish the Minister once a month with the reasons why any detainee shall not be released.	
(3) Any detainee may at any time make representations in writing to the Minister relating to his detention or release.	
(4) The Minister may at any time order the release of any detainee.	In section 6(5), the courts are expressly forbidden either to review anything done by the police under this section or to order the release of any detainee.
(5) No court of law shall pronounce upon the validity of any action taken under this section or order the release of any detainee.	
(6) No person, other than the Minister or an officer in the service of the State acting in the performance of his official duties, shall have access to any detainee, or shall be entitled to any official information relating to or obtained from any detainee.	In section 6(6), detainees shall be completely cut off from the world – no lawyers, family or medical people have the right to see them.
(7) If circumstances so permit, a detainee shall be visited in private by a magistrate at least once a fortnight.	

The Ploughshare: Preamble and Bill of Rights
of the South African Constitution of 1996

COMMENTS BY ALBIE SACHS	'THE PLOUGHSHARE' CONSTITUTION OF THE REPUBLIC OF SOUTH AFRICA, 1996
The Preamble and Founding Provisions are written in language that is accessible and self-explanatory. Instead of proclaiming the naked power of the State, it sets out the humane and egalitarian values which are binding on the State in all its exercises of power.	**Preamble** We, the people of South Africa, Recognise the injustices of our past; Honour those who suffered for justice and freedom in our land; Respect those who have worked to build and develop our country; and Believe that South Africa belongs to all who live in it, united in our diversity. We therefore, through our freely elected representatives, adopt this Constitution as the supreme law of the Republic so as to: + Heal the divisions of the past and establish a society based on democratic values, social justice and fundamental human rights; + Lay the foundations for a democratic and open society in which government is based on the will of the people, and every citizen is equally protected by law; + Improve the quality of life of all citizens and free the potential of each person; and + Build a united and democratic South Africa able to take its rightful place as a sovereign state in the family of nations. May God protect our people. Nkosi Sikelel' iAfrika. Morena boloka setjhaba sa heso. God seën Suid-Afrika. God bless South Africa. Mudzimu fhatutshedza Afurika. Hosi katekisa Afrika.

(continued)

COMMENTS BY ALBIE SACHS	'THE PLOUGHSHARE' CONSTITUTION OF THE REPUBLIC OF SOUTH AFRICA, 1996
	Chapter 1: Founding Provisions, Republic of South Africa The Republic of South Africa is one sovereign, democratic state founded on the following values: a. Human dignity, the achievement of equality and the advancement of human rights and freedoms. b. Non-racialism and non-sexism. c. Supremacy of the Constitution and the rule of law. d. Universal adult suffrage, a national common voters roll, regular elections and a multi-party system of democratic government, to ensure accountability, responsiveness and openness.
	Chapter 2: Bill of Rights This Bill of Rights is a cornerstone of democracy in South Africa. It enshrines the rights of all people in our country and affirms the democratic values of human dignity, equality and freedom . . .
Six of the eight constitutional rights to freedom and security of the person that John would have today were violated by his captors.	*12. Freedom and security of the person* 1. Everyone has the right to freedom and security of the person, which includes the right – a. not to be deprived of freedom arbitrarily or without just cause; b. not to be detained without trial; c. to be free from all forms of violence from either public or private sources; d. not to be tortured in any way; and e. not to be treated or punished in a cruel, inhuman or degrading way. 2. Everyone has the right to bodily and psychological integrity, which includes the right – a. to make decisions concerning reproduction;

(continued)

COMMENTS BY ALBIE SACHS	'THE PLOUGHSHARE' CONSTITUTION OF THE REPUBLIC OF SOUTH AFRICA, 1996
	b. to security in and control over their body; and c. not to be subjected to medical or scientific experiments without their informed consent. . .
Every single one of the seventeen constitutional rights of arrested or detained persons that John would have enjoyed today were violated by his captors.	**35. Arrested, detained and accused persons** 35.1. Everyone who is arrested for allegedly committing an offence has the right – a. to remain silent; b. to be informed promptly (i) of the right to remain silent; and (ii) of the consequences of not remaining silent; c. not to be compelled to make any confession or admission that could be used in evidence against that person; d. to be brought before a court as soon as reasonably possible, but not later than (i) 48 hours after the arrest; or (ii) the end of the first court day after the expiry of the 48 hours, if the 48 hours expire outside ordinary court hours or on a day which is not an ordinary court day; e. at the first court appearance after being arrested, to be charged or to be informed of the reason for the detention to continue, or to be released; and f. to be released from detention if the interests of justice permit, subject to reasonable conditions. 35.2. Everyone who is detained, including every sentenced prisoner, has the right – a. to be informed promptly of the reason for being detained; b. to choose, and to consult with, a legal practitioner, and to be informed of this right promptly;

(continued)

COMMENTS BY ALBIE SACHS	'THE PLOUGHSHARE' CONSTITUTION OF THE REPUBLIC OF SOUTH AFRICA, 1996
	c. to have a legal practitioner assigned to the detained person by the state and at state expense, if substantial injustice would otherwise result, and to be informed of this right promptly; d. to challenge the lawfulness of the detention in person before a court and, if the detention is unlawful, to be released; e. to conditions of detention that are consistent with human dignity, including at least exercise and the provision, at state expense, of adequate accommodation, nutrition, reading material and medical treatment; and f. to communicate with, and be visited by, that person's (i) spouse or partner; (ii) next of kin; (iii) chosen religious counsellor; and (iv) chosen medical practitioner. 35.3. Every accused person has a right to a fair trial ...
Instead of allowing security personnel to terrorize all and sundry, these provisions set out the values that are binding on them and that subordinate them to the public authorities and the law, including international law.	**Chapter 11: Security Services** **198. *Governing principles*** The following principles govern national security in the Republic: a. National security must reflect the resolve of South Africans, as individuals and as a nation, to live as equals, to live in peace and harmony, to be free from fear and want, and to seek a better life. b. The resolve to live in peace and harmony precludes any South African citizen from participating in armed conflict, nationally or internationally, except as provided for in terms of the Constitution or national legislation. c. National security must be pursued in compliance with the law, including international law. d. National security is subject to the authority of Parliament and the national executive.

APPENDIX 3
PRINCIPLES FOR THE
POLITICAL APPLICATION
OF PSYCHOTHERAPY

These eight guiding principles were developed over years of practice at the Medical Foundation through the guiding inspiration of Helen Bamber, some of whose expressions will be found in this text. I drafted these principles in policy documents to guide our choice of personnel and our delivery of services, and saw to their publication. Today they are carried forward by Freedom from Torture (the agency's new name), the Helen Bamber Foundation, the Traumatic Stress Clinic and other agencies in the field. They were originally given by Helen Bamber and me, in a joint presentation under the title, 'Torture as the Perversion of a Healing Relationship', to the Annual Meeting of the American Association for the Advancement of Science, Boston, Massachusetts, 14 February 1988, in a panel convened for the AAAS Committee on Scientific Freedom and Responsibility by Dr (now Professor) Richard Mollica. The document was published by Diana Miserez in *Refugees, the Trauma of Exile* (Martinus Nijhoff Publishers, 1988) and then in *Trauma and Uprooting* (Matador, 2020), pp. 92–106. I am grateful to Richard Mollica for providing the original public platform, and to Diana Miserez for publishing it and for the release of copyright so it can be reissued here.

1. A Human Rights Commitment

Torture is a social, political and moral problem that arises on co-ordinates of time and geography that are frequently planned as a political strategy at local and global levels. Whenever it is applied on a systematic basis, torture has historical precedents and well-designed social consequences. In these cases it is usually associated with other major features of political instability, and the individual sequelae of torture are therefore often difficult to disentangle from trauma associated with other man-made calamities like warfare; political conquest and dispossession; concentration camps; solitary confinement and other forms of imprisonment; exile, deportation and refugee status in a foreign land. Meaningful progress in rehabilitative work with survivors requires an understanding, by all concerned, that such work is part of a broader human rights commitment, addressed to these issues. In the face of these injustices, therapeutic neutrality is meaningless. Clients do better in therapy when they know that their therapist is aware of these human rights issues and when it is possible to share with clients the fact that therapeutic help is part of the organization's broader commitment to social justice.

2. The Principle of Positive Intervention: A Commitment to Rehabilitation with Individuals and Families

Many of those we see have suffered extensive physical trauma. In these and in all other cases of torture there is massive psychic trauma, which, if unattended, will almost certainly be compounded rather than alleviated over time. We work to the principle of positive intervention through medical attention and through sustained and structured emotional support in all those cases where people express a need that allows us to engage with them in constructive terms.

Where physical trauma is implicated, the principle of positive intervention begins from a medical consultation. We find that this plays a part in legitimizing help-seeking behaviour across a wide range of cultures. As a specialist in physical disorder, the physician has a direct and practical role to play, as well as an indirect symbolic one in helping to restore to individuals the privacy and integrity of their own bodily processes. The separation of body from mind is nowhere less appropriate than in the treatment of torture, where the body has been abused to gain access to the mind. An integrated physical and psychosocial approach is developed from this basic principle of positive intervention involving the combined endeavours of a multi-professional team.

The concept of cure is in many cases inappropriate. Such post-traumatic sequelae are not the conditions of an illness so much as a form of bondage through which the torturer ensures that his interventions will last over time.

The rehabilitative aim is centred on the purpose of freeing victims rather than 'curing' them. Damage is in many cases profound and extensive, but with almost everyone that comes to our attention there is something constructive that can be be done. There are always questions to be asked as to what constitutes a resolution to the ultimate violation of someone's personal world: What does it mean for someone to get better, when wilful cruelty has caused lasting damage? And what counts as healing?

3. An Organizational Commitment

Separate individual treatments and discrete, unrelated resources are less useful than the resources of a team. Survivors' feelings of grief, rage and helplessness need a containing environment where staff can accept and work with them.

A young man spoke of the process of 'decompensation' – the abreaction of profound trauma – not long after arriving in London from his home in Central America where he had been tortured and had seen others suffer. Until he was seen at the Medical Foundation some months later, there was no one who could encompass the terms of his anguish. And so, he told us, 'the forest was my doctor'. He would visit a nearby patch of beech forest where he would run about, cry and shout in great distress, relieving pent-up emotions. The Medical Foundation, he said later, 'took over from the forest'. Survivors need a relationship with a community rather than with a specific treatment, and it is only in a therapeutically structured community that staff can feel sufficiently supported by one another to endure their repeated exposure to extreme experience. There are always questions to be asked here about what this experience does to the staff who undergo this work, what they get out of it and how are they best supported.

4. Survival as a Creative Act

People's responses to stress are influenced by their own appraisal of the situation and their capacities to process the experience, to attach meaning to it and to incorporate it in their belief systems. Resilience in adversity is not only a strategy for coping but also a creative challenge. People's developmental histories, cognitive set, attachment and affectional base, their relationship network and prior experience of mastery and self-confidence through challenge and adaptation, are all determining factors in their reactions to massive trauma. In the range of therapies offered, we have found it essential to make contact with a person's prior forms of adjustment, and to reactivate internal and adaptive strategies for further recovery

We have been profoundly impressed by the dignity of those who survive torture and by the importance they attach to transcending the victim identity and to reacquiring a sense of agency and creative endeavour in their lives. We have come to regard the services we offer as aids for the remarkable powers of self-renewal that our clients bring to us. Ordinary social relationships contain those agencies for change that can, when tapped, release profound self-healing, regenerative resources. We see our professional skills as a means towards this end.

Mustafa, the teacher mentioned in the Epilogue, described how by teaching others he had found himself able to survive. Group therapy played an important role in his subsequent rehabilitation, for it helped him to rediscover strengths and resources in himself that the needs of others drew from him. He had lost most of what he loved and valued, and a sense of inconsolable loss pervaded the clinical picture. He was startled by the growing recognition in the group that he had not lost the capacity to be of use to others, and after this discovery he was able to rebuild his life. There are intriguing questions to be raised here as to how many other cases of psychotherapy show progress when survival, self-renewal and personal transformation arise through similar dynamics of self-creation.

5. Survival as a Process of Bearing Witness

Disaster imposes a sense of isolation on each survivor. The reduction of this isolation must be a central part of the process of recovery if people are to make genuine adjustments. The sustained and structured emotional support available at the Foundation has the aim of sharing with survivors an acceptance that they have each witnessed disaster of incomprehensible magnitude. Many come to see that the testimony they provide in the process of bearing witness carries a responsibility towards the past that is one of the keys towards adjustment in the future. This can become one of the most powerful antidotes to the guilt of survival. The telling of stories and the recounting of narrative has become an integral and engaging aspect of the Foundation's life. The question to be asked here is, in how many other such cases of psychotherapy should we regard the evidential content of the patient's narrative as something like testimony that can be built upon as it is written up? In this case, the therapist's role is akin to that of the oral historian.

6. Torture as a Perverted Form of Intimacy

Torture frequently involves an intimate and intense relationship between an individual and one or several others. The body and mind of the victim are a focus for concentrated attention, either in the form of an onslaught or assault, or in a process that is sustained over time and repeatedly applied. Injury thus arises in a direct and personal relationship whose purpose is the deliberate destruction of bodily and psychic integrity. Where the body is the primary site of attack, it is the torturer's point of access to the victim's identity and mind, and every physical scar leaves an emotional scar.

7. Torture as a Secular Inquisition

Torture has always been an instrument of war. It is today once again the means for maintaining a particular kind of 'peace', and to achieve social control through coercion or terror the state has established itself as a secular inquisition in many countries. The suffering of the individual is thus the torturer's access to the community. The victims of torture are always individuals, but never individuals alone. For every person detained, there are mothers and fathers, brothers and sisters, wives and children who wait. Torturers deprive the community of its individuals. Just as significantly, they deprive the individual of community by attacking the trust and coherence that make the fabric of any society.

As a personal and intimate violation, the torture process 'borrows' from the prototype of a healing relationship between a person and their doctor, confessor or counsellor. But in doing so it perverts the benign intentions of the healing relationship to induce the very state from which the healer is committed to free their patient. This can leave the victim maimed, incapacitated, disabled, cowed, and dispossessed of information; or the victim can be forced to witness or participate in such action against others.

8. The Reclamation of Space and Time

The majority of those tortured do not survive. The testimony of those who do, seen in agencies like ours, casts a shadow upon us all. Koestler's account of his time in detention awaiting execution during the Spanish Civil War is given in the Epilogue. He described himself and his fellow inmates as 'men without shadows'. We see our responsibility, partly, in reclaiming time and space for those who have suffered the loss of both. We attempt to help those who have lived 'without shadows' to discover a voice with which to speak of themselves. A young man, consumed by intensely injured emotions that followed torture and exile said, 'I've lost my life, I've lost my plan. When you have a plan for life and the base is broken, nothing is left. I wanted to build my future and have an education, but now everything is lost.' Another person talked about becoming 'zero.' First, he had been a student; and he would have become an economist, he said, or perhaps even a lawyer. But now, he said, 'I have become a zero.' Sometimes, he said, he did not want to live: 'If you aren't happy, if you aren't glad in the world then you might [as well] die.' Then he laughed and said that he still had his youth and his freedom, and he wanted to make a new beginning.

We find that as people begin to speak for themselves, they can reclaim time and space. Like the people described above, they recover from the consequences of torture and rediscover an entitlement to a lifespan that the process was intended to destroy. When people who have endured a nightmare begin to talk about survival, it behoves us all to take account of what they have to say. The poet Anna Akhmatova writes that if you listen to her, 'You will hear thunder':

Almost in an Album
You will hear thunder and remember me
and think – she wanted storms.
The horizon will be hard crimson
and the heart will burn as before.

That's how it will be on that Moscow day,
when I leave the city for ever
and rush to where I long for,
still leaving my shadow among you.

And so it is with the perversion of human relationships. The damage done in hours, days or months remains in the bodies and minds of those who survive. Torment is internalized, and profound injuries are either disavowed at great personal expense, or are lived out through biological and psychological processes, until such time as an audience is found that can bear to pay attention. To listen, however, one must be ready to 'hear thunder'.

BIBLIOGRAPHY

Books and Journals

Abrahams, L. 1977. *The Celibacy of Felix Greenspan.* Chicago: Academy Publishers. Reissued 1993.

———. 1978. *Bosman At His Best: A Choice of Stories and Sketches, Culled by Lionel Abrahams.* Cape Town: Cape Town Human and Rousseau.

———. 1982. *Chaos Theory of the Heart and Other Poems.* Cape Town: Jacana Press.

———. 1988. *The Writer in the Sand.* Cape Town: Ad. Donker.

———. 1995. *A Dead Tree Full of Live Birds.* Johannesburg: Snailpress.

Akhmatova, A. 1988. 'Almost in an Album'. In *Selected Poems*, translated by Richard McKane. London: Bloodaxe Books.

Alexander, N. 2014. *Interviews with Neville Alexander: The Power of Languages and the Languages of Power.* Edited by B. Busch, L. Busch and K. Press. Durban: University of KwaZulu Natal Press.

Alleg, H. 1958. *The Question.* London: John Calder. Reprinted by University of Nebraska Press, 2006, with new Foreword, Introduction and Afterword.

Arenstein, R., and R.W. Johnson. 1991. 'Rowley Arenstein, friend of Mandela, supporter of Buthelezi, talks to R.W. Johnson'. *London Review of Books*, Vol. 13, No. 4.

Armah, Ayi Kwei. 1968. *The Beautyful Ones Are Not Yet Born.* London: Heinemann African Writers.

Barnard, A. 1992. *Hunters and Herders of Southern Africa.* Cambridge: Cambridge University Press.

Beissert, C. 2013. *Beautiful: Translations from the Spanish – The Poetry of Lorca and Neruda.* Cullowhee, NC: New Native Press.

Belton, N. 2012. *The Good Listener: Helen Bamber – A Life Against Cruelty.* London, Faber and Faber.

Bernstein, H. 1968. *The World That Was Ours.* London: Heinemann.

———. 1994. *Rift: The Exile Experience of South Africans.* London: Jonathan Cape.

Bizos, G. 1989. *No One To Blame: A Personal Account of Some Inquests into Deaths in Detention under Apartheid.* Cape Town: David Phillips Publishers.

Blacking, J. 1973. *How Musical Is Man?* Seattle: University of Washington Press.

Bosman, H.C. 1969. *Cold Stone Jug.* Johannesburg: Human and Rousseau.

Brand, D., and C. Gevers. 2015. *South African Constitutional Law in Context.* Cape Town: Oxford University Press.

Breytenbach, B. 1984. *The True Confessions of an Albino Terrorist.* Johannesburg: Taurus.

Brutus, D. 1969. *Letters to Martha*. London: Heinemann African Writers Series.

Bunting, B. 1986. *The Rise of the South African Reich*. South Africa: Mayibuye Books.

Campbell, R. 1930. 'African Moonrise' and 'Horses on The Camargue', in *Adamastor: Poems by Roy Campbell*. London: Faber and Faber, pp. 60 and 84.

Camus, A. 1955. *The Myth of Sisyphus*. New York: Alfred Knopf. Reissued Vintage 2018.

Carlson, J. 1973. *No Neutral Ground*. London: Quartet Books.

Chrust, J. (ed.). 1977. *Keidan Memorial (Yizkor) Book* (Yiddish edition). Reissued in English, 2018. Israel and USA: Keidan Association.

Clingman, S. 1998. *Bram Fischer: Afrikaner Revolutionary*. Cape Town: David Philip Publishers.

Coleman, M. 1998. *A Crime Against Humanity: Analysing the Repression of the Apartheid*. Johannesburg: Human Rights Committee; Belville: Mayibuye Books, University of the Western Cape; Cape Town: David Philip Publishers.

Cope, J. 1982. *The Adversary Within: Dissident Writers in Afrikaans*. Cape Town: David Philip.

Cronin, J. 1987. *Inside*. London: Jonathan Cape.

Currie, I., and J. de Waal. 2005. *The Bill of Rights Handbook*, 6th edn. Cape Town: Juta Academic Publishers.

de Vos, P., and W. Freedman (eds). 2014. *South African Constitutional Law in Context*. Cape Town: Oxford University Press.

Dlamini, J. 2020. *The Terrorist Album: Apartheid's Insurgents, Collaborators and the Security Police*. Cambridge, MA: Harvard University Press.

Ellis, S. 1998. 'The Historical Significance of South Africa's Third Force'. *Journal of Southern African Studies* 24(2): 261–99.

Erasmus, P. 2021. *Confessions of A Stratcom Hitman*. Cape Town: Jacana Media.

Fachler, D. 2013. 'The John Schlapobersky Affair'. *Jewish Quarterly* 68(3): 10–14.

Fanon, F. 1961. *The Wretched of the Earth*. New York: Grove Press.

Farbstein, R. 1998. 'Diaries and Memoirs as a Historical Source: The Diary and Memoir of a Rabbi at the "Konin House of Bondage"'. Translated by Naftali Greenwood. *Yad Vashem Studies* Vol. XXVI, pp. 87–128.

First, R. 1965. *117 Days: An Account of Confinement and Interrogation under the South African 90-Day Detention Law*. London: Penguin. Reissued by Virago Modern Classics with Introduction by Gillian Slovo, London, 2010.

Fučik, J. 1948. *Notes from the Gallows*. New York, New Century Publishers. Reprinted London: Gibbs Smith, 1990.

Fugard, A. 1993. 'The Island', in A. Fugard, *The Township Plays*. Oxford: Oxford University Press, pp. 193–227.

Garson, P. 2020. *Undeniable: Memoir of a Covert War*. Cape Town: Jacana.

Gerlach, W. 2000. *And the Witnesses Were Silent: The Confessing Church and the Jews*. Lincoln: University of Nebraska Press.

Gibbon, P. (1908) 2008. 'The Veld', in E.H. Crouch (ed.), *A Treasury of South African Poetry and Verse*. London: Franklin Classics, pp. 64–65.

Gobodo-Madikizela, P. 2003. *A Human Being Died That Night*. London: Portobello.

Green, T. 2007. *Inquisition: The Reign of Fear*. London: Macmillan.

Hijuelos, O. 1989. *The Mambo Kings Play Songs of Love*. New York: Farrar Straus and Giroux.

Hikmet, N. 2002. *Poems of Nazim Hikmet*. Translated by Randy Blasing and Mutlu Konuk. New York: Persea Books. (Revised 2nd edn.)

———. 2005. *Poems of Nazim Hikmet*. Translated by Randy Blasing and Mutlu Konuk. New York: Persea Books (Revised 2nd edn, 2002).

International Defence and Aid Fund (IDAF). 1970. 'South Africa: Trial by Torture – The Case of the 22'. London.

Johnstone, F.A. 1976. *Class, Race and Gold: A Study of Class Relations and Racial Discrimination in South Africa*. London: Routledge and Keegan Paul.

Katz, S. (ed.). 2016. *Turning Points: Crowd-Writing. The Amazing True Adventures of Totally Normal People*. London: CreateSpace Independent Publishing Platform.

Klausen, S. Forthcoming 2021. 'Pining for Purity: Miscegenation, Apartheid and the Immorality (Amendment) Act (1950) in South Africa 1950–1985', in Dagmar Herzog and Chelsea Shields (eds), *Colonialism and Sexuality*. New York: Routledge.

Koestler, A. 1937. *Spanish Testament*. Left Book Club Edition. London: Victor Gollancz Press.

———. 1957. *Reflections on Hanging*. Reprint edition 2019. Athens, GA: University of Georgia Press.

Krige, U. 2010. *Briewe van Uys Krige uit Frankryk en Spanje* [Letters from Uys Krige from France and Spain]. Cape Town: Hemel and See Books.

Krog, A. 1999. *The Country of My Skull*. London: Vintage Books, Random House.

Laing, R.D. 1968. *The Politics of Experience and The Bird of Paradise*. Harmondsworth: Penguin. Reissued Penguin 1990.

Lee, R., and I. DeVore (eds). 1995. *Kalahari Hunter-Gatherers: Studies of the !Kung San and their Neighbours*. Cambridge, MA: Harvard University Press.

Lerer-Cohen, R., and S. Issroff. 2002. *The Holocaust in Lithuania, 1941–1945: A Book of Remembrance*. New York: Gefen Publishing House.

Levinsonas, J. 2006. *The Shoah (Holocaust) in Lithuania*. Vilnius: The Vilna Gaon Jewish State Museum of Lithuania.

Lewin, H. 1976. *Bandiet: Seven Years in a South African Jail*. London: Penguin.

Lifton, R.J. 1986. *The Nazi Doctors: Medical Killing and the Psychology of Genocide*. New York: Basic Books.

Madikizela-Mandela, W. 2014. *491 Days: Prisoner Number 1323/69*. London: Modern African Writing Series.

Mandela, N.R. (ed.). 1965a. *Nelson Mandela Speaks*. London: South African Studies – African National Congress.

———. 1965b. *No Easy Walk to Freedom: Articles, Speeches and Trial Addresses of Nelson Mandela*. Edited by Ruth First. London: Heinemann.

———. 1973. *No Easy Walk to Freedom: Articles, Speeches and Trial Addresses of Nelson Mandela*. Second edition, edited and Foreword by Ruth First. New York: Basic Books.

———. 1994. *Long Walk To Freedom: The Autobiography of Nelson Rolihlahla Mandela*. London: Little, Brown and Company.

Mandela, N.R., S. Venter and Z. Dlamini-Mandela. 2010. *The Prison Letters of Nelson Mandela*. New York: Norton.

Mandy, N. 1984. *A City Divided: Johannesburg and Soweto*. London: Macmillan.

Mapanje, J. (ed.). 2002. *Gathering Seaweed: African Prison Writing*. London: African Writers Series.

Marshall, P. 1994. *Around Africa: From the Pillars of Hercules to the Straights of Gibraltar*. New York: Simon and Schuster..

Merton, R. (1948) 1990. *The Seven Storey Mountain*. New York: Harcourt Brace. Reissued by SPCK Classics, London, 1990.

Miserez, D. 1988. *Refugees, the Trauma of Exile*. Dordrecht. London and Boston: Martinus Nijhoff Publishers.

———. 2020. *Trauma and Uprooting*. Leics., UK, Matador.

Mtshali, O. 1972. *Sounds of a Cowhide Drum*. Johannesburg: Renoster Books. Reissued as *Sounds of a Cowhide Drum: Imisondo Isigubhu Sesikhumba senkomo*. Cape Town: Jacana, 2012.

Newitt, M. 1995. *A History of Mozambique*. Bloomington: Indiana University Press.

Niemöller, M. 2000. 'First They Came for the Communists', in W. Gerlach, *And the Witnesses Were Silent: The Confessing Church and the Jews*. Lincoln: University of Nebraska Press, p. 47.

O'Brien, K. 2011. *The South African Intelligence Services: From Apartheid to Democracy 1948–2005*. London: Routledge.

Orwell, G. 2003. 'A Hanging', in *Shooting an Elephant and Other Essays*. London: Penguin.

Oshry, R.E. 1995. *The Annihilation of Lithuanian Jewry*. New York: Judaica Press.

Paton, A. (1949) 2002. *Cry the Beloved Country: A Story of Comfort in Desolation*. London: Penguin. Reissued by Vintage, London, 2002.

———. 1968. *The Long View*, edited by E. Callan. London: Pall Mall.

Plaatje, S.T. 1916. *Native Life in South Africa*. London: P.S. King and Son.

Pogrund, B. 1991. *Sobukwe and Apartheid*. New Jersey: Rutgers University Press.

———. 2006. *How Can Man Die Better: The Biography of Robert Sobukwe*. Cape Town: Jonathan Ball Publishers.

Rosenthal, N. 2014. *The Gift of Adversity*. New York: Jeremy P. Tarcher/Penguin.

Sachs, A. 1968. *Stephanie on Trial*. London: Harvill Press.

———. 1969. *The Jail Diary of Albie Sachs*. London: Sphere. Reprinted by Africa Book Centre, London, 1978.

———. 1990. *The Soft Vengeance of a Freedom Fighter*. Oakland: University of California Press. Reissued by Souvenir Press, 2014.

———. 2009. *The Strange Alchemy of Life and Law*. Oxford: Oxford University Press.

———. 2016. *We the People: Insights of an Activist Judge*. Johannesburg, Witwatersrand University Press.

———. 2018. *Oliver Tambo's Dream*. London: African Lives Press.

Sampson, A. 1987. *Black and Gold: Tycoons, Revolutionaries and Apartheid*. London: Pantheon.

Schlapoberksy, J. (ed.). (1986) 1990a. *Selected Papers of Robin Skynner, Vol 1: Explorations with Families: Group Analysis and Family Therapy*. London: Routledge.

——— (ed.). (1987) 1990b. *Selected Papers of Robin Skynner, Vol 2: Institutes and How to Survive Them: Mental Health Training and Consultation*. London: Routledge.

———. 1993. 'The Language of the Group: Monologue, Dialogue and Discourse in Group Analysis', in D. Brown and L. Zinkin (eds), *The Psyche and the Social World*. London: Routledge, pp. 211–31 (reissued by Jessica Kingsley Press, London, 2000); and in J. Schlapoberksy, 2016, *From the Couch to the Circle*. London: Routledge, pp. 112–34.

———. 1995. 'Forensic Psychotherapy: The Group-Analytic Approach', in C. Cordess and M. Cox (eds), *Forensic Psychotherapy*. London: Jessica Kingsley, pp. 227–44.

———. 1996. 'The Reclamation of Space and Time: Psychotherapy with Survivors of Torture and Organised Violence'. Presentation at The Political Psyche Conference, Institute for Contemporary Arts, London, 1993. Issued in *Medical Foundation Proceedings*.

———. 2001. 'The Social World of the Forsaken Psyche'. *Group Analysis* (December) 34(4): 485–500.

———. 2002. 'My Father's Uncle Played the Mandolin: Reflections on the Killing Fields of Europe'. *Mikbatz: The Israeli Journal of Group Psychotherapy* 7(1): 68–75.

———. 2005. 'Refugee Survivors of Organised Violence and Torture: A Group Work Approach', in *The UK Government Department of Health Textbook on Mental Health Services for Refugees*. Embargoed In Press.

———. 2012. 'Introduction' in I. Harwood, W. Stone and M.W. Pines (eds), *Self-Experiences in Group Revisited: Affective Attachments, Intersubjective Regulations, and Human Understanding*. Psychoanalytic Enquiry Book Series. New York: Taylor Francis, pp. 1–7.

———. 2014. 'Resonanz und Reziprozität in privaten und öffentlichen Beziehungen' [Resonance and reciprocity in groups and in society]. *Gruppenpsychotherapie und Gruppendynamik* 50(4): 269–87.

———. 2015a. 'On Making a Home amongst Strangers: The Paradox of Group Therapy'. 39th Foulkes Lecture, May 2015. *Group Analysis* (December) 48(4): 406–32.

———. 2015b. 'Group Psychotherapy in the United Kingdom: Report for Special Edition'. *International Journal of Group Psychotherapy* 65(4): 565–76.

———. 2016a. *From the Couch to the Circle: Group-Analytic Psychotherapy in Practice*. New York: Routledge.

———. 2016b. 'Street Children in South Africa: Four Short Stories', in S. Katz (ed.), *Turning Points: Crowd-Writing. The Amazing True Adventures of Totally Normal People*. London: CreateSpace Independent Publishing Platform, pp. 256–76.

———. 2017. 'Group Analysis on War and Peace', in G. Ofer (ed.), *Bridge Over Troubled Water: Conflicts and Reconciliation in Groups and Society*. London: Karnac, pp. 19–50.

——— (ed.). 2020. *Malcolm Pines Collected Papers in Psychoanalysis and Group Analysis*. London: Routledge (In Press).

Schlapobersky, J., and H. Bamber. 1988. 'Rehabilitation Work with Victims of Torture in London: The Reclamation of Time and Space', in D. Miserez (ed.), *Refugees, the Trauma of Exile: The Humanitarian Role of Red Cross and Red Crescent*. Dordrecht, Boston, London. Martinus Nijhoff Publishers, pp. 206–22.

Schlapobersky, J., and M. Pines. 2000. 'Group Methods in Adult Psychiatry', in M. Gelder et al. (eds), *The New Oxford Textbook of Psychiatry*. Oxford: Oxford University Press, pp. 1350–68.

———. 2010. 'Group Analysis and Group Analytic Psychotherapy', in V. Tschuschke (ed.), *Gruppenpsychotherapie und Gruppendynamik*. Stuttgart: Thieme, pp. 264–68.

Schlapobersky, J., J. Cilasun, M. Papanastasiou and A. Thomas. Forthcoming. 'The Large Group In Training', *Group Analysis*.

Serote, M.W. 1972. *Yakhal'Inkomo: The Cry of Cattle at the Slaughter: Poetry*. Johannesburg: Renoster Books. Reissued by Ad. Donker, Cape Town, 1983.

———. 1974. *Tstelo*. Johannesburg: Renoster Books.

———. 1976. *No Baby Must Weep*. Johannesburg: Renoster Books.

———. 1978a. 'When Lights Go Out', in *Behold Mama, Flowers*, pp. 69–70. Johannesburg: Ad. Donker.

———. 1978b. *To Every Birth Its Blood*. Johannesburg: Ravan Press. Reissued by Picador Africa, 2004.

———. 1982. *Selected Poems*. Cape Town: Ad. Donker.

———. 1984. *Come and Hope with Me*. Cape Town: David Phillip Publishers.

———. 1993. *Third World Express*. Cape Town: David Phillip Publishers.

Sharansky, N. (1988) 1998. *Fear No Evil: The Classic Story of One Man's Triumph over a Police State*. New York: Perseus.

Sherbersky, H. 2020a. 'Spotlight'. *New Psychotherapist* 73 (Spring): 49–50.

———. 2020b. '"Treating This Place Like Home": An Exploration of the Notions of Home within an Adolescent In-patient Unit, and Subsequent Implications for Staff Training'. Doctoral thesis, University of Exeter, UK.

Shimoni, G. 2003. *Community and Conscience: The Jews in Apartheid South Africa*. Boston: Brandeis University Press.

Shlapobersky-Strichman, R. 2011. 'From Darkness to Light', in S. Abramovich and Y. Zilberg (eds), *Smuggled in Potato Sacks: Fifty Stories of the Hidden Children of the Kovna Ghetto*. London: Vallentine Mitchell, pp. 231–40.

Sikakane, J. 1977. *Window on Soweto*. London: International Defence and Aid Fund.

Suttner, R. 2011. *Inside Apartheid's Prison*. Melbourne: Ocean Press. Reissued by Jacana, Cape Town, 2017.

Thompson, L. 2000. *A History of South Africa*. New Haven, CT: Yale University Press.

Thornberry, C. 2004. *A Nation Is Born: The Inside Story of Namibia's Independence*. Winghoek: Gamsberg Macmillan Publishers.

Tolstoy, L. 1873. *Anna Karenina*. Translated by Richard Pevear and Larissa Volochonsky. Reprinted by Penguin Classics, London, 2003.

Tutu, D. 1999. *No Future Without Forgiveness*. London: Rider.

Twiss, M. 2002. *The Most Evil Men and Women in History*. London: Michael O'Mara Books.

Van Onselen, C. 1982. *New Babylon New Nineveh*. Johannesburg: Jonathan Ball Publishers.

Wheatcroft, G. 1986. *The Randlords: The Men Who Made South Africa*. London: Atheneum Books.

Whitechapel, S. 2003. *Flesh Inferno: Atrocities of Torquemada and the Spanish Inquisition*. London: Creation Books.

Wordsworth, L. 2006. 'Lines Composed a Few Miles above Tintern Abbey', in *The Collected Poems of William Wordsworth*. London: Wordsworth Poetry Library.

Zobel, J. 1950. *Black Shack Alley*. Paris: Présence Africaine. Reissued by Penguin Classics, London, 2020.

Web Sources

'Apartheid General's Wife Commits Suicide'. 2013. iol.co.za. Retrieved May 2020 from https://www.iol.co.za/news/south-africa/apartheid-generals-wife-commits-suicide-100418.

'Apartheid Legislation 1850s–1970s'. 2011/2019. South African History Online. Retrieved May 2020 from https://www.sahistory.org.za/article/apartheid-legislation-1850s-1970s.

'Asimbonanga by Johnny Clegg (With Nelson Mandela)', 1999. youtube.com. Retrieved May 2020 from https://www.youtube.com/watch?v=BGS7SpI7obY.

B'nai Avraham and Yehuda Laib Family Society (BAYL). Bulletin 74. Retrieved May 2020 from https://bayl.org/wp-content/uploads/2020/09/BAYL-Bulletin-Vol.-74-Sept.-2020.pdf.

'Coetzee's "Fairy Tales" – The Mail & Guardian 11/09/1998': Retrieved 1 December 2020 from https://mg.co.za/article/1998-09-11-coetzees-fairy-tales/\.

Dumile Feni, in 'The Constitutional Court Art Collection', Constitution Hill Living Museum. Retrieved May 2020 from https://www.constitutionhill.org.za/pages/constitutional-court-art-collection.

'Facing Death … Facing Life – David Khumalo filmed by Ingrid Gavshon'. Retrieved 20 October 2020 from https://www.idfa.nl/en/film/98915cd3-e2c3-459f-baec-f0e03 4555ae5/facing-death-facing-life.

'Frank Dutton'. Retrieved 8 January 2021 from https://en.wikipedia.org/wiki/Frank_Dutton.

Gosschalk, B. 2017. 'Obituary', *Guardian*, 13 April. Retrieved May 2020 from https://www.theguardian.com/world/2017/apr/13/bernard-gosschalk-obituary.

Hijuelos, O. 1989. 'The Mambo Kings Play Songs of Love'. Retrieved May 2020 from https://www.goodreads.com/review/show/1259686926.

'Immorality Act No. 23 of 1957'. P. O'Malley, Nelson Mandela Foundation: O'Malley, The Heart of Hope website. Retrieved May 2020 from https://omalley.nelsonmandela.org/omalley/index.php/site/q/03lv01538/04lv01828/05lv01829/06lv01884.htm.

'Institute for Justice and Reconciliation'. 2020. Retrieved May 2020 from https://ww.ijr.org.za/.

'Itzhak Unna Appointed Ambassador to SA'. Retrieved October 2020 from http://www.jta.org/1974/03/11/archive/ israel-names-full-ambassador-to-south-africa'.

John Blacking. 2020. wikipedia.org. Retrieved May 2020 from https://en.wikipedia.org/wiki/John_Blacking.

Leveson, M. 2004. 'Obituary: Lionel Abrahams'. *English Academy Review* 21(1): 177–79. Retrieved May 2020 from https://doi.org/10.1080/10131750485310151a.

'Lightning Bird'. Retrieved May 2020 from https://en.wikipedia.org/wiki/Lightning _bird.

'Lionel Abrahams: Mischievous Guru of South African Letters'. 2000. Obituaries, *Independent*, 9 June. Retrieved May 2020 from https://www.independent.co.uk/news/obituaries/lionel-abrahams-730543.html.

'List of Deaths in Detention'. 2011/2019. South African History Online. Retrieved May 2020 from https://www.sahistory.org.za/article/list-deaths-detention.

'"More than a Shop" – Fanny Klenerman and the Vanguard Bookshop in Johannesburg'. 2019. The Heritage Portal. Retrieved May 2020 from http://www.theheritageportal.co.za/article/more-shop-fanny-klenerman-and-vanguard-bookshop-johannesburg.

'Natives (Abolition of Passes and Coordination of Documents) Act No 67 of 1952'. P. O'Malley, Nelson Mandela Foundation: O'Malley, The Heart of Hope website. Retrieved May 2020 from https://omalley.nelsonmandela.org/omalley/index.php/site/q/03lv0 1538/04lv01828/05lv01829/06lv01853.htm.

'Nelson Mandela's Inauguration Speech as President of SA', given 10 May 1994. South African Government News Agency, 10 May 2018. Retrieved 22 May 2020 from https://www.sanews.gov.za/south-africa/read-nelson-mandelas-inauguration-speech-president-sa. Also available to view at https://www.youtube.com/watch?v=t3OrcQ18JtY.

Niemöller, M. 'First They Came for the Communists'. Poetic prose. Retrieved 23 May 2020 from https://en.wikipedia.org/wiki/First_they_came_…

Orwell, G. 2003. 'A Hanging', in *Shooting an Elephant and Other Essays*. London: Penguin. Retrieved 23 May 2020 from https://en.wikipedia.org/wiki/A_Hanging.

'Peter Marshall'. Retrieved 28 December 2020 from: https://wn.com/_peter_marshall_ (author)/Peter_Marshall/_Peter_Marshall.

'Prohibition of Political Interference Act, 1968' (Act No. 51), also known as the 'Prohibition of Improper Interference Act', later renamed 'The Prohibition of Foreign Financing of Political Parties Act'. wikipedia.org. Retrieved May 2020 from https://en.wikipedia .org/wiki/Prohibition_of_Political_Interference_Act,_1968.

'Remembering and Learning from the Past: The 1976 Uprising and the African Working Class'. Libcom.org, 29 June 2013. Retrieved May 2020 from https://libcom.org/ library/remembering-learning-past-1976-uprising-african-working-class.

Robert F. Kennedy's 'Day of Affirmation Address'. 1966. Retrieved May 2020 from https://en.wikipedia.org/wiki/Day_of_Affirmation_Address.

Schlapobersky, J. 2015. 'On Making a Home amongst Strangers: The Paradox of Group Therapy'. 39th Foulkes Lecture, May 2015. Retrieved 22 April 2020 from https:// groupanalyticsociety.co.uk/39th-foulkes-lecture-may-2015.

'Senzenina' by Cape Town Youth Choir (formerly Pro Cantu Youth Choir). 2010. Retrieved May 2020 from https://www.youtube.com/watch?v=5fDU1PYWT8A'.

Serote, Mongane, Wally. Retrieved 20 October 2020 from https://en.wikipedia.org/wiki/ Mongane_Wally_Serote.

Sherbersky, H. 2020. 'Spotlight'. *New Psychotherapist* 73 (Spring): 49–50. Retrieved 22 April 2020 from https://www.psychotherapy.org.uk/ukcp-news/new-psychotherapist/ new-psychotherapist-issue-73-spring-2020/.

Thamm, Marianne. 2020. 'Alleged Apartheid-Era Criminals Must Account – and There Are Many in Happy Retirement'. Daily Maverick, South Africa, 25 June. Retrieved 26 June 2020 from https://www.dailymaverick.co.za/article/2020-06-25-alleged-apa rtheid-era-criminals-must-account-and-there-are-many-in-happy-retirement/.

'The Appointment of Judges'. 2011/2016. South African History Online. Retrieved May 2020 from https://www.sahistory.org.za/article/appointment-judges.

'The Constitutional Court Art Collection' Constitution Hill Living Museum Retrieved May 2020 from https://www.constitutionhill.org.za/pages/constitutional-court-art-collection.

'The Use of Torture in Detention' (Refers to Rooi Rus Swanepoel), P. O'Malley, Nelson Mandela Foundation: O'Malley, The Heart of Hope website. Retrieved May 2020 from https://omalley.nelsonmandela.org/omalley/index.php/site/q/03lv01538/04lv 01828/05lv01993/06lv02002.htm.

'Third Force'. Retrieved 3 December 2020 from https://en.wikipedia.org/wiki/Third _Force_(South_Africa).

'Tribute to Bill Ainslie'. 2006. Afronova Modern and Contemporary Art. Retrieved May 2020 from https://web.archive.org/web/20200809193654/https://www.afronova. com/exhibitions/tribute-to-bill-ainslie/..

'Truth and Reconciliation Commission (South Africa)'. 2020. wikipedia.org. Retrieved May 2020 from https://en.wikipedia.org/wiki/Truth_and_Reconciliation_Commis sion_(South_Africa).

'Truth Body Hears Testimony on Deaths in Detention', 29 April 1996. South African Press Association. Retrieved May 2020 from https://www.justice.gov.za/trc/media/ 1996/9604/s960429g.htm.

Tutu, D., et al. 1998. 'Truth and Reconciliation Commission of South Africa Report, Vol. 3', 29 October. Vol. 3, Chapter 6, Sub-section 20, page 568, paragraphs 153–70. Retrieved December 2020 from https://www.justice.gov.za/trc/ report/finalreport/ Volume%203.pdf. See also 'https://sabctrc.saha.org.za/reportpage.php?id=13472&t =%2Bswanepoel+&tab=report'.

INDEX

CPSIA information can be obtained
at www.ICGtesting.com
Printed in the USA
BVHW091834140621
609554BV00014B/587